CONTENTS

CONTENTS

Sixth Day

Seventh Day

Eighth Day

THE MOORS MURDERS

THE TRIAL OF MYRA HINDLEY
AND IAN BRADY

With an Introduction
and Edited by

JONATHAN GOODMAN

MAGPIE BOOKS LTD
London

This edition first published by Magpie Books Ltd in 1994,
a division of Robinson Publishing

Magpie Books Ltd
7 Kensington Church Court
London W8 4SP

First published as The Trial of Ian Brady and
Myra Hindley in 1973, then published as The Moors Murders,
by David & Charles Publishers Plc, 1986 and 1987.

ISBN 1 85813 539 7

A copy of the British Library Cataloguing in
Publication Data is available from the British Library.

Printed and bound in Great Britain by
HarperCollins Manufacturing, Glasgow

THE MOORS MURDERS

Ninth Day
Evidence for the Defence

Tenth Day

Eleventh Day

Twelfth Day

Thirteenth Day

Fourteenth Day

INTRODUCTION

The whole of anything is never told:
you can only take what groups together.
Henry James

Murder for pleasure is almost invariably a solitary vice; indeed, until late in 1965, when the activities of Ian Brady and Myra Hindley were brought to light, one would have needed to pore over very dusty records to find an exception to prove the rule that killing for entertainment's sake is the most unsociable crime of all.

Brady and Hindley were voyeurs, écouteurs, of their own corruption. Enlarging the Freudian pleasure principle, they derived at least as much satisfaction from the shadow of their deeds as from the deeds themselves: from the salacious nostalgia of looking at photographs showing their own intimacy and the obscene contortions of a frightened child; from listening to a tape recording of the child's pleas to be allowed to return to her mother; from hearing another child read a newspaper account of the search for one of their murder victims; and from visiting, and taking others unknowingly to visit, a secret cemetery on a Pennine moor.

Ian Brady, the bastard son of a tea-shop waitress and a man he never knew, was born in a Glasgow maternity hospital on 2 January 1938, and while still a baby was given into the care of foster-parents, a couple with four children of their own who lived in a tenement in the Gorbals slums. His mother visited him frequently, and it seems that she paid for his upkeep, for the foster-parents could not have afforded the neighbours' description of him, when he was five or six, as 'the smartest wee lad in the street'; on Sundays he wore a frilly silk shirt and a kilt, and on weekdays black velvet trousers.

But the little boy's impeccable appearance was deceptive. Before he was nine, when he moved with his foster-parents to a council house on the Pollok Estate just outside the city, he had gained a reputation for cruelty, not only to animals and insects, but also to children weaker than himself. Some twenty years later, people who were at primary school with Brady, their memories perhaps overcoloured by time and newspaper head-lines, spoke of his acts of cruelty. One of them was quoted as saying:

> The cats weren't worth bothering with after he'd finished with them. He always carried a flick-knife, and was a great one for a carry-on. He once tied me to a steel washing-post, heaped news-papers round my legs and set fire to them. I can still remember feeling dizzy with the smoke before I was rescued.

In 1949, at the age of eleven, Brady started attending Shaw-lands Academy in Glasgow. According to a classmate, he was 'a boy who didn't like company, but nae dunderhead'. He was already interested in, if not yet obsessed with, nazism:

> He read all kinds of books about the nazis and never stopped talking about them. Even when we were playing war games, he made a great point of being a 'German' . . . . When Ian used to shout 'Sieg heil!' and give the nazi salute, people would laugh.

The same classmate also noted that Brady usually had plenty of pocket money, an affluence that may be explained by his appearance at Glasgow Sheriff Court in 1951 on charges of housebreaking and attempted theft, for which he was put on probation for two years. In July of the following year he was admonished on similar charges at Govan Court. Leaving school in 1953, when he was fifteen, he worked for a few months as a butcher's assistant, then as a teaboy in a shipyard. In November 1954 he again appeared at Glasgow Sheriff Court, this time on nine charges of housebreaking and theft, and received two years' probation, a condition of the order being that he returned to his mother, who was now married and living at Moss Side, a grimy suburb of Manchester.

Brady's step-father found him a job as a porter at the Man-chester fruit market, where he himself worked; but the wages were low, the temptations many, and at the city magistrates' court in November 1955 Brady was convicted of stealing lead seals from banana boxes. He was sent to quarter sessions for sentencing, and received a two years' term of Borstal training, which he served at Hull and Hatfield.

On his release, in November 1957, he returned to his mother and step-father, who were now living at 18 Westmorland Street in Longsight, a Manchester suburb contiguous to, and no less depressing than, Moss Side. (The owner of the house has the dubious, and perhaps unique, distinction of having been land-lady to two unconnected murderers; she owns two other houses in the street, and at one of these, No. 10, a tenant was Alfred Bailey, who in 1964 was sentenced to life imprisonment for the murder by strangulation of a six-year-old girl.)

Between April and October 1958, Brady was employed to roll barrels and clean out vats at a brewery close to Strangeways Prison. Before being sent to Borstal, he had been a fairly heavy drinker, so it would be false to assume an occupation syndrome from the fact that during and after the time he worked at the brewery he often drank to excess, receiving a fine in June 1958 for being drunk and disorderly. At the end of the year he went back to work at the fruit market: but for only a few months. During this time—either from a desire to 'better himself' or because, although tall and wiry, he lacked the strength for heavy manual work—he applied for several office jobs, and was eventually taken on as a stock clerk at Millwards Merchandise Ltd, a small chemical distributing firm in Levenshulme Road, Gorton; he started there, at a salary of £12 a week, in February 1959.

He was a good worker, careful and neat, and his employers' only complaints were of his unpunctuality and brief but frequent absences when he slipped out of the office to place bets, always for small amounts and usually each-way, with a local bookmaker. He rarely said more than a few words to the other office workers; during the lunch break he sat alone in his small office overlooking a yard filled with empty chemical drums and carboys and, after hurrying through a meal usually consisting of cheese and whisked raw eggs, read books on nazi war crimes and criminals. (His other main literary interest, erotic sadism, was apparently restricted to after-office hours.) He sometimes spent the lunch break writing orders to record dealers for tapes of German marching songs, speeches by nazi leaders, and evidence at the

Nuremburg war crimes trials; these orders, written in over-large handwriting, often ended with the words 'Thank you, Meine Herren' above the signature.

In January 1961, when Brady had been working at Millwards for nearly two years, a tall, unnaturally blonde girl called Myra Hindley joined the firm as a shorthand-typist.

Like Brady, she had had a disturbed childhood. The daughter of a mixed, Catholic-Protestant, marriage, she was born in Gorton on 23 July 1942. After the birth of her sister Maureen in 1946, she was sent to live with her grandmother in another part of Gorton. Although a reasonably bright child (her IQ rating was 109), she lacked the discipline that a normal home life might have provided. She was allowed to stay out later than other children of her age, and often played truant from school. She failed to pass the 11-plus examination, and in her first year at a modern secondary school her report card read:

Progress and conduct	satisfactory
Personality	not very sociable
Attendance	consistently unsatisfactory

The characterism of 'not very sociable' did not apply to her relations with classmates, however: they remember her as 'funny and always singing', and as 'a comedienne, making up ditties and telling jokes'.

In June of 1957, her last year at school, she saw a boy drown in a reservoir. The experience seems to have been traumatic: she organised a collection for a wreath and took a day off from school to attend the funeral; immediately afterwards, encouraged by an aunt and uncle, she embraced the Roman Catholic faith, taking the name 'Veronica' and attending mass regularly.

During the period between leaving school and joining Millwards, she had a succession of office jobs, all with local firms, none lasting more than a few months. Most evenings she spent at cinemas and dance halls. When she was seventeen she became engaged to a childhood friend, but broke it off after a year because, she said, 'he is too childish and we're not saving enough money for marriage'.

It was at this time, if not before, that she became interested in Germany; she began to read books about that country, and early in 1961 obtained an application form for joining the NAAFI so that she could work there. But soon afterwards, still undecided as to whether or not to apply, she was sacked from her job because of absenteeism. The following week, she started work in the stock office at Millwards.

The laws of probability had been defied. It was a millions-to-one chance that brought Brady and Hindley together, to draw from one another, and to exacerbate, a taste for wickedness. Only a slight deviation in the course of either of their young lives would have kept them apart; would have prevented the formation of a synergy, a sum of evil far greater than its parts; would have averted several murders and saved a large expenditure of public money in the name of retribution.

From the first moment she saw him, Hindley was attracted to Brady. She made no secret of her fascination, but Brady (who, so far as is known, had never had a girl-friend—a boy-friend either, for that matter) virtually ignored her for almost twelve months, perhaps in the belief that the subtle sadism of disregard gave more satisfaction than would a normal, or even abnormal, sexual relationship.

In her first year at Millwards, Hindley kept a diary. Most of the entries were notes of hairdressing appointments for root toning and pink and blue rinses, or reminders of relatives' birthdays, or sums to show how she had spent her weekly wages of £8.50. But scattered among the mundane words and figures were references to Brady:

Ian looked at me today. . . . He smiled at me today. . . . The pig—he didn't look at me. . . . He ignored me today. . . . I wonder if he'll ever take me out. . . . I almost got a smile out of him today. . . . Ian wore a black shirt and looked smashing. . . . He is a loud-mouthed pig. . . . I love him.

At last, just before Christmas 1961, she was able to write:

Eureka! Today we have our first date. We are going to the cinema.

But her joy must have been constrained by the knowledge that the film chosen by Brady for the first date was as important to him as the date itself. The film was *Trial at Nuremburg*, whose subject was nazi war atrocities.

From now on, however, their relationship quickly ripened, and by the spring of 1962 they were inseparable. Instead of going home for lunch, Hindley brought sandwiches to the office and joined Brady at his desk, where they read aloud to one another from his books on nazism. Having shown sufficient delight in accounts of the extermination and mass burial of Jews, Hindley was allowed to borrow, for home reading, items from Brady's growing library of books on the history and practice of torture.

There was a marked change in Hindley's appearance and attitude. To coincide with Brady's pet-name for her of 'Myra Hess', and to imply a substance to their conjoined sexual fantasies, she dyed her hair to the extremity of blondeness, exaggerated her small mouth with crimson lipstick and, away from the office, wore sham-suede jackets and leather boots. Before taking up with Brady, she had often spoken of her wish to marry and had shown a love for children in many acts of generosity and in volunteering to baby-sit for neighbours. But now she sneered at marriage, dubbing it 'conventional hypocrisy' and telling a friend: 'I'll never get engaged or marry anybody, because Ian and I have a very good understanding with one another.' Her reaction to a neighbour's pregnancy was the question: 'Why don't you do something to shift it?'

Brady had bought a secondhand motor-cycle, and every night, after having a meal with his mother and step-father, he drove the couple of miles to the diminutive, dilapidated house in Bannock Street where Hindley lived with her grandmother, a woman in her seventies whose lack of interest, let alone inquisitiveness, in what went on under her own roof was, to say the least of it, unusual. Night after night the grandmother sat in the kitchen, the television turned on, her mind turned off, while upstairs two sane people conditioned themselves to commit insane acts; she ignored even the racket of marching songs and nazi speeches, just as she ignored the complaints of neighbours at the volume of the recordings—just as later, in a different house, she would ignore a boy's screams and the thump of his falling body.

In 1963 Hindley passed her driving test and, acting on Brady's advice, bought an old mini-van. It seems clear from a letter that Brady wrote to her that they were planning a robbery and had discussed the need for an escape-car: 'Let's capitalise on the situation [of having a car]. I shall grasp this opportunity to view the investment establishment [a bank?] situated in Stockport Road next Friday. I will contact you before then to give other details.' Nothing came of this plan, nor of a similar plan for which Brady tried to enlist the assistance of some ex-Borstal acquaintances.

Brady's driving license did not cover four-wheeled vehicles, and he never applied for an extension of the license. Hindley drove him to and from work and did all the driving on their several trips into the surrounding countryside and when they spent a summer holiday in Scotland; also, pandering to his fascination with railway stations, she often drove him to the main-line stations in Manchester and sat in the parked car for sometimes an hour or more while he wandered around. (He said that he went to the railway stations because he 'enjoyed looking at people', but in the light of a subsequent event, a more sinister purpose may be surmised.)

In September 1964, as a result of slum clearance, Hindley's grandmother was given the tenancy of 16 Wardle Brook Avenue, a two-bedroomed council house on the Hattersley overspill estate outside Manchester. Among the modern conveniences of the house was a cigarette machine which was refilled with packets and emptied of coins every Sunday; Hindley, especially, found this useful, since she was a heavy smoker.

Brady moved into the new house, to share Hindley's bedroom, early in 1965. Among the belongings that he brought with him were the paraphernalia of photography, including a developing tank and an enlarger. These last two items were specially necessary, for many of his indoor photographs were not the sort he could have given to a high-street chemist for processing. Some showed Hindley, wholly or partly undressed, in obscene poses; others, taken with the aid of a remote-control gadget, were of her and Brady in the act of coition or entwined in eccentric embraces. There was also a set of photographs of a little girl, naked and gagged, which transcended pornography.

Apart from trades-people, there were few callers at the house in Wardle Brook Avenue. The most frequent visitors were

Hindley's sister, Maureen, and her husband, David Smith, who had been married in August 1964 when she was eighteen and he was sixteen. The day after the wedding, Brady and Hindley had taken the couple on a trip to Bowness in the Lake District. Brady already knew Maureen quite well, as she had been working at Millwards for about a year, but it seems that he had met Smith no more than once or twice, and then only briefly. The drive to the Lake District was the first of many such outings, which usually ended back at the Smiths' home, with the sisters sharing a bed while the man and the boy stayed talking and drinking into the small hours, eventually to fall asleep in their chairs.

Brady knew that between October 1959 and October 1964, Smith had been convicted on three occasions for violent, spur-of-the-moment crimes and once for housebreaking, when three other cases were taken into consideration, and this may explain why, after a few meetings, he began to take the boy into his confidence, first of all showing off his books and extolling the vices of his favourite author and idol as a pioneer of perversions, the Marquis de Sade, and then offering to lend Smith any of the volumes that pricked his fancy.

Later, in the spring of 1965, Brady turned their discussions towards crime—talking generally, testing Smith's reactions, before inviting him to take part in the armed robbery of a bank. He said that he had kept watch on several banks and had compiled detailed notes on their security arrangements. This Smith believed; but he was less convinced by Brady's claim that he had two revolvers, a 0·38 Smith & Wesson and a 0·45 Webley, together with ammunition. To prove that not only did he have the guns (Hindley had bought them from members of a rifle club which she had joined), but also that he was able to fire them with some degree of accuracy, Brady arranged a shooting display on a remote part of Saddleworth Moor, which lies to the north-east of Manchester, close to the Pennine Way. While the two girls sat in the car, he fired some rounds at makeshift targets and allowed Smith to try a few shots, afterwards retrieving the spent shells. As they walked back to the car, Brady asked Smith if he was impressed. Smith said that he was.

Brady and Hindley took the Smiths to the moors on several other occasions, once at eleven o'clock at night. The Smiths enjoyed these outings, but not half as much as their companions, who obtained a macabre, and almost certainly orgastic, pleasure from the knowledge that they were picnicking within a covert graveyard of their own making.

In July 1965 the Smiths moved into a council flat less than a quarter of a mile from Wardle Brook Avenue. Before, when they were living at Gorton, they had always visited Brady and Hindley by invitation. Now they were soon made to realise that unexpected calls were not welcomed; within a few weeks of moving to Hattersley, Maureen Smith was twice turned away from her grandmother's house, first by her sister, then by Brady.

Soon after taking possession of the new flat, David Smith went through one of the frequent periods of unemployment which he ascribed to 'regular tonsillitis'. Hearing of this, Brady again spoke of his plan for a robbery, and Smith agreed to 'case' a local bank. (It appears that, all along, his only quibble with the plan was Brady's insistence on the carrying of guns with live ammunition.) He spent a morning watching a bank, and provided Brady with notes of what he observed.

On 25 September, as was by now usual on Saturdays, Brady and Hindley spent the evening with the Smiths. According to David Smith (in his deposition):

Myra and Maureen stayed up until about 1.30 am. They then went to bed, leaving myself and Brady in the living room. . . . We discussed the bank job and how the guns would have to be used with live bullets, then he asked me if I was capable of murder. I just gave him a blank look.
He then said: 'I've done it'. He said he had done three or four. He was drunk so I didn't pay much attention. . . . He asked if I believed him. I just looked at him blankly as if I did and I didn't. I wasn't interested.
He then went on to describe how he did it. He said that there were two ways. The first one was to wait in a car in a street chosen beforehand until the right one came along. He would then get out of the car and murder him. He said he didn't like that method very much. He said it took too long just preparing. . . . The second method was to go out in a car and pick somebody up and take them back to Wardle Brook Avenue, and he did it there. He said he buried the body on the moors. He said he would pick up people between the ages of sixteen and twenty. He chose that age group because they were always listed as missing by the

police. He said he had photographs to prove it, but he would not let me see them.

He said that before he killed anyone he used to take a drug. It was Pro-Plus. His books were always removed from the house, and all photographs and tape recordings. I can't remember him saying anything else that night about the killing. I did and I didn't believe him.

The following Saturday, 2 October, there was another late-night session:

The conversation about murders started up again. Brady said: 'You don't believe I am capable of it, but it will be done.' He said he wasn't due for another one for three months, and this one would not count. . . . We had had a few bottles of wine to drink—about six—and I was more interested in what I was drinking.

Three days later, early in the evening of Tuesday, 5 October, Brady called on Smith and asked him to parcel up the books he had lent him, together with other 'off-beat' items, including Smith's own collection of pornography and an exercise book in which Smith noted his favourite quotations and paraphrased the ostensible philosophies of celebrated perverts. According to Smith, Brady offered no explanation for this request; and again according to Smith, Brady was not asked for one. The same evening, Smith made up the parcel and carried it round to 16 Wardle Brook Avenue. Brady took the parcel upstairs, and came down a few minutes later with two suitcases. As he and Smith helped Hindley to put the cases in the back of her car, he quipped: 'Don't drop them or they'll blow us all up.' Leaving Smith to walk home, Brady and Hindley drove off towards Manchester Central Station.

According to Smith: 'They had not told me what they were going to do with the suitcases, but I had an idea.'

Disposal of the suitcases was part of the preparation for committing a murder. The plan, proved and improved by experience, was impeccable; all that was left to chance was the choice of victim, and this was the least important consideration in the scheme of things. For Brady, the motive on this occasion was more blurred than usual: there was pleasure in killing, of course—a pleasure that would linger in the mind and stimulate the senses; but this time there was, too, the motive of personal aggrandisement. David Smith 'did and didn't' believe that Brady had the ability to kill. He had to be *made* to believe. Evidence was needed.

At ten minutes past six on Thursday morning, 7 October, an emergency call from a telephone box on the Hattersley council estate was received at Hyde Police Station. The caller, David Smith, said that he and his wife were in fear of their lives. A motor patrol officer set off at once, but within a minute or two of his leaving, there was a second call from Smith, who sounded even more frantic than before; terror emphasised his natural slight stammer as he pleaded for protection 'for me and Mo'.

The couple, found cowering in the shadow of the telephone box, were driven to the police station, and David Smith talked to detectives for several hours. As one of the detectives commented afterwards: 'What he said sounded like a nightmare, but it was not the sort of nightmare that anyone in his right mind could possibly dream.'

At 11.30 last night I was at home with my wife. Me and my wife were in bed, but we were awake. . . .
Myra, that's my wife's sister, knocked on our flat door and I let her in. She seemed normal at the time. . . . She, Myra that is, was there only about ten minutes at the most, and then she asked me to walk home with her to 16 Wardle Brook Avenue, as she was a bit scared of walking about on the estate in the dark. I'd got dressed after I got out of bed . . . and I left our flat with her about a quarter to twelve midnight, or about that time. . . .
We got almost to Myra's house. I intended to leave her there, then she said: 'Ian has a few miniature wine bottles for you. Come and collect them now.'
As we approached the front door, Myra stopped walking and she said: 'Wait over the road, watch for the landing light to flick twice.' I didn't think this was unusual because I've had to do this before, whilst she, Myra, went in to see if Ian would have me in. He's a very temperamental sort of fellow. I waited across the road as Myra told me to, and then the landing light flicked twice, so I walked up and knocked on the front door. Ian opened the front door and he said in a very loud voice for him, he normally speaks soft: 'Do you want those miniatures?' I nodded my head to show 'yes' and he led me into the kitchen, which is directly opposite the front door, and he gave me three miniature bottles of spirits and said: 'Do you want the rest?'

When I first walked into the house, the door to the living room—which was on my right, standing at the front door—was closed. After he'd put the three bottles down in the kitchen, Ian went into the living room and I waited in the kitchen. I waited about a minute or two, then suddenly I heard a hell of a scream; it sounded like a woman, really high-pitched. Then the screams carried on, one after another, really loud. Then I heard Myra shout: 'Dave, help him,' very loud. . . .

When I ran in, I just stood inside the living room, and I saw a young lad, about seventeen years old. . . . He was lying with his head and shoulders on the couch, and his legs were on the floor. He was facing upwards. Ian was standing over him, facing him, with his legs on either side of the young lad's legs. The lad was still screaming. He didn't look injured then, but there was only a small television light on, the big light was off. Ian had a hatchet in his hand, I think it was his right hand, it was his right hand, he was holding it above his head, and then he hit the lad on the left side of the head with the hatchet, I heard the blow, it was a terrible hard blow, it sounded horrible.

The young lad was still screaming, and the lad half fell and half wiggled off the couch, on to the floor, on to his stomach. He was still screaming. Ian went after him and stood over him and kept hacking away at the young lad with the hatchet. I don't know how many times he hit the lad with the hatchet, but it was a lot, about the head, about the neck, you know that region, the shoulders and that. . . .

I felt my stomach turn when I saw what Ian did, and some sick came up and then it went down again. I couldn't move. When he, Ian that is, was hacking at the lad, they got close to me, and one of the blows Ian did at the lad grazed my right leg. I remember, Ian was swinging about with the hatchet, and one blow grazed the top of Myra's head. . . .

After Ian stopped hitting the lad, he was lying on his face, with his feet near the door. I could hear like a gurgling noise in the lad's throat. . . . Ian got a cover off one of the chairs and wrapped it round the lad's head. I was shaking, I was frightened to death of moving, and my stomach was twisting. There was blood all over the place, on the walls, fireplace, everywhere.

Ian never spoke a word all this time, and he got a cord, I think it was electric wire, I don't know where he got it from, and he wrapped it round the lad's neck, one end of the cord in one hand, one end in the other, and he then crossed the cord and pulled and kept pulling until the gurgling stopped in the lad's throat. All the time Ian was doing this, strangling the lad, Ian was swearing; he was saying: 'You dirty bastard.' He kept saying that over and over again.

Myra was still there all this time, just looking. Then Ian looked up at Myra and said something like: 'It's done. It's the messiest yet. It normally only takes one blow.'

Myra just looked at him. She didn't say anything at all. Ian got up then, the little light was still the only one on, and he lit himself a cigarette, after he'd wiped his hands on a piece of some material. Then Ian turned the big light on, and he told Myra to go into the kitchen and get a mop and bucket of warm water, and a bowl with soapy water in it and some rags.

Myra did that and Ian turned to me then and said: 'Your stick's a bit wet,' and he grinned at me. The stick he meant was a stick I'd taken with me when I went with Myra from our place. It's like a walking stick, and the only thing I can think is that when I rushed into the living room at first I'd dropped it, because it was lying on the floor near the young lad. . . .

Then Myra came in with the bowls of water and that. She didn't appear upset, and she just stepped over the young lad's body and placed the bowls of water and that on the carpet in front of the fireplace.

Then Ian looked at me like, and said: 'Give us a lift with this mess.' I was frightened and I did what he said and I helped to clean the mess up. . . . No one spoke while this was going on, then after we'd cleaned most of it up, Ian—he was speaking to Myra—said: 'Do you think anybody heard the screams?' Myra said: 'Yes, me gran did. I told her I'd dropped something on my toe.' Then Myra left the living room.

While she was out, Ian offered me a bottle of wine. . . . The young lad was still lying on the floor. Myra came in with a white bed sheet. I think Ian had told her to get one. And a lot of pieces of polythene, fairly big they were, and a large blanket. . . . Ian told me to get hold of the lad's legs, which I did, and Ian got hold of the lad's shoulders and we lifted him into the sheets and blankets. The only reason I did this was out of sheer bloody fear. Then Ian came out with a joke. He said: 'Eddie's a dead weight,' and both Ian and Myra thought it was bloody hilarious. I didn't see anything to laugh about. . . .

On the stick I had, the one I mentioned to you, there is some bound string, and Ian took the stick and unwound the string. He cut it into lengths, about two or three foot in length, and he gave me one end, and he tied the lad's legs up in a funny way, so that the lad's legs were together and bent up into his stomach. Then Ian carried on tying the lad up; it was like a maze of bloody knots. . . .

I had to help him while he folded the corners of the sheet together, with the lad in the middle, and then he tied the corners together. Then he made me do the same with him with the polythene sheets, and last of all came the blanket. He didn't tie that—it was like a kind of cradle. Myra was mopping up all this time. Then Ian told Myra: 'Go upstairs and hold your gran's door to,' and then he said to me: 'Lift your end up,' and between us we carried the young lad upstairs into Myra's bedroom and we put him down near the window.

Then we came downstairs and I saw a wallet lying on the floor. Ian picked it up and pulled out a green sort of card and said: 'That's his name. Do you know him?' I looked at the card and saw the name Edward Evans. I didn't know him. I saw a pair of shoes lying on the living room floor as well as the wallet, and Ian picked them up, and a couple of letters that were lying there, and put them in a shopping bag. He picked the hatchet up, gave it to me and said something like: 'Feel the weight of that. How did he take it?' I said nothing and gave it him back. I was frightened of him using it on me.

He put the hatchet in with the rest of the things, and he took them upstairs. Myra was still cleaning up, and by this time the house was looking something like normal. . . .

Then Ian went on to describe how he'd done it. How, he said, he'd stood behind the settee looking for some miniatures for me, and the lad Eddie was sat on the settee. He said: 'I held the axe with my two hands and brought it down on his head.' Myra said: 'His eyes registered astonishment when you hit him.' Those are the exact words she said.

Ian was complaining because he'd hurt his ankle and they'd have to keep the lad's body upstairs all night, and he wouldn't be able to carry the lad down to the car because of his ankle. Myra suggested that they use my wife's and my baby trolley to carry the lad's body into their car. Well, it's Myra's car. I agreed straight away. I'd have agreed to anything they said. We arranged to meet where Myra works in Manchester tonight, that's Thursday, at five o'clock. . . .

After we had cleaned up Evans's blood, Myra made a cup of tea, and she and Brady sat talking. She said: 'Do you remember that time we were burying a body on the moors and a policeman came up?' Then she drew me into the conversation and said: 'I was in the mini with a body in the back. It was partitioned off with a plastic sheet. Ian was digging a hole when a policeman came and asked me what the trouble was. I told him I was drying my sparking plugs and he drove off. I was praying that Ian wouldn't come back over the hill whilst he was there.'

. . . I said I'd better be off, I wanted to go and they let me go, and I ran all the way home. They were both unconcerned. I let myself into the flat right away, woke Maureen up and had a wash. . . . I didn't tell her what had happened and I got in bed. It was about three to half past in the morning then. I couldn't get to sleep. I kept thinking about the lad, about the screams and the gurgling he was making. I got up after a bit, put the light on, woke Maureen up and told her all about it. Then she got up, she was crying and upset, and we sat down and tried to decide what to do. . . . It got to about six o'clock. We decided it was the best time to go out, there were milkmen and that knocking about, so I armed myself with a carving knife and a screwdriver, in case I meet Ian and Myra. Maureen came with me and we walked to the telephone kiosk in Hattersley Road West and telephoned the police. That's it. . . .

David Smith also told the police, among other things, about Brady's firearms, so at 8.15 am, before knocking at the back door of 16 Wardle Brook Avenue, Superintendent Robert Talbot, the head of the police division in which Hattersley is situated, took the precaution of borrowing a bread roundsman's white overall to hide his uniform jacket.

Hindley came to the door, and Superintendent Talbot asked her if her husband was at home. She said she was not married. Revealing his uniform, Talbot asked if there was a man in the house. 'There is no man here,' she said. Talbot then pushed past her into the kitchen, and Hindley at once said: 'He is in the other room in bed.' Followed by Detective Sergeant Alexander Carr, the superintendent walked into the living room.

Brady, wearing only a vest, was lying on a divan bed. He was writing a letter to a director of Millwards, saying that he had injured his ankle and was unable to come to work. He continued to write, glancing up only when Talbot asked him his name.

The superintendent said that he was investigating a report that an act of violence had taken place in the house.

'There was nothing wrong here,' Hindley claimed.

Leaving Detective Sergeant Carr in the living room with Brady, the superintendent went upstairs, accompanied by Hindley. He found the grandmother in bed in the front room. The other bedroom door was locked, and when he asked Hindley for the key, she told him that she had left it at work and that it was inconvenient for her to go for it.

They returned to the living room. Talbot said that he was not leaving until he had searched the bedroom, and eventually Hindley said to Brady: 'Well, you'd better tell him.'

'There was a row last night,' said Brady. 'It's in the back bedroom.' He told Hindley to hand over the key, and she took it from her handbag and gave it to the superintendent.

By now, other policemen had arrived. Talbot and Carr went upstairs and unlocked the bedroom door. Beneath the window of the sparsely furnished room was a body wrapped in a blanket. Some books had been thrown on top of the bundle, and beside it on the floor were a carrier bag and a stick, both saturated with blood.

The victim was soon identified as Edward Evans, a seventeen-year-old apprentice machinist who had lived at Ardwick, Manchester. It appears that he was homosexual. He had left home early on the Wednesday evening, telling his mother that he was going to a football match at Old Trafford. He was last seen at seven o'clock in a public house in the centre of Manchester, close to a railway station where he could have caught a train to the football stadium.

Brady and Hindley were driven to Hyde Police Station and interviewed separately. Brady stated that he had met Evans in Manchester and taken him back to the house. 'We had an argument and we came to blows. After the first few blows the situation was out of control. . . . Eddie kicked me at the beginning on my ankle. There was a hatchet on the floor and I hit Eddie with it.' He said that Smith was at the front door when the argument started; Hindley had called him into the living room and he had joined in the fracas, hitting Evans with a stick and kicking him. Brady made no mention of having strangled Evans: 'When Dave and I began cleaning up the floor, the gurgling stopped.'

Hindley refused to say very much, but most of what she did say conflicted with Brady's statement. Whereas Brady admitted being in Manchester the night before, she claimed that they had bought some wine at a nearby off-licence: 'Then we went up to Glossop and sat talking for ages. It was just a normal evening out before all this happened. It was the same as hundreds of other evenings out.' She repeatedly said: 'Ian didn't do it. I didn't do it. David Smith is a liar.' At subsequent interviews she added little to this story, refusing to answer questions unless she were allowed to see Brady.

At mid-day Detective Chief Superintendent Arthur Benfield, who had been appointed head of Cheshire CID only six days before, went with the Home Office pathologist, Dr Charles St Hill, to the house in Wardle Brook Avenue. Dr St Hill made a preliminary examination of the body, which was then taken to the mortuary, where a post-mortem revealed that Evans had died from a fractured skull his death accelerated by strangulation by ligature. There were fourteen lacerations of the scalp, which could have been caused by the hatchet found in the carrier bag in the back bedroom. Dr St Hill also observed widespread bruising on the back of the head and across the shoulders, and several 'defence wounds' on the arms and hands. There were indications (trouser fly buttons undone; fibres in the region of the anus which bore similarities to fibres found in the living room) that some form of sexual activity had taken place.

The police began to search the house. Among the articles they took away were the two loaded revolvers and a quantity of ammunition; numerous photographs and negatives; books about Germany and nazi atrocities during World War II; and a notebook containing doodles, sketches and a jumbled list of names in Brady's handwriting.

On the parcel shelf in Hindley's car, which was parked outside the house, the police found a wallet containing sheets of paper divided into columns of words and abbreviations. Brady admitted to Chief Superintendent Benfield that the wallet was his; the notes, he said, were 'the plan for the disposal of Eddie'. He insisted that this 'disposal plan' was prepared after Evans was killed, but careful analysis of the entries convinced the police that the plan referred to a premeditated murder. Most of Brady's explanations for the words and abbreviations were probably true—'ALI' meant alibi, 'POLY' stood for polythene sheets, 'PRO-P' for Pro-Plus tablets, and 'HAT' for hatchet—but his assertion that 'P/B' stood for Penistone Burn, a place on the moors, was soon shown to be certainly false.

Forensic examination of the living-room carpets revealed no trace of blood, and this negative finding seemed to provide a further indication that the murder of Evans was planned: the only way the carpets could have escaped being stained was if they had been taken up before the boy was brought to the house and replaced after the living room was cleaned. David Smith insisted, however, that, according to his recollection, the carpets were on the floor the whole time. This conflict between expert forensic opinion and the word of an eye-witness remains one of the minor mysteries of the case.

Smith had told the police about the early-morning conversations during which Brady boasted that he had committed three or four murders and buried the bodies on the moors. While a squad of uniformed policemen and detectives ransacked the house, scraping plaster from the walls, removing the floorboards, and digging up the garden, the investigation spread out: house-to-house inquiries were made on the Hattersley estate and in Gorton, all known associates of Brady and Hindley were interviewed, and information was sought at places where they had lived or worked. At the height of the investigation, the police team consisted of officers from Cheshire, Lancashire, the West Riding of Yorkshire, Derbyshire, Manchester City, and the newly-formed No. 1 Regional Crime Squad.

As a result of the house-to-house inquiries, the police interviewed a twelve-year-old girl who lived next door but one to 16 Wardle Brook Avenue. With her mother's consent, she had spent several evenings with Brady and Hindley, who had given her wine and spirits to drink; she had been on trips to the moors with them, one of the last occasions being on Christmas Eve, 1964, when they had stayed there until past midnight. Some time in January 1965 (probably New Year's Day), Brady had recorded a conversation between Hindley and the child, part of which referred to a report in a local newspaper of the search for Lesley Ann Downey, aged ten, who had disappeared from a fairground near her home in Ancoats, Manchester, on Boxing Day.

The police drove the neighbour's child to Saddleworth Moor, and she pointed out the area where Brady and Hindley had taken her; it was around Hollin Brown Knoll, on the A635 road between the villages of Greenfield and Holmfirth. Police officers immediately began to search the area, continuing through the night with the aid of arc lamps. At three o'clock in the afternoon of the following day, Saturday, 16 October, the remains of Lesley Ann Downey were found buried in the peat about 90yd from the road. The body, which was naked, was lying on its right side with the legs doubled up towards the abdomen. The child's clothes and a string of beads were in the grave. A post-

mortem examination was conducted by Dr David Gee, lecturer
in forensic medicine at Leeds University, but the body, having
lain in the damp peat probably for nine months, was too decomposed for the cause of death to be established.

On 20 October, Detective Chief Inspector John Tyrrell made
an important discovery while searching through some of Hindley's possessions. Hidden in the spine of a white prayer book
called *The Garden of the Soul*, a souvenir of her first communion,
were two left-luggage tickets for articles deposited at Manchester
Central Station. The abbreviation 'P/B' in the disposal plan was
now explained: the letters stood, not for Penistone Burn, as
Brady had pretended, but for prayer book.

The tickets were for the two suitcases taken from the house on
the night before the Evans murder. As well as books belonging
to Brady and Smith, the suitcases contained coshes, wigs, masks,
notes on the security arrangements of banks and company
offices, a large collection of photographs and negatives, and two
tape recordings. Among the photographs were nine that showed
Lesley Ann Downey, naked and with a scarf tied over her
mouth, posed obscenely.

One of the tape recordings bore the voices of Hindley and the
neighbour's child talking about the newspaper report. The other
recording, the ultimate horror in Brady and Hindley's contract
of depravity, was of Lesley Ann Downey pleading with them
not to undress her but to allow her to go home: 'I have got to
get home before eight o'clock. . . . I will get killed if I don't.
. . .' Several times during the recording, both Brady and Hindley
could be heard ordering the child to put something—a gag,
perhaps—in her mouth. The recording ended as if it were a
radio programme, with Christmas music faded in and growing
in volume. This music helped the police to fix the time of the
recording as round about Christmas 1964, when the child had
disappeared.

During a long interrogation, Brady said that he knew of the
tape recording; he also admitted taking the photographs of
Lesley Ann Downey in the back bedroom at Wardle Brook
Avenue. His story was that two men had brought the child to
the house for the purpose of taking the photographs: 'One [of
the men] stayed outside. I don't know him. The other man I do

know. . . . She left the house with the man who brought her.
. . . I'm not saying who it is. I know his name. I've met him in
Manchester and he goes into Liston's Bar.'

Hindley was more specific. She asserted that Lesley Ann
Downey had been brought to the house by David Smith and
taken away by him after the photographic session. (At the trial
both Brady and Hindley tried to put the blame for the murder
on Smith, and a half-hearted and quite unsuccessful attempt was
made to implicate a schoolfriend of Smith's as the 'other man'.)

Twenty-two of the photographs found in the suitcases were
of moorland scenes, some showing Brady or Hindley, others
the scenery alone. It struck the detectives as odd that Brady had
considered it necessary to remove such seemingly innocent
pictures from the house before the Evans murder. Bearing in
mind Smith's statement that Brady had told him that he had
'photographic proof' of earlier murders, the police enlisted the
aid of farmers, shepherds and members of rambling and rock
climbing clubs to identify the scenes, and within days each
photograph had a twin photograph taken by the police.

One of Brady's photographs showed Hindley holding a puppy
under her coat; she was crouching on one knee and looking down.
The identical scene was located by the police on Thursday, 21
October, 373yd from the grave of Lesley Ann Downey and on
the opposite side of the A635. When Inspector John Chaddock
removed a stick that he had plunged into the ground to indicate
the spot, there was a strong smell of decomposition. The police
carefully scraped away the soil to reveal a body lying in a twisted
position, the lower limbs facing downwards while the upper
part of the trunk and the head were turned to the left. The body
was fully clothed, but the trousers and underpants were rolled
down to the thighs, indicating sexual interference. As in the
case of Lesley Ann Downey, the post-mortem examination
(conducted by Professor Cyril Polson, professor of forensic
medicine at Leeds University) failed to reveal the cause of death.
The face was unrecognisable, but the body was identified from
the clothing as that of John Kilbride, a twelve-year-old boy
who had disappeared from a market near his home at Ashton-
under-Lyne almost two years before, on 23 November 1963.

The discovery of the body of John Kilbride shocked the police but did not surprise them, for they had come across the boy's name in Brady's notebook. Asked to explain its presence on a page that contained sketches and other names, Brady lied that it was the name of someone he had known in Borstal.

A significant piece of evidence came to light when the police checked the records of vehicles used by Hindley. She had not owned a car in November 1963, but on the day when John Kilbride disappeared she had hired a Ford Anglia. The foreman at the garage remembered that when the car was returned the following morning, 'It looked as if it had been through a ploughed field.' He had thought to himself: 'Who's going to touch for the job of washing that?'

To establish the approximate date of the photograph of Hindley crouching over the grave, the dog (a mongrel called Puppet, which also appeared in several of the indoor photographs, contributing to their obscenity) was taken to a veterinary surgeon so that its present age could be estimated. The dog had to be anaesthetised while its teeth were X-rayed, and it died during the examination. When Chief Superintendent Benfield broke the news to Hindley, she lost control and screamed: 'You fucking murderer!' But this was her last show of emotion; during her many interviews she admitted virtually nothing, and the police came to realise, both from her refusal to answer questions and from her general demeanour, that she was the tougher member of the 'evil partnership'.

The detectives engaged on the case suspected that at least two other bodies were buried on the moors. In July 1963 a sixteen-year-old Gorton girl disappeared on her way to a dance; her home was two doors from where David Smith then lived, and she was known to Hindley. At the time of her disappearance, trenches to take gas pipes were being dug on the moors; the pipes were laid by the beginning of September, two months later. One of the photographs of Hindley on the moors bore a striking similarity, in dress, stance and facial expression, to the photograph of her beside the grave of John Kilbride. In the former photograph her gaze was directed at a spot covered by the gas pipe, and the detectives found it hard to resist the conclusion that if they had received permission to have this stretch of pipe deflected, another body might have been found.

In July 1964, almost exactly a year after the girl's disappearance, an eleven-year-old boy left his home near the University of Manchester to stay the night with his grandmother. His mother, who was going to a bingo hall, walked a short distance with him. If he took the normal route to the grandmother's house, he must have passed the corner of Westmorland Street where Brady then lived and where, at that time of the evening, Hindley might easily have been waiting to drive him to Gorton. The boy never arrived at his grandmother's, and is still missing.

Before the passing of Sydney Silverman's *Murder (Abolition of Death Penalty) Act*, which came into operation on 9 November 1965, the police held a trump card in murder cases in which other killings were suspected; playing on the theory of 'the more the madder', the accused might be induced to reveal other crimes to support a plea of insanity, which, if accepted, would substitute life in a mental institution for death on the gallows. The Moors case was the first case of mass murder under the new Act ('Silverman's Folly', as some policemen, the polite ones, refer to it). In Chief Superintendent Benfield's words: 'There was no question of capital punishment in the Moors case. Brady and Hindley were not fools, so why should they admit any more? If they did, there might be no possibility of release in the future.'

As a result of the publicity attached to the case, the police were almost inundated with telephone calls and letters, many of them referring to suspicious incidents witnessed on the moors during the past two or three years. People were asked to report to mobile police posts on roads over the moors, one each in Cheshire, Yorkshire and Derbyshire, where particulars were taken of the incident; they were then asked to lead the police to the spot, which was ringed with a yellow dye and later searched. Before long, the moors looked like a plantation of giant marigolds; but, although 400 reports were investigated, nothing of significance to the murder case was found.

An RAF photo-reconnaisance unit took a series of aerial photographs of the area, which showed clearly where the ground had been disturbed. Again, each place was located, marked and searched. The only bodies found were those of animals.

The days, the weeks, passed, and the search became a race

against time. Winter comes early to Saddleworth, which is 1,600ft above sea level, and winter is the season to stay away from the moors, a time of foul weather in a place where earlier winters have precluded shelter; the ground is often covered with snow, and is almost always threaded with ice, making it rock-hard.

The search was called off in November. Already the bright yellow circles, symbols of the investigators' thoroughness and perseverance, were flecked with snow and being brushed away by the wind.

The municipal borough of Hyde—which has been described, amusingly but unjustly, as 'an S-bend with chip shops'—is tacked to the eastern suburbs of Manchester as if as an after-thought. It was here, in the magistrates' court, a place of dark panelled walls surmounted by a white domed ceiling, that the committal proceedings were held in the case of The Queen against Ian Brady and Myra Hindley.

The chairman of the Bench was a woman who served on several local committees for the public good, and thus had earned herself an MBE. The popular press decided that she was newsworthy, not because of her personality, intelligence or standing in the community, but because of the excessive collec-tion of almost identical toque hats which she wore, a different toque each day, during the proceedings. There were two other lay magistrates, one a retired confectioner, the other a retired trade union official.

The task of the magistrates to decide whether or not there was a *prima facie* case for Brady and Hindley to answer was really no task at all. On 21 December 1965, at the end of an eleven-day hearing of evidence which the prosecution witnesses had already given to the police and which most of them would have to give again at Chester Assizes, the two accused were formally com-mitted for trial (an object which, in Scotland, would have been achieved as efficiently, far less expensively, and without squan-dering many people's time, by the Lord Advocate's weighing-up of evidence contained in statements [precognitions] taken in private by a procurator fiscal).

The magistrates had been faced with a far more difficult

decision on the first day, when David Lloyd-Jones and Philip Curtis, representing Brady and Hindley respectively, had pleaded for the committal proceedings to be held *in camera*. In Curtis's words:

> Magistrates have always been entitled as examining justices to sit in private if they wish. What are the advantages of sitting in open court and having the whole of the evidence reproduced in such a way that it will make it impossible for any juryman ever to come to this case without preconceived notions of what the case against the accused is?

It would be incorrect to suggest that, in ruling against the defence submission, the magistrates were swayed by their egos—by even an unconscious wish to elevate their names from the limbo of local press reports into the lurid limelight of the front pages of national newspapers. All one may say is that there was a serious defect in a system which allowed lay magistrates to decide whether publicity for committal proceedings was right or wrong, and which presented the temptation to some magistrates to make a choice between what seemed right in their own interests and what was right in the interest of justice.

(The defect was cured by the *Criminal Justice Act 1967*, ss. 1–4, which, in addition to reducing the time and effort spent on committal proceedings, limited the scope of press and broadcasting coverage to the barest outline, and allowed full publicity only when a defendant requested it or was not sent for trial. As in 1958, when the Tucker Committee had recommended rather less stringent restrictions, a number of journalists supported their arguments in favour of publicity by quoting Lord Hewart's dictum on visible justice; but one thing is certain, and that is that Lord Hewart did not mean that justice should manifestly and undoubtedly be seen to be done in order to boost newspaper sales, which was the sole reason why the prosecution evidence in sensational cases was reported twice over—once pre-trial, once again at trial.)

As much, perhaps more, publicity was given to the proceedings at Hyde as to the trial, and there can be no doubt that this was prejudicial to the accused. To say that Brady and Hindley would have been convicted anyway, pre-trial publicity or not, is to say that there should be one law for the obviously guilty and one law for those whose guilt requires some effort to prove. The prejudice was aggravated by the way in which certain newspapers censored the non-salacious testimony and by the way in which the reports were presented, with headlines, sub-headings and bold or italic type emphasising specially ghoulish or sexy aspects. For these newspapers, probably the highlight of the proceedings was when Lesley Ann Downey's mother shouted at Hindley from the witness box: 'You beast! You killed my little girl and you sit there staring at me. . . . You tramp!'

The extravagant nationwide coverage ruled out a defence request for a change of venue for the trial, and made it difficult, perhaps impossible, to find twelve people unaware of, and un-affected by, the publicity, who were yet worthy of serving on the jury.

Every decade has at least one 'crime of the century', and in the sixties this label was attached to the Moors case. If ticket touts had turned some of their profiteering energies from the sporting and theatrical to the legal, then the trial, which opened in the spruced-up No 2 Court at Chester Castle on 19 April 1966, would have provided very rich pickings indeed. Only sixty seats were available to the public, and for these a queue formed in the early hours of each of the fourteen days of the trial. The public was outnumbered by a motley, many-tongued corps of reporters, augmented by a pack of authors, each of whom was hoping, as someone commented, to turn the 'crime of the century' into a Book of the Month. Security precautions reduced the usual number of public seats: the gallery was speckled with policemen on the look-out for signs of disturbance and for known troublemakers who might have evaded the screening process in the courtyard; the front row of seats, directly behind the dock, was kept empty. There were other precautions, the most spec-tacular of which was a shield of reinforced glass at the sides and back of the dock: a 'draught excluder', the police called it.

The case was tried before Mr Justice Fenton Atkinson—the son of a judge, Sir Cyril Atkinson—who had been appointed to the Queen's Bench in 1960.

Sir Frederick Elwyn Jones, QC, MP, the Attorney-General led the prosecution, the first time that the senior law officer had taken part in a murder trial since the case of Dr John Bodkin Adams at the Old Bailey in 1957. Elwyn Jones (whose knowledge of nazi war crimes and criminals was probably more extensive than even Brady's, since he had served on the British prosecution team at Nuremburg) had to be in London on several days during the trial, once for the opening of parliament, at other times for cabinet discussions on the Rhodesia crisis, and his role was then assumed by William Mars-Jones, QC (now a High Court Judge), an efficient and perseverant silk who had prosecuted in the Lime fraud case, Carmarthen, 1962, a trial which lasted fifty-five days, at that time the longest criminal trial this century. Junior Crown counsel was R. G. Waterhouse.

Brady was defended by Emlyn Hooson, Liberal MP for Montgomeryshire, who had taken silk six years before, when, at the age of thirty-five, he was the youngest QC since David Maxwell-Fyfe in 1934. Hooson led David Lloyd-Jones, who had represented Brady at the Hyde committal proceedings.

By a poignant coincidence, on the first day of the trial, Hindley's counsel, Godfrey Heilpern, QC, learned that his sister-in-law, the manageress of a Salford dress shop, had been murdered. Consequently, he had to be absent from court on the day of David Smith's cross-examination, which was conducted by his junior, Philip Curtis, who had been Hindley's counsel at Hyde.

Four women were called to serve on the jury, but Mr Hooson and Mr Heilpern each made two peremptory challenges of them so as to form an all-male jury.

Brady was charged with the murders of Edward Evans, Lesley Ann Downey and John Kilbride. At the committal proceedings, Hindley had been charged with two murder counts —Evans and Downey—plus a third count of harbouring Brady while knowing that he had murdered Kilbride; but before trial, she was also charged with a fourth count—the murder of Kilbride. Like Brady, she pleaded not guilty to all the charges.

While the evidence of David Smith furnished the Crown with the corner-stone of their case, there also existed a wealth of circumstantial evidence which alone, by its cumulative power, was capable of sending both the accused to prison for life. It must be borne in mind, however, that prison for life often means far less than the words seem to threaten. The legal definition of 'life', its meaning in terms of years, is inexact, affected as it is by many factors—for example, the circumstances and number of crimes of which the prisoner is found guilty; his behaviour before the crime, after arrest, and while serving sentence; the shifting whims and beliefs of politicians, penologists, and people whose names inspire respect or, at least, ensure the publication of their letters to *The Times*.

In the cases of Brady and Hindley, the defence could not possibly hope for acquittals; prison terms were inevitable. But there was a faint hope that reasonable doubt could be implanted in the minds of the jury as to whether the accused were guilty on all counts. If the jury were to find them guilty of some, not all, of the charges, their chances would be improved of serving only a fraction of the lifetime penalties which the Crown clearly sought to have imposed.

Defence counsel concentrated their main attack on David Smith, the Crown's strongest yet most vulnerable witness, treating him as an accomplice in the murder of Edward Evans, and suggesting that it was he who had killed Lesley Ann Downey and John Kilbride. It was a simple matter to discredit Smith as a person, but as a witness he was virtually incontrovertible; allied with the natural arrogance of semi-education was the knowledge that he was 'in the clear', for he gave evidence on the understanding that no proceedings would be taken against him in respect of any statements he had made to the police. He not only answered most of the defence questions with swaggering ease but often answered back (Mr Hooson's sarcastic 'And you're a man in the habit of holding a stick in your hand all the time?' was met with the cutting irony of 'But I'm not in the habit of witnessing murder, sir').

The defence was handed what the judge called 'a stick with which to beat Smith' by the revelation that since November 1965 he had received an average of £15 a week from the *News of the World*, and that this newspaper (slogan: 'All human life is here') had promised him a lump sum of at least £1,000 for the use of his name on a series of articles that would appear only if Brady and Hindley were convicted. Clearly, 'this quite extraordinary arrangement' (the judge's words again) might have caused him to fabricate evidence against the accused.

As it happened, Smith's first statement to the police, made before the *News of the World* approached him, was rather more prejudicial to the accused—Hindley especially—than the evidence Smith gave at the trial. The contagious effect of his interviews with the newspaper's representatives was to supplant simple words and phrases in the statement with gaudy-coloured imagery (the plain 'Ian' of the statement became a 'butcher' from the witness box, and Evans's body became a 'rag doll'), but it seems that there was also a sub-editing influence on his memory. The Attorney-General was able to cut short the defence attack by applying for the statement (which the jury had not heard) to be compared with Smith's evidence; this, of course, was the last thing the defence wanted, and, on the tacit understanding that there would be no further reference to the possible effects of the newspaper's compact with Smith, the judge refused the application.

It is surprising that no action was taken against the *News of the World*. The fact that Smith's evidence was, in some respects, diluted in comparison with his statement does not mean that the newspaper's influence was negative, or even benign to the defence. Who can be sure that if there had been no implied financial incentive to ensure conviction, Smith would not have examined the statement, and his conscience, more closely so as to be sure that any errors that might have crept into the statement were not repeated as evidence? The inglorious history of 'cheque-book journalism' is almost as old as the press itself, and there are several instances of newspapers being fined for contempt of court. (The best-remembered example, perhaps, relates to the second 'Crumbles case' [Patrick Mahon], 1924, when three newspapers were charged, and one of them, the *Evening Standard*, was fined £1,000 for hiding a witness and then allowing her story to appear while the case was *sub judice*. Passing sentence, Lord Hewart wondered if, 'with unlimited enterprise and wealth, we may reach a time when witnesses on both sides will be bound by contract and lodged by this or that newspaper'.)

The *News of the World*'s interference in the Moors case was condemned by the Press Council, which also issued a Declaration of Principle (*Appendix 2*); but any hope that the Council's words were in any way a deterrent to chequebook journalism must be tempered by the knowledge that in 1963 the Council condemned the *News of the World* for publishing the life story of Miss Christine Keeler, the star witness in the Stephen Ward case, and that five or six years later the same newspaper published a revised version of Miss Keeler's memoirs.

For much of the time that Brady and Hindley were in the dock—he in a chain-store suit of unassuming grey, she usually wearing a black and white jacket and skirt, her hair silver-lilac at the start of the trial, melon-yellow at the end—their behaviour seemed to imitate the way they must have spent the days at Millwards. There was an air of casual efficiency about them. The copious notes they made were flicked from the pads, passed across the rail of the dock, forgotten; it was the practised motion of an invoice being handed over for checking. Occasionally, and especially at the approach of an adjournment (in their terms, lunch-break or knocking-off time), they nudged one another, to offer a mint-sweet from a tube, or to share a smile when a witness's remark jogged a memory of some out-of-office-hours experience.

Brady went into the witness box three times: twice during legal arguments in the jury's absence, and notably once to give evidence in his own defence, on which occasion he was examined for eight and a half hours. The relentless cross-examination by the Attorney-General caused Brady to tell lie after lie—lies at times so blatant and reckless as to seem like a burlesque of untruthfulness. He admitted that if the blows from the hatchet caused Edward Evans's death then it was he who had killed him, but he denied premeditation; he maintained stoically that he had played no part in the other two murders. There were periods of the cross-examination when Brady gave quite detailed answers, and when he argued with the Attorney-General over trivial points that to him, lacking the perspective of morality, were more relevant than the fact of murder itself; then, realising the hopelessness of his case, the uselessness of lengthy denials ('My train of thought now is that I will be convicted anyway'), he answered in as few words as possible. He slipped up just once, and that was not during cross-examination, but in examination-in-chief: while describing Lesley Ann Downey's visit to the house—a visit which, he said, was arranged by Smith and was for the sole purpose of photographing the child—he told Mr Hooson: 'After completion, *we all got dressed* and went downstairs.'

Hindley was in the witness box for nearly six hours. Only in minor respects did her evidence conflict with Brady's. She said that she was 'horrified' at the killing of Evans, and that her treatment of Lesley Ann Downey, recorded on the tape, was 'indefensible', 'cruel'—mere words to her, perhaps, ingredients of what the Attorney-General called 'counterfeit shame', yet in a case that extended the dimensions of evil, even a semblance of regret was welcome.

Closing speeches and the judge's summing-up occupied most of the last three days of the trial. The summing-up, precise yet colloquial, deliberately low-keyed (as was Mr Justice Fenton Atkinson's whole handling of the trial), was spoken directly to the jury, and so quietly that people in the well of the court had to lean forward to catch all that was said. The two accused made no effort to hear, and at one point Brady appeared to be asleep.

The jury retired at twenty minutes to three on Friday, 6 May. At five o'clock they returned to pronounce Brady guilty of all three murders, and Hindley guilty of the murders of Edward Evans and Lesley Ann Downey; she was found not guilty of the murder of John Kilbride, but guilty of harbouring Brady, knowing that he had committed the crime.

Asked if he had anything to say before sentence was passed, Brady again revealed his obsessional regard for detail. In anyone else, it might have seemed pathetic. 'No,' he said; then, referring to a question which the jury had interrupted their deliberations to ask: 'Except the revolvers were bought in July 1964.' Hindley had nothing to say.

Mr Justice Fenton Atkinson, as quietly as ever, passed concurrent life sentences ('the only sentences which the law now allows') for each of the murder charges, and a sentence of seven years, also concurrent, for the charge against Hindley of being an accessory after the fact.

Brady did not appeal. On 17 October the Criminal Division of the Court of Appeal dismissed Hindley's appeal, which had been argued on the ground that she should have been tried separately (*Appendix 1*). Giving judgment, Lord Chief Justice

Parker said that the Court was satisfied that there was no miscarriage of justice:

> There was, no doubt, in this case a danger of grave prejudice from the fact that that man was a really terrible murderer and that she had throughout admitted a very close association with him, taking part in all his activities and, indeed, being in the house, if not in the room, on the occasion of two of the murders. . . . [But] that was a prejudice which was inevitable, and was there just as much, if not to a greater extent, if she were tried separately. . . . The evidence against her was overwhelming.

Brady, at his own request, is serving his sentence under rule 43 of the Prison Regulations, which restricts contact with other prisoners. Until August 1971, when he was moved to Parkhurst on the Isle of Wight, he was kept in the maximum security 'E' wing of Durham Prison. At one time virtually the sole occupants of this wing were child murderers. Keeping company with Brady was John Straffen, the shambling lunatic who is in prison only because no mental institution is secure enough to guarantee his confinement, also Raymond Morris, the murderer of Christine Darby at Cannock Chase in 1967, who developed so intense a hatred of Brady that he several times tried to wound or scald him. Three child murderers: one of them, Brady, a sadist with homosexual tendencies, the second hopelessly insane, and the third a libidinist. It would require some ingenuity to devise a more sinister trio than this—or, for the two sane prisoners, an existence more comparable to hell; here was the near-reality of Sartre's *Huis Clos*.

Brady has petitioned the Home Office to allow him to see Hindley, who he claims is his common-law wife. He has emphasised later applications by fasting, and in the spring of 1971 went for more than two months without taking solid food.

Hindley, too, it is reported, claims a common-law alliance. Her pleasures are circumscribed in Holloway, but she appears to accept the bounds. She reads a lot, chiefly books that assist her endeavours to pass O-level examinations, and has acquired a delicate skill, almost akin to art, at embroidery and crocheting. Within the last year or so she has returned to the Roman Catholic faith, confessing her sins and patching a wall of her cell with pictures of favourite saints.

When Lord Stonham was under-secretary at the Home Office, he visited Hindley and was much impressed by her quiet manner and intelligence. Afterwards, he was quoted as saying that he was worried that a person like her could be in prison—a sentiment that was reversed by William Mars-Jones, who spoke for the majority by saying that he would be worried if she were not.

CHESTER SPRING ASSIZES, 1966

THE CASTLE, CHESTER
Tuesday, 19 April 1966
and succeeding days

BEFORE
MR. JUSTICE FENTON ATKINSON
(and a jury)

THE QUEEN
against

IAN BRADY
and
MYRA HINDLEY

THE ATTORNEY-GENERAL (THE RIGHT HON. SIR FREDERICK ELWYN JONES, QC, MP), MR W. L. MARS-JONES, QC, and MR R. G. WATERHOUSE appeared on behalf of the Crown

MR H. E. HOOSON, QC, MP, and MR D. T. LLOYD-JONES appeared on behalf of the accused Brady

MR G. HEILPERN, QC, and MR P. CURTIS appeared on behalf of the accused Hindley

FIRST DAY

Before arraignment (in the absence of the jury) MR HOOSON, for Brady, made three submissions, with MR HEILPERN, for Hindley, concurring:

1. As a rule of practice, in a case of murder two or more persons should not be charged in the same indictment. (Authorities cited in support of the submission: Archbold, paragraphs 130, 131, 2547; R *v.* Jones [1918], No 13 Criminal Appeal Reports; R *v.* Large, No 27 C.A.R.; R *v.* Davis, No 26 C.A.R.; Connelly *v.* The Director of Public Prosecutions, 1964 Appeal Reports. Authorities cited against the submission by THE ATTORNEY-GENERAL: R *v.* Grondkowski, 1946 K.B. Reports; R *v.* Buggy [1961], No 45 C.A.R.)

2. The second and third counts in the indictment (the murders of Lesley Ann Downey and John Kilbride) were not founded on the same facts as the first count (the murder of Edward Evans), and were not a series of offences of the same or similar character.

3. If the Judge ruled against the first two submissions, he should still hold that Brady would be embarrassed in his defence by reason of being charged with three offences on the indictment, and as a matter of discretion should order that there should be a separate trial on the first count.

(Authorities cited in support of the second and third submissions: Makin *v.* The Attorney-General of New South Wales, 1894 Appeal Cases; R *v.* Ball, 1911 Appeal Cases; R *v.* Thompson, 1918 Appeal Cases; R *v.* Noor Mohamed, 1949 Appeal Cases.)

MR JUSTICE FENTON ATKINSON: I am satisfied that the Kilbride and Downey evidence is admissible in the case of Evans, and vice versa, and the evidence in any one of the three deaths is admissible in the other two; and having considered it, I can see no sufficient reason for the exercise of my discretion in directing that these charges should be tried separately.

I have a further application from Mr Heilpern for a separate trial for his client, Hindley, on the ground that a lot of the evidence against Mr Hooson's client, Brady, is not admissible against Hindley. I have thought about that a great deal, but giving the best consideration I can, considering the evidence and the interests of justice as well as the interests of the accused,

I think it right that these two charges should be tried together as one trial.

Mr Attorney-General, I do not know whether you take the view that there is a great deal of detail in the depositions that should be cut out on the grounds that it is wholly irrelevant or merely prejudicial.

THE ATTORNEY-GENERAL: There is one aspect of that matter which it might be convenient for me to raise now in the absence of the jury, and that is the evidence of the conversation between Smith and Brady about the plan for a bank robbery. In my submission it is an admissible and relevant part of the prosecution's case, in that it explains the presence of Smith at the scene of the murder and shows a part of the process by which the accused was seeking to involve Smith in the murder.

MR JUSTICE FENTON ATKINSON: I think all that is admissible evidence. I was thinking of trips to the Lake District, and so on, which have no relevance whatever.

THE ATTORNEY-GENERAL: The relevance of the Lake District visit is that it leads to the first critically important conversation, and it is part of my case that this accused had been corrupting this young man, Smith, by insidious advice and generous hospitality soon after the wedding. I will not lead it in any detail, but I fear I may have to lead that evidence.

MR JUSTICE FENTON ATKINSON: What about the books?

THE ATTORNEY-GENERAL: They are merely included in the evidence because of the evidence that Smith was told by Brady to bring any incriminating material he had before the murder. As to the books, what I had in mind was only the one passage from De Sade which Smith says Brady read out to him.

MR JUSTICE FENTON ATKINSON: You are not asking the jury to read *Justine*?

THE ATTORNEY-GENERAL: No, my Lord, I have suffered the agony of having to read that myself.

MR JUSTICE FENTON ATKINSON: It is not a very edifying exhibit, is it?

(*Mid-day adjournment*)

THE CLERK OF ASSIZE: Ian Brady and Myra Hindley, the first count of the indictment is against each of you, that on or about the seventh day of October, 1965, in the County of Chester, you murdered Edward Evans. How say you, Ian Brady, are you guilty or not guilty?

BRADY: Not guilty.

THE CLERK: How say you, Myra Hindley, are you guilty or not guilty?

HINDLEY: Not guilty.

THE CLERK: The second count is against each of you, that on a day unknown between the twenty-sixth day of December, 1964, and the seventh day of October, 1965, in the County of Chester, you murdered Lesley Ann Downey. How say you, Ian Brady, are you guilty or not guilty?

BRADY: Not guilty.

THE CLERK: How say you, Myra Hindley, are you guilty or not guilty?

HINDLEY: Not guilty.

THE CLERK: The third count is against each of you, that on a day unknown between the twenty-third day of November, 1963, and the seventh day of October, 1965, in the County of Chester, you murdered John Kilbride. How say you, Ian Brady, are you guilty or not guilty?

BRADY: Not guilty.

THE CLERK: How say you, Myra Hindley, are you guilty or not guilty?

HINDLEY: Not guilty.

THE CLERK: The fourth count is against you, Myra Hindley alone, that well knowing that Ian Brady had murdered John Kilbride on a day unknown between the twenty-third day of November, 1963, and the seventh day of October, 1965, you did receive, comfort, harbour, assist and maintain the said Ian Brady. How say you, Myra Hindley, are you guilty or not guilty?

HINDLEY: Not guilty.

The jury was called. Four women jurors were challenged (two by MR HOOSON, *two by* MR HEILPERN), *and their places were taken by male jurors. The jury was sworn.*

THE ATTORNEY-GENERAL *opened the case on behalf of the Crown. (The opening speech was a straightforward narrative of prosecution evidence contained in depositions taken at the committal proceedings;*

the salient points are dealt with in the Introduction to this volume, and it would be an unnecessary recapitulation to print the speech.)

SECOND DAY   *Wednesday, 20 April*

THE ATTORNEY-GENERAL *concluded his opening speech.*

EVIDENCE FOR THE PROSECUTION

DETECTIVE CONSTABLE DEREK LEIGHTON, *official photographer to the Cheshire Constabulary, testified as to photographs he had taken of the exterior and interior of 16 Wardle Brook Avenue; of the body of Edward Evans before and after the coverings had been removed; and of objects, including the hatchet, in the immediate vicinity of the body in the back bedroom. (Witness not called at trial; evidence read from deposition.)*

HAROLD BESWICK, *surveyor in the employ of Manchester Corporation, gave evidence as to plans he had made of 16 Wardle Brook Avenue and of the Hattersley estate, showing the position of Underwood Court (where the Smiths lived) and the telephone call box, Hyde 3538, from which David Smith telephoned the police. (Evidence read.)*

LESLIE WRIGHT, *assistant street lighting superintendent for Hyde Corporation, proved plans of street lighting on the Hattersley estate:* 'If anyone were making a journey from Underwood Court to Wardle Brook Avenue after 11.30 pm, the road on which they would travel would, generally speaking, be in darkness.' *(Evidence read.)*

MAUREEN SMITH *(called 'out of sequence', as she was in an advanced state of pregnancy), examined by* MR MARS-JONES: I am nineteen. I am the wife of David Smith and the only sister of Myra Hindley. She was brought up by our grandmother, and I was brought up by our parents. We were good friends. I first discovered that my sister was going out with Ian Brady just before Christmas, 1961. I met him at my gran's, at 7 Bannock Street, Gorton. From that time on, I saw quite a lot of the two of them. For about a year, from June 1963 to 1964, I was working at the same place as my sister and Brady. During 1963, I saw Brady at my gran's house almost every night.

Now at this time, in 1963, did you and your sister ever have any conversation about where she did her shopping, or part of it?—Yes, at Ashton market.

Did she tell you how frequently she went shopping in Ashton market?—Yes, every Saturday.

Did she tell you what sort of things she bought?—She used to buy diamond-patterned nylons, tinned soup and tinned food, you know.

Where did you gather that she was doing her shopping in 1964?—Still in Ashton-under-Lyne market until she moved to Hattersley in September 1964.

Were you married to David Smith on 15 August 1964?—Yes.

Where did you go on the day after the wedding?—To the Lake District at Windermere. In Myra's car.

Was that at someone's invitation?—Yes, Brady's

Where did you go on your return to Manchester?—To 7 Bannock Street.

After that occasion did you visit your sister and the accused, Brady, from time to time, and did they visit you?—Yes.

And were there occasions when they stayed the night?—Yes.

When they stayed the night, where did your sister sleep?—She used to sleep with me.

Where would the menfolk sleep?—Downstairs in their chairs.

Can you give us some indication of how often you went out together in the van?—About every three weeks.

To what sort of places did you go?—To the moors.

Do you know what particular moor or moors you went to?—It was Saddleworth Moor.

What would happen?—Brady used to go off with David and leave Myra and I.

Do you remember Boxing Day, 26 December 1964, Mrs Smith?—Yes.

Were you with your husband throughout the whole of that day?—Yes.

Could he have had time to get to Wardle Brook Avenue at any stage of that day?—No.

Now, on New Year's Eve 1964, did you have visitors?—Yes, Brady and Myra.

On the occasion of that visit did your sister tell you anything about where she had been on Christmas Eve?—Yes. To the moors with Brady.

Did she say what they had done?—She said they had taken blankets with them and were going to stay the night. She said they changed their mind, it was too cold.

I want to ask you about an occasion when your sister came to the house, and there was some reference made to Mrs Downey. Can you first of all tell us about what date that was?—It was about February 1965.

Will you tell my Lord and the jury what your recollection is of what was said, and by whom?—It was about Mrs Downey offering a reward of £100 to anybody who could give any information as to where her daughter, Lesley, was. I said to Myra: 'Her mother must think a lot of the child,' and she just laughed.

Do you know where the Greenfield reservoir is?—Yes.

Do you remember any occasion when you went up on the moors at night when your husband and the accused, Brady, left the car?—Yes. It was about half-past eleven on 24 April 1965.

What happened after you had stopped?—We got out of the car and Brady said he was going to show David the reservoir. He said it looked nice with the moon shining on it . . .

MR JUSTICE FENTON ATKINSON: Mrs Smith, we are adjourning now, and you are to be back tomorrow morning. You are a witness giving evidence, so you must not discuss this case with anybody. You will be free to go after tomorrow morning when you have finished your evidence.

THIRD DAY   *Thursday, 21 April*

MAUREEN SMITH, *recalled; examined by* MR MARS-JONES:

Do you remember, towards the end of October of last year, being taken in a police car out into the country?—Yes.

Did you know what road the car was travelling along?—The Greenfield–Holmfirth road.

Do you remember the police car stopping at a certain spot?—Yes.

Had you stopped at that spot on any previous occasion?—Yes, when we went out with Myra and Brady.

Was this something which happened every time you went out with them, every other time, or only rarely?—Only rarely.

Now I want to ask you some questions, Mrs Smith, about Tuesday, 5 October 1965—that is to say, two days before you went to Hyde police station. Was your husband, David, home with you the whole of the evening?—Until eight o'clock.

What happened at eight o'clock?—He went round to Myra's with some books wrapped up in newspaper.

When did you next see him?—About half-past eight, back in the flat at Underwood Court.

I come to Wednesday now, the 6th October of last year. Did your husband stay in that evening, or not?—He went out to my gran's for some tea. I asked him to go.

Would that be about eight o'clock?—Yes.

Did your husband take anything with him?—I don't think so.

MR JUSTICE FENTON ATKINSON: Had he some letter from the housing authority?—Yes, he had a letter.

MR MARS-JONES: How long was he away?—About a quarter of an hour.

Did he go out again?—He stayed in the flat until he went to bed. About eleven o'clock.

Now, some time after you had gone to bed, was there a ring on the front door telephone?—Yes, about half an hour afterwards.

Who got up?—Me.

And having answered the telephone, did you recognise the voice of the caller?—Yes, it was Myra.

Did you let her into your flat?—Yes.

Did she say something to you?—She said she wanted to give me a message to give to my mother. To tell her that she would see her at the weekend, and she could not get up there before.

What did you say to that?—I asked her why she had come round so late, and she said it was because she had forgotten earlier on and she had just remembered. I asked her why she had not got the car, and she said because she had locked it up.

Now, during this conversation, was there someone else in the room besides you and Myra?—David. He came in just as Myra arrived.

How was he dressed at that time?—He had his jeans and vest on, that's all.

How did the conversation go after that?—She asked David, would he walk her round to 16 Wardle Brook Avenue because all the lights were out.

What was said then?—David said he would, and he got ready. Then he said he would not be two minutes, and then they both left.

Did he take anything with him?—Yes, a walking stick.

Was that a usual thing or an unusual thing?—The usual thing.

Can you remember Myra, your sister, coming round as late as that before this occasion?—No.

When did you next see your husband, David?—A quarter to three.

What was he looking like?—He was white and he was scared.

Did you get up?—Yes, I made him a drink of tea.

What did he do?—He was having a wash.

What happened after that?—He was sick.

Did you both leave the house later?—Yes, about ten to six.

Did David have something with him when he went?—A knife and a screwdriver.

Where did you go to from the flat?—To the telephone box.

Cross-examined by MR HOOSON:

Was your husband employed in August 1964, when you were married, Mrs Smith?—Yes.

How long did he remain in that employment? Was it until just after the new year of that year?—Yes.

Since then has he been unemployed most of the time?—Yes.

Does he take jobs and keep them for a week or two, and then he is unemployed?—No, he keeps them for two months.

When he has been unemployed, what have you lived on?—On dole money.

When you moved to this flat, what was the rent?—£2 7s od [£2.35] a week.

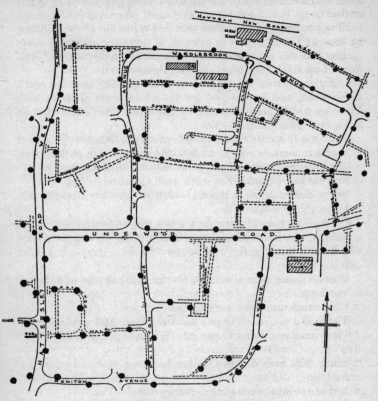

Plan of Hattersley Estate
(The black circles indicate street lamps)

Do you remember my Lord asking you if you had a note left by the rent man?—Yes.

Just have a look at that, please. (*Exhibit produced to the witness.*) Does that read: 'Mr Smith, I want £14 12s 6d [£14.63] at the Town Hall on Saturday or I shall take legal proceedings. Mr Page is doing his job and if that dog is not out of the building by tonight I shall have you evicted. If there are any more complaints of teddy boys and noise I shall take further action.' And printed on it is 'Rent Man'. Is that right?—Yes.

Did you write on the back of it: 'Dear sir, My husband and I are at work, and because we are not on the best of terms with Mr Page I shall personally deliver the rent to the Town Hall on Saturday—Mrs Smith'?—Yes.

You took this note round on Wednesday, 6 October. Was your husband in work or out of work?—He was at work at that time.

For how long had he been at work?—Since February.

And he had continued at work until October?—Yes.

When did he leave that work?—He left the work on the 6th.

Were you at work?—Yes.

If you were both at work, how was it that you owed £14 12s 6d arrears of rent?—Because I was not turning up much money, and Dave was not going out regular. We were paying out other debts.

Was he going once a week?—No, he just had one odd day off in the week.

How much were you earning between you?—£13.

You had not money to pay on 6 October, had you?—No.

How were you going to pay it?—We were going to ask Dave's dad.

Since that sixth day in October has your husband worked at all?—No.

But are things much easier, money-wise?—Yes.

He has a great deal of money now, has he not?—Yes.

Where does he get it?—Must I answer that question?

MR JUSTICE FENTON ATKINSON: Yes.

THE WITNESS: Well, he has been getting it off his dad.

MR HOOSON: How much off his dad?—About £10 a week.

Is that the only place where he has been getting money?—No.

Where else has he been getting it?—From a newspaper.

When did he first start getting money from a newspaper?—About November.

When you say that Dave had left work on 6 October, he had left work before that evening when he went round to the house?—No, he was in work until 7 October.

Are you quite right in what you said to my Lord and the jury that your husband was at work from February 1965?—Yes.

What was he doing?—Making rubber.

When your husband did not go to work, did he ever give a reason?—He had overslept.

Tell me, Mrs Smith, in September of last year, 1965, did you separate from your husband?—Yes.

Why?—Because I was pregnant and he did not want a baby. We had just lost one.

How long did you stay away from him?—Just for one night.

Had he beaten you at all when he found that you were pregnant?—No.

Used he often to go out on his own and leave you in the flat?—Not very often.

How often was it?—Only about twice out of the week.

Do you remember Boxing Day, 1965?—Do you mean last year? We stayed in, I think, as far as I know. I cannot remember.

You have been giving evidence to the jury about Boxing Day, 1964, which is a year earlier. You do not remember what you did on that day either, do you?—Yes, I do. We had a baby then, and when you have a baby you do not go out much.

You often used to leave the baby with your mother and go out, did you not?—At weekends.

And other nights?—Sometimes.

Why is it that you can remember Boxing Day, 1964, and not Boxing Day, 1965?—Because on Christmas Eve, 1964, we had a party. On Christmas Day we did not go out, and on Boxing Day we did not go out.

Did you not go to the Three Arrows on Boxing Day, 1964?—Yes.

How often did you go to the Three Arrows?—Every weekend.

Then how do you know you went on Boxing Day?—Because we went on Boxing Day because we did not go on Christmas Day.

I want to ask you about Wednesday, 6 October. Dave went round to your grandmother's house about 6.30, did he not?—Yes.

In fact, he went round three times that night?—Twice.

He went at 6.30 first of all, and came back about 7 to 7.30? Just think.—Yes, that is right.

And then he went again at about 8 o'clock?—Yes.

When he went round at 6.30 he took this note about the rent with him?—Yes.

MR HOOSON: My Lord, I should make it clear that matters that my learned friend is going to cross-examine to, I am going to adopt, but as a matter of convenience I leave it to him.

MR JUSTICE FENTON ATKINSON: That seems very sensible.

Cross-examined by MR HEILPERN:

Mrs Smith, I would like to know a little more about your financial arrangements.—There is not a lot to tell.

Let us just see, shall we? At the beginning of October 1965, you and your husband were desperately short of money?—Yes.

What did you work as?—A part-time machinist.

How much were you paid?—£4 10s [£4.50] a week.

How much did your husband earn?—About £8.

He hardly worked at all in the previous months, did he?—No.

As you told my learned friend, since these matters have arisen you are very well off financially?—Yes.

Tell me a bit more about it, would you? Are you part and parcel of this financial arrangement with the newspaper?—Yes. Whatever we get we share.

What are you getting?—Sometimes £10 a week, sometimes £15, sometimes £20.

Who decides?—David.

What does he do?—He just asks, can he have a bit more.

Does the financial arrangement stop there, or is there going to be a very large sum of money coming?—There is going to be a very large sum of money. It depends on syndication.

That means it is not only one newspaper, but a body of newspapers?—Yes, that is what syndication means.

Mrs Smith, I do not suppose it is very easy for you to remember details over the last year or so, is it?—No.

I want to ask you about the evidence you gave of the conversation with your sister about Ashton market. Ashton market is a very considerable distance away, is it not? Over six miles, I understand?—Yes.

Of course, very much nearer to where she was then living were other shops, other stores, other supermarkets?—Yes.

Do you know a supermarket close to where she lived called Adsega's? Is that in Cross Street, Gorton?—Yes.

There is nothing magic about diamond mesh pattern stockings, you can get them anywhere?—Yes.

I suggest to you that you got a little confused in your account, and that the place she went regularly to on Saturdays was the supermarket at Adsega's?—No, she used to tell me she had gone to Ashton market.

What is there so enthralling about Ashton market as compared with other markets?—She said things were cheaper there, and there were nicer things.

I want to go now to the night of 6 October 1965. Your husband took the note from the rent man with him when he went out?—For the first time. He said he was going to show it to Ian.

Did he want Ian's assistance in raising the money?—No. To get some advice as to whether we should get rid of the dog or whether we should keep it.

Are you telling my Lord and the jury that having received this urgent demand for money, your husband took the note to Ian Brady without any idea that he was going to ask him for help in raising this money?—It was because Ian knew about dogs.

The fact is that you were desperate for money?—Yes.

And that is why he went down to see Ian, is it?—No, not as far as I know.

Are you not in your husband's confidence?—He told me he had taken it round to Ian's to ask him about the dog, so I believed him.

Would you mind explaining what is meant by this in the note: 'If there are any more complaints of teddy boys and noise—'? (*Witness interrupts:*) Because the night before that, David had seen two people that he knew, and one had nowhere to go and it happened to be raining, so he let him stay the night. He left next morning, and the caretaker of the flats happened to see him.

This talks about 'teddy boys'?—There were two of them.

Now let us go on to the later hours, shall we? Some time about half-past eleven the buzzer went?—Yes.

Are you saying that you were both in bed?—Yes.

I suggest to you that that is not right, to start with?—That is right.

Do you say it was you who answered the telephone?—Yes.

It was your husband, was it not?—It was me that answered the telephone.

As soon as the buzzer went, at all events, your husband got out of bed?—No. I got out of bed and looked out of the window. He asked me who it was, and I said: 'It can't be Myra because the car isn't there.'

I merely asked you the fact; I did not ask about any conversation. All that I want to make clear is that before Myra arrived at the door of the flat, your husband was already out of bed?—Yes.

He was partly dressed?—Yes.

It was your husband who opened the door to Myra, was it not?—It was me.

I must suggest to you that in fact there was a conversation, although you may not have been there, between Myra and your husband to this effect: 'Will you slip round? Ian wants you'?—Not unless I was not there. I did not hear her say that, and I was there.

To which he replied: 'Right, I will get my shoes on'?—No.

Then there was a further conversation about this note?—I do not know.

Would you try to think? It is important.—I can't remember.

You have been telling us a lot of very tiny details that you remember. Try to remember this.—Dave asked her, could he have the note back, and she said: 'I have left it in the car.'

The note was produced, was it not?—No.

Your husband had brought it back with him?—No, he said Ian had kept it.

I suggest that you asked your husband to produce it, and you said: 'Show Myra the note'?—She said: 'Ian showed me the note,' and David asked her if she had it with her, and she said 'No'.

So there was a conversation about the note and the contents of it?—No, except for asking if he could have it back.

Are you saying that there was no conversation about what was in that note?—She asked where we were going to get the money from.

We are getting it by easy stages. Do you remember your husband's answer?—He said he was going to ask his dad for it.

And Myra said: 'Are you going to try and get a tap off my dad?'—I don't remember her saying that.

Did he not reply: 'Are you joking? I couldn't get a ha'penny out of him'?—Not that I can remember.

There is just one last matter I want to ask you about, Mrs Smith. You have told my Lord and the jury of some conversation you had with your sister relating to the disappearance of the child Downey. Had you mentioned that sort of thing to anybody else?—Yes, I mentioned it to my mother.

I am suggesting to you that you are confusing it with what you said to your mother?—No, to Myra. She had had a lot to drink, and that is why she laughed.

Had you had a certain amount to drink?—No, about three glasses of wine.

Did that make you at all sleepy or confused?—No.

Just one general question on your trips to the moors. In answer to my learned friend this morning, you said that you were taken up by the police, and the car stopped at a particular place, and you had stopped there before, but only rarely?—Yes.

You have stopped, I suppose, at dozens of places?—Well, it is all the same to me, the moors.

You may have stopped almost anywhere on the moors, but you do not really recall now?—No.

MR HOOSON: I understand that the last witness and the next witness have been brought here together and lunched together. I think that would be highly undesirable today, my Lord.

MR JUSTICE FENTON ATKINSON: Someone, I think, will arrange that they are not in contact over the adjournment until after he has given his evidence.

MR HOOSON: I am obliged, my Lord.

(*Mid-day adjournment*)

DAVID SMITH, *examined by* MR MARS-JONES: I was born on 9 January 1948. I live with my wife, Maureen Smith, at 18 Underwood Court, Hattersley. From about 1954 until about April last year I lived with my father at 13 Wiles Street, Gorton. After April 1965 I stayed at my grandfather's house at Aked Street, Ardwick, and at my mother-in-law's at 20 Eaton Street, Gorton. I moved to the flat at Underwood Court on 23 July 1965.

Look at the jury when you give your answers, please. Do you remember the day after you got married? There is no dispute about this apparently: you went up for the day to Windermere?—Yes.

On the way back, were you in the back of the van with Brady?—Yes.

Do you remember any reference being made either by you or by Brady to the subject of work?—Yes, sir. We had had quite a bit to drink. He just asked me what was my idea of work, and he said he was not too keen on it. It was just something to pass the time away, something that had to be done.

Do you remember an occasion early in 1965 when the question of work was again raised?—The only occasion that I can remember is when Brady asked me what I thought the ideal robbery was, and I told him a large supermarket using a removal van—a large van—and he laughed, and he mentioned a bank and said that was the only really big job worth going after—a bank; and nothing much more was said.

Was that subject mentioned again on a later occasion?—On lots of occasions it was mentioned very slightly, and a little later on I got interested in it. We agreed on robbing a bank, the three of us. He instructed me to keep a watch on one certain bank.

What did that involve?—I was driven down to a specified bank and told what to do, and I had to take notes of certain things—of arrivals and departures for a good three hours—and then meet him again and tell him what I had taken down.

Do you remember, in October of last year, being taken up to the moors in a police car?—Yes.

Was the police car stopped at some point?—Yes.

Where was that place?—Just where the two graves were of Downey and the lad.

Had you been there before?—Only once.

Tell us about the one occasion when you had been on this one side of the road where the reservoir is?—Well, it was Ian and Myra, myself and my wife Maureen. We were in the mini driving down the road, and Ian told her to stop the car. He said: 'It's only the reservoir but it looks nice with the moon shining on it. Shall we get out of the van?' Ian and myself walked off towards this reservoir. He told me to stop and he pointed out the reservoir, and we stayed there about ten minutes.

Did you see anything on that occasion?—Only the reservoir.

What about graves?—He was falling all over, but he seemed to know where he was. There was another occasion when we went past it. It was done for the purpose of testing guns.

Where did you go for that purpose?—On the moors, just a few miles past the graves.

Now was there any conversation between you and Brady about the use of those guns?—Yes, sir.

How long before the night when Evans was killed?—Roughly about four or six months before.

MR HOOSON: I do not see the relevance of a conversation four to six months earlier, unconnected with the events which we are investigating.

MR JUSTICE FENTON ATKINSON: Members of the jury, would you mind retiring?

The jury was absent from the court for twelve minutes (and the witness, DAVID SMITH, for part of that time), while the admissibility of the evidence was argued.

MR HOOSON *submitted that the evidence regarding the conversation was inadmissible because it had no relevance to any issue before the jury, and that even if it had slight relevance, its prejudicial effect was so great that it should be excluded.*

MR MARS-JONES *argued that the evidence was relevant because (a) it showed the way, and the fact, that Brady first raised the subject of killing; (b) it provided a possible motive for Brady's murder of Evans, namely, that he could kill a man in cold blood and was therefore a powerful ally in the proposed bank robbery; (c) it explained why Brady dared to murder Evans in the presence of Smith ('Having implicated Smith so fully in the proposed bank robbery . . . it was a very powerful deterrent for preventing*

Smith going to the police and telling what he had seen.'); (*d*) *it explained why Brady had told Smith about the murders that had already been committed, and the burial on the moors.*

MR JUSTICE FENTON ATKINSON: Mr Hooson, I am against you. I think all this side of the case is relevant as showing the background which existed between these two on the vital day of 6 October.

MR HOOSON: I am obliged, my Lord.

MR MARS-JONES: While the jury are absent, might I sound your Lordship on this point? There is at a later stage the question of the books. It is not my intention to put any books before the jury. I propose to deal with one book from which an extract was read.

MR HOOSON: It would become admissible in any event in re-examination, so I do not propose to take any objection.

MR JUSTICE FENTON ATKINSON: That solves that problem. But we are not going to have any lists? I suppose the titles are more sinister than the contents, if you were foolish enough to buy them.

MR MARS-JONES: I have not read any, my Lord.

MR JUSTICE FENTON ATKINSON: One was enough for me. Let us have the jury back.

MR MARS-JONES: Mr Smith, you were saying before the jury retired that there had been a conversation some four to six months before Evans was killed. Will you tell my Lord and the jury your recollection of that conversation? Don't go too fast.

MR JUSTICE FENTON ATKINSON: Just go at your own speed. Do not bother about me.

THE WITNESS: We were talking about the robbery and what sort of robbery it would be, and the way we were going about it, and what risks we would have to take, and Brady mentioned that guns would be carried, one by Myra and one by himself, and that they would be loaded with live ammunition. He called it a safeguard, an insurance, in case there was any obstruction, and then they would be used with the live ammunition in them.

What did you say?—I did not object to the carrying of the guns, but I did object to the use of live ammunition. I said I preferred blanks. He waved it aside by just laughing.

MR JUSTICE FENTON ATKINSON: Members of the jury, I want you to follow this: this evidence is not being called to show that Brady is just a bad man, a potential bank robber or something of that sort, but it really forms the background leading to various conversations to which this witness is going to testify, and lies behind what was the position between these two when you get to the evidence of 6 October. You must not use this against Brady by saying: 'He is a chap who might rob a bank and therefore would murder three children.' That is very different. I know you understand that.

MR MARS-JONES: Do you recognise these two guns? (*Exhibits produced to the witness.*)—Yes, sir. I have seen Brady use them, and I have used them myself.

Can you recall when was the next conversation between you and Brady, which was of significance in connection with this case?—He gave me instructions that whenever they decided to do the job at the bank, all writing materials, books, and things like that, were to be moved; and if I had any I was to let him have them so that he could dispose of them.

Now I want to go to Saturday, 25 September of last year, which is about a fortnight before Edward Evans was killed. On that evening did you stay up talking with the accused, Brady? —Yes. He mentioned the bank—what would happen if someone obstructed us, like, and that the guns would be used to move them, stop the obstruction. He mentioned that the bullets would have a mark on them. He asked me what my reaction would be if this was to happen. We had been drinking for a good four or five hours, and I thought it was the drink talking, and I looked at him and waited for him to carry on. He went on to say—he asked me if I was capable of using a gun or of murder.

What did you do or say?—I was the listening party, he held the stage, he was doing the talking. He went on to say that he had killed three or four people. This just convinced me that it was the beer talking. He leaned back and he said: 'You don't really believe me.' I must have smiled at him. Getting a bit tired, I was. And then he said: 'It will be done,' and a matter of a quarter of an hour later we were both asleep.

Did he give any indication as to how they had been killed?— I don't think it was on that occasion. He said the ages of the people were between fifteen and twenty-one, and the reason he gave was because when the police received missing-person reports between those ages they did not pay all that much attention. And he went on to say that he waited in the car until somebody came along, and then he just got out and did it. And another way he mentioned, the way he preferred, was to go out in the car, wait in a place and pick somebody up, and take them back to the house and do it in the house. He preferred that way because any evidence against him was in the house, and he could get rid of it in his own time.

Did he at any time before the Evans killing occurred say what had happened to persons he had killed?—Yes, he said they were buried on the moors.

Was anything said about the preparations which he made before he attempted to kill?—Yes, that was mentioned. All his clothes would be brushed and cleaned and inspected, everything would be listed that he had on, and he said he took a drug, Pro-Plus, as a stimulant.

Was anything said to you about photographs?—He mentioned that he had photographic proof of his killings.

Now I want you to come, if you will, to Saturday, 2 October, which was the Saturday before Evans was killed. Was there any mention of the subject which had been raised on the previous Saturday?—Yes. He mentioned roughly what he had mentioned the week before, and I didn't believe him. He just leaned over and said: 'I have killed three or four and I'll do another one, but I'm not due for another one for three months. But it will be done and it won't count.'

I want you to come to Tuesday, 5 October of last year, the day before Evans was killed. You mentioned instructions that had been given about certain books that you had. Did anything happen to those books on that Tuesday before the killing?—Yes. I wrapped them up and took them round to Wardle Brook Avenue.

Why did you take them round on that day?—Because Ian had asked for them.

About what time did he ask for those books?—I think it was round about six or seven o'clock.

When you got into the house in Wardle Brook Avenue, what

happened to your parcel?—It was taken off me by Myra. She placed it on the living-room table.

What happened then?—Ian came downstairs. Myra told him that I had brought it round, and he just took it upstairs. After about two minutes he came down with two suitcases. Those were taken outside and handed over to Myra and placed in the mini-van. Then they drove away.

Was anything said when you were getting these suitcases into the mini-van?—I picked one of them up, and as I handed it over the wall to Myra, Ian said: 'Whatever you do, don't drop it, or it will blow us all up.'

Who was driving the van when it was driven off?—Myra.

Have you ever seen anyone else drive it?—No.

Now I want to come back to the subject of the books. Was there a particular book which you and the accused had a discussion about?—Yes, sir. *The Life and Ideals of the Marquis de Sade*.

Was there any occasion when he read any part of it to you?—Yes.

(*Exhibit produced to the witness*.) Can you find in that book the part that was read to you? Just look, please, at page 140 to start with: do you recognise that?—Yes.

Who does that book belong to?—This was Ian's.

Is there a mark on it at that page?—Yes, I think I put that.

Does the passage read as follows? 'Should murder be punished by murder? Undoubtedly not. The only punishment that a murderer should be condemned to is that which he risks from his friends or the family of the man he has killed. "I pardon him," said Louis XV to Charolais, "but I also pardon him who will kill you." All the bases of the law against murderers is contained in that sublime sentence. (Salic Law punished murder with a fine.) In a word, murder is a horror, but a horror often necessary, never criminal, and essential to tolerate in a republic. Above all it should never be punished by murder.'—Yes.

How long before Evans was killed was that read out to you?— I cannot say exactly—about three weeks.

What had been said on the subject of the Marquis de Sade?— Ian had said that he was an admirer of his works, he enjoyed reading them. He said he was a good author and they were good books.

All the books that you took across to 16 Wardle Brook Avenue, who did they belong to?—A few of them were mine.

How did you come to acquire those?—I was recommended to buy that type of book by Ian.

Mr Smith, I want you, if you will, to deal with the events of Wednesday, 6 October. What was the first occasion that you went to 16 Wardle Brook Avenue?—It would be round about eight o'clock or a quarter to eight. I went round there with a note about our dog that I had received from the rent man. I showed Ian Brady the letter. He studied it and just said: 'There is nothing you can do about it.'

When you got there, what was he doing?—He was just getting ready to go out.

What about Myra?—Myra was doing her hair.

When you left, did you see what happened to the two accused? —They drove away in the car.

Was your wife at home when you got back?—Yes.

What time did you go to bed?—It would be about eleven o'clock.

What was the next thing that happened?—Just after 11.30 the inter-com rang.

What happened then?—My wife answered it. She came to the bedroom and told me who it was. I got out of bed. I put on my jeans, a pair of socks, and a pair of mocassins, and a waistcoat, and I went into the living room, and a knock came on the door. Maureen let Myra into the flat, and she was more or less talking to Maureen, she wasn't talking to me. I was stroking the dog. She said she had come round over something to do with a message for her mother, and she said: 'Will you walk me round to Wardle Brook Avenue, because all the street lights are out.' So I put my coat on, and I walked over and took my walking stick—my dog stick—and I walked out of the flat with Myra.

Do you recognise that? (*Stick produced to the witness.*)—Yes, sir, that is my stick.

Was it any different on that night to what it is now?—Yes. That part of it *there* had about four inches of string bound round it, and there was a little loop to put my wrist in to hold it.

When you got to a place somewhere near the house, what happened?—Myra stopped walking and she said: 'While you're here, Ian's got some miniature wine bottles and you might as well have them. Just wait over the road and I will switch the landing light three times, and you will know that he is not doing anything, and you can come up.'

I want you to say in your own words, at your own pace, the whole story from then on.—Well, I was waiting less than half a minute and the landing light flicked on and off three times. I knocked on the door and it was opened by Ian. Before I could say anything, he said in a loud voice: 'Have you come for those wine bottles?' I said 'Yes'; so with that he walked straight into the kitchen. He placed three wine bottles by a small table next to the stove, and he said: 'Do you want the rest of them?' I said 'Yes', and he went into the living room. It was a matter of ten seconds, maybe, then all of a sudden I heard a very loud scream, very loud, and it sort of went on. Just before it died out another scream followed it. And then I heard Myra shout out: 'Dave, help him.' I did not know what was going on. I ran out of the kitchen and into the living room, and I just froze, I stopped dead. My first thoughts were that Ian had hold of a life-sized rag doll and was just waving it about. The arms were going all over. Then it dawned on me that it was not a rag doll. It fell against the couch not more than two feet away from me. My stomach turned over. It was half screaming and groaning. The lad was laid out on his front and Ian stood over him with his legs apart with an axe in his right hand. The lad groaned and Ian just lifted the axe over his head and brought it down upon the lad's head. There were a couple of seconds of silence and the lad groaned again, only very much lower. Ian lifted the axe way above his head again and brought it down. The lad stopped groaning then. He was making a gurgling noise like when you brush your teeth and gargle with water. Ian placed a cover over his head. He had a piece of electric wire, and he wrapped it round the lad's neck and began to pull it; and he was saying: 'You fucking dirty bastard,' over and over again. The lad just stopped making this noise and Ian looked up and said to Myra: 'That's it. It is the messiest yet.' He just stood up then and he told Myra to go and get some old rags, soapy water in a bucket, and also a mop.

Just pause there. Now, when you got into the room, when all this first started, did you see anybody else there?—Yes, Myra.

Can you tell us whether the accused, Myra Hindley, was there from the time you first saw her when you got into the room, until it was all over, when he said: 'It is the messiest yet'?—I could not swear to that.

What happened to your dog stick?—I dropped it.

Did you at any time use that stick on Evans?—No, sir.

Did you kick him or offer him any other kind of violence from start to finish?—No, sir.

Will you tell us what kind of impression Brady created upon you as you watched him?—Well, I have seen butchers working in shops showing as much emotion as he did when they were cutting up sheeps' ribs. He was very calm indeed. He was not in a frenzy—no frenzy at all.

I want to go back to your story. Will you tell the jury, please, what happened next?—Myra went out of the room to get the rags and cleaning-up water. Ian picked up the axe and walked over to me, and he said: 'Just feel the weight of that. How did he take it?' I held it in my hand and just nodded at him. He took it back and placed it on the hearth. There was a small coffee table next to the fireplace on which there was a bottle of wine, and he picked that up and took a mouthful and passed it to me. I took a mouthful. Then he lit a cigarette and Myra came in. He asked Myra if she thought anybody had heard anything, and she said her gran had shouted downstairs, and Myra had shouted up that she had dropped the tape-recorder on her toe. We set about, all three of us, rubbing the walls down and the floor. He was really going to work on it, rubbing round the door and round the top of the door. He then told Myra to get something. I don't know whether she was upset. Myra went into the kitchen, but she came back with some blankets and some big sheets of polythene. She gave them to Ian and he laid them on the floor. We lifted Evans up and placed him on them. Ian picked the string off the handle of my stick, and then Ian and myself tied Edward Evans up, his body. We then covered him up with the sheets of polythene, and he was carried upstairs into the bedroom. After all the cleaning was done, the house was really spotless, and Myra went into the kitchen and brewed a pot of tea. I sat on one end of the couch and Ian on the other end. Myra sat next to the fireplace in her gran's chair, the armchair, and she had her feet on the mantlepiece top, and we had tea. Myra said to Ian: 'You should have seen the look on his face—the blow registered in his eyes.' Ian then went between the sofa and the wall—there is a fairly good gap—and he came up behind the sofa and showed how he raised the axe above his head and brought it down, and he said he was amazed because Evans had half raised himself and then plopped, and he was amazed because it should only take one blow. And Myra said: 'Do you remember the time we were on the moors and we had that body in the back?' Ian just looked at her. She went on: 'The time when the policeman came up.' She smiled and she looked at me then. She was talking to me and she said: 'I was sat in the mini-van alone, and Ian was over the ridge and he was digging a grave, and then the police car stopped and the policeman walked up to me and said: "What's the trouble?".' She said she was praying that he didn't walk over the top, and she said to him: 'My plugs are wet and I'm just drying them out,' and the policeman went away. Then Ian was sat there rubbing his ankle, and he said: 'I have knocked my ankle again.' Myra sort of shrugged, and he was complaining because he would not be able to move the body of Evans that night. Myra then turned round and said to me: 'You have a pram, don't you, Dave?' I did have a pram, and I told her it was at my grandfather's in Ardwick. I agreed to meet them after work next day and get the pram and bring it back. This is about three o'clock. I said: 'I will have to be going now,' and they nodded. I ran all the way home.

I have asked you about one or two matters which arise in the account you have given. Do you know, one way or the other, whether there were any rugs on the floor when all this was going on?—Yes, sir.

There were?—Yes, sir.

We have seen how eventually the body was found with the knees up and the head down, almost done up into a ball. Who worked out the method of tying him up?—Brady.

Did you notice anything about Edward Evans's clothing?—Yes, sir. His jeans' zip was down.

Was it partly down or fully down?—It was all the way down.

When you got ready to lift him, did Brady say anything?—He just looked up as we took the strain, and he turned round and said: 'Eddie's a dead weight.' That struck Ian and Myra as a joke and they started laughing.

Did you feel it was funny?—No. I was sick. My humour is not that bad.

What did you see done with the axe?—It was put in a shopping bag.

Did Brady put anything else inside that bag?—A wallet, and the shoes next, all in the same bag.

Did he take anything out of the wallet?—He just pulled out a green card and he showed it to me, and it was printed 'Edward Evans' and what looked like an insurance number and 'apprentice engineer' under it, and he then placed it back.

What did you do after you got home?—I went into the bedroom with Maureen. We got into bed. She turned the light off and I just got up and turned it on again and told her.

Where did you go when you left the flat?—We went down the road for the telephone, and I made a 'phone call to the police. I think it was about six o'clock. We did not want to hang about, I wanted to speed them up a bit, so we waited for a few minutes and then I made another call. Eventually, the police car arrived, and we were driven to Hyde police station.

Did you go anywhere near 16 Wardle Brook Avenue on Boxing Day, 1964?—No, sir.

Had you ever seen or heard of Lesley Ann Downey before her pictures appeared in the papers?—No, sir.

Have you ever seen a boy called John Kilbride?—No, sir.

MR MARS-JONES: I think that is all I wish to ask this witness in chief.

MR HOOSON: I think it is desirable, my Lord, that the cross-examination should be all in one, starting first thing in the morning.

(*The witness retired.*)

POLICE CONSTABLE JOHN ANTROBUS *of the Cheshire Constabulary, employed on motor patrol duties, testified that, on 7 October 1965, he had driven to a telephone call box in Hattersley Road West, arriving there at 6.15 am.* 'I was approached by David Smith, who was accompanied by his wife. He was very agitated and very upset. I drove them to Hyde police station, where they were dealt with by other officers.'

EDITH EVANS *testified that her son, Edward Evans, left home between 6.15 pm and 6.30 pm on 6 October 1965; he said that he was going to a football match at Old Trafford, Manchester. The following day, she identified the body of her son at Hyde public mortuary.*

GEORGE SMITH, *licensee of Auntie's Bar, Oxford Road, Manchester, gave evidence of seeing Edward Evans in the bar at about seven o'clock in the evening of 6 October 1965.* 'I had known him about three or four months. It was very unusual for him to come in on his own. When I last saw him, he was alone.'

POLICE SUPERINTENDENT ROBERT TALBOT *of the Cheshire Constabulary, in charge of the Stalybridge Division*: At 8.20 am on Thursday, 7 October 1965, as a result of information received from David Smith, I went with other police officers to 16 Wardle Brook Avenue. I borrowed a white coat from a bread roundsman, also a basket, in order to get near the premises without arousing suspicion.

I knocked at the back door, and Myra Hindley opened it. I said to her: 'Is your husband in?' She replied: 'I haven't got a husband.' I said to her: 'I am a police superintendent, and I have reason to believe there is a man in this house.' I opened the white coat to show my uniform. She replied: 'There is no man here.' I said to her: 'I am not satisfied. I want to come in.' I walked into the kitchen and she said: 'He is in the other room in bed.'

I was then joined by Detective Sergeant Carr, and we went into the front room, where I saw Ian Brady lying on a divan bed. He was undressed except for a vest and was writing. I said: 'I have received a report that an act of violence took place in this house last night, and we are investigating it.' Myra Hindley said: 'There was nothing wrong here.' Brady sat silent. I said to her: 'Who lives in this house?' She said: 'My gran—she is upstairs in bed—myself and Ian.' I said to her: 'I am going to search the house. Have you any objection?' She said: 'No.'

I went upstairs with Myra Hindley, where I saw a bedroom which was occupied by the grandmother. I tried the door of the remaining bedroom and found it to be locked. I said to Myra: 'What is in this room?' She replied: 'I keep my firearms in there and I always keep this door locked.' I said: 'Can I have the key?' She replied: 'It is at work.'

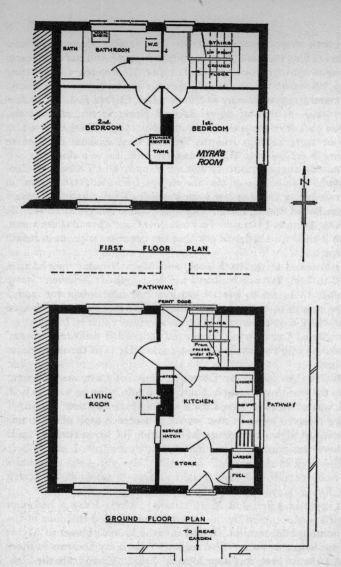

Floor plan of 16 Wardle Brook Avenue

I then went downstairs with her, and in the presence of Brady I said: 'There is a locked room upstairs, and I will have to search it. Have you got the key here?' Brady did not reply, but Myra said again: 'It is at work.' I said: 'Will you get your coat on, and we will take you by car to work and bring you back.' She replied: 'I don't want to go. It's not convenient.' I said: 'I am afraid you must get the key. I am not leaving this house until I have searched that bedroom.' She then became silent and looked at Brady for some time. I again requested her to go and get her coat, and she looked at Brady again and said: 'Well, you had better tell him.' Brady then stood up and said: 'There was a row last night. It's in the back bedroom. Give them the keys.' Myra gave me a bunch of keys.

I went upstairs and unlocked the door and saw that the room was furnished with a single bed, wardrobe, table and chair. Underneath the window, on the floor, was a bundle wrapped in a dark-coloured blanket. I went to it and saw the shape of a human foot sticking out of the bundle. There were some books lying on top of the body. There was a carrier bag beside the body, which contained, amongst other things, a hatchet. A stick was lying on the floor.

Sergeant Carr then joined me in the bedroom. We both went downstairs. Sergeant Carr said to Brady: 'We have found a body in the back bedroom, and I am taking you to Hyde police station for further inquiries to be made.' He cautioned Brady, who nodded his head and said: 'Yes, I know.'

I immediately sent for Dr Ellis of Hyde to examine the body, and he arrived shortly afterwards and pronounced life extinct. I examined the bedroom and found two loaded revolvers; each gun was fully loaded.

FOURTH DAY   *Friday, 22 April*

DAVID SMITH, *recalled. Cross-examined by* MR HOOSON:
Smith, have you received an undertaking by the prosecution that you will not be prosecuted in respect of any offence disclosed by you in your statements?—Yes, sir.

Is it right that you have entered into an arrangement with a newspaper whereby you will have a very large sum in certain eventualities?—Yes, sir.

And do the certain eventualities include the conviction of Brady and Hindley?—I should imagine that would be the —

So you have a vested financial interest, have you not, and have had since November, in their conviction?—Yes.

Do you mind telling us the name of the newspaper with whom you have entered into this arrangement?—No, sir.

Well, I am asking you to tell us.—(*No answer.*)

MR JUSTICE FENTON ATKINSON: Come on. You know the name. Tell it to us.—I don't know if the newspaper would wish me to do that.

They may have some questions to answer about this. Who are they?—I'm sorry, sir. I can't answer that.

MR HOOSON: Who told you that you could not answer that?— I would like to see —

Who told you that you could not answer that?—Nobody told me.

Answer it, then.—I can't answer that question, sir.

Why?—I don't think the newspaper wishes to be involved in it.

Tell me why you cannot answer that question. You have been receiving their money.—(*No answer.*)

MR JUSTICE FENTON ATKINSON: You must tell us.—I can't answer that question, sir.

MR HOOSON: You heard my Lord say you must tell us.—I refuse to answer the question unless I have the sanction of the newspaper.

What do you mean, 'have the sanction of the newspaper'? You are here to give evidence in a case, not to obey the directions of a newspaper.—I am not obeying any directions of a newspaper.

MR JUSTICE FENTON ATKINSON: Mr Hooson, it seems to me that there is no point in taking steps against him for contempt of court in refusing to answer, because you have got to ask him about a lot more relevant matters. But Mr Attorney, is this not a matter which requires investigation?

THE ATTORNEY-GENERAL: My Lord, the investigation will take place immediately.

MR JUSTICE FENTON ATKINSON: It sounds to me like a gross interference with the course of justice. (*To* MR HOOSON:) I think you should pass on to something else.

MR HOOSON: I pass on from that name, but I want to ask you this: is the arrangement for you to supply information for articles to be written about this case?—Information is involved in it.

Was there a ghost writer?—I don't know.

You see, you used phrases yesterday—you talked about 'a body like a rag doll': those were not your phrases, were they?—Yes.

At the time that we are concerned with, 6 October, you were very hard up, were you not?—I was short of money.

For example, on that day you were not working?—That is correct.

How did you live when you were unemployed?—Off my father, mostly.

I want to question you about the events of the night of 6 October—just on your version for the moment. You described how you heard a scream. You went into the living room and saw Brady wielding an axe and an object on the floor. What did you do to stop it?—I didn't do anything. I've said this all along. I didn't do anything.

Just have a look at that stick, will you? (*Exhibit produced to the witness.*) The lower two-thirds of that stick was the following morning wet with blood.—Yes.

On that stick were hairs from Edward Evans's head?—Yes.

Can you explain how they got there?—I should imagine it was some time in the struggle his head struck the stick, which wasn't in my hand.

You have been very prone to violence yourself, have you not?—I have a police record of violence.

Let us take this year. In March did you attack a boy with a chain?—I was provoked extremely and the police did not take any action.

It has been suggested in this case that Brady was corrupting you. You did not know Brady, for example, as a young boy, at the age of eleven, in 1959? You were convicted of wounding with intent then, were you not?—I was attacked.

I want you to look at your own notebook. (*Exhibit produced to the witness.*) Is it divided into three parts: in the first part there is a list of books; then some notes in the second part and some extracts from the books; but the third part, are they notes of your thoughts and reflections?—Could I just read it for a moment?

Have you had a look at them?—I am still reading it.

MR JUSTICE FENTON ATKINSON: I think he has read it now.

MR HOOSON: Are those your own notes, reflections of your views on life?—I was beginning to write a book.

Just look at page 23. You refer to: 'Three authors, three books, three different dates, all writing about sexual pleasure in perversion. . . .' I do not want to go through all this stuff with you. Then you go on, about the fourth sentence: 'Every man or woman is one of two things, a masochist or a sadist, only a few practise what they feel. . . .' Are those your views?—Well, they do practise what they feel.

Look at the next page: 'Perversion is the way a man thinks, the way he feels, the way he lives. People are like maggots, small, blind, worthless fish bait. . . . Rape is not a crime, it's a state of mind. Murder is a hobby and a supreme pleasure.'—That is not entirely mine. That is what I could surmise as the meaning of the Marquis de Sade.

'God is a disease, a plague, a weight around a man's neck.' Are those your views?—Yes.

'A disease which eats away his instincts. God is a superstition, a cancer, a man-made cancer, which is injected into the brain in the form of religion.' Those are your views?—On the subject of religion.

'You live for one thing, a supreme pleasure in everything you do. Sadism is the supreme pleasure.'—There again I was surmising the words of de Sade.

'Look around. Watch the fools doing exactly what their fathers did before them. The Book, they live by the Book.' These were your views, were they not?—A number of them.

We see in the earlier part that you copied a long list of books, then you made private notes. Then you have got extracts from two or three books—from *Justine*, *The Carpetbaggers*, *Eternal Fire*—and then you write your own notes, and I have only quoted parts of them today. Did you take the view that murder was a hobby?—No, sir.

Well, why did you write it?—I was just writing down my view of what de Sade was trying to put over.

Are you telling the jury that your views on religion, on God, and so on, in those passages are your own?—I think every man has his own views on religion, and they are my own.

But do I understand you to mean that your views on religion, and so on, *here*, are your own, but your views on murder and sadism are not your own?—That is correct.

You had books on violence and perversion before you ever met Brady?—Not on perversion, no. I had the normal kind of books.

You had books on violence before you met Brady?—Not solely dealing with violence, no.

Look at the second part of this document. There is an extract beginning with the words: 'Should murder be punished with murder? Undoubtedly not,' and so on. When did you write that out?—After Brady read it to me.

I suggest that Brady never read it to you.—You are mistaken. Brady did read it to me.

You did not like work?—I don't think anybody likes work.

I am not concerned with what anybody else thinks. What did you think? You did not like work?—I enjoy certain kinds of work.

Why were you usually out of a job?—I usually got sacked.

For what reason?—Sickness. Mostly tonsillitis.

And your employers generally sacked you because of tonsillitis?—Not because of tonsillitis, but because I had it so regular.

Regular tonsillitis. I see. Did you ever tell Brady of the thoughts that you had written here?—No.

You told us that your views on people written here were your own. Now all that is left in this document are your views on murder and sadism?—These are not my views.

Let us see if you are really going to try and maintain this. 'Every man and woman is one of two things, a masochist or a sadist. Only a few practise what they feel, the remainder, because some organisation says it is wrong and they fear some mighty indestructible force, rather sit back and rot away until the end. These people enjoy what they are told to enjoy, they feel the way they are taught to feel, they live the way they are taught is the proper way of living; they breed the way one man tells them to breed. They live by laws that were made thousands of years ago, and they fear the God they are taught is kind and loving.' Are those your views up to there?—They are my views about people.

Let us take the very next sentence: 'People are like maggots, small, blind, worthless fish bait.' You have already told us those were your views?—Yes.

So it is the one sentence which is not your view: 'Perversion is the way a man thinks, the way he feels, the way he lives'?— And the one about rape.

I am coming to that. 'Rape is not a crime, it's a state of mind.' Was that your view?—No, sir.

Then you say: 'Murder is a hobby and a supreme pleasure.' Whose views are those?—I should imagine de Sade's.

Did you accept that view?—No, sir.

You disputed it?—I didn't accept it or dispute it.

Do you mind telling the jury why you pick those two or three sentences out as not your views when the rest are?—When reading a book that I don't understand, I always try and re-write it so that I can understand what the author is trying to put over.

Towards the latter part of 1964, did you have discussions with Brady about how to get money without working?—Yes.

Did you tell Brady that you could make money by selling pornographic photographs?—No, sir.

You are smiling. Why smile?—Because it is the first I have ever heard of it.

Did you have a discussion at some time when you thought that you could raise some money by what you described in your words as 'rolling a queer'?—No.

What does it mean?—Robbing a homosexual. I should think nearly everybody knows what that means.

I suggest to you that towards the end of 1964 you were very keen on making money by selling pornographic photographs?— No, sir.

And that you suggested to Brady, as you knew he had got a camera, that he might take some, and he agreed?—No, sir.

Did you not say that you could get a girl to pose?—No.

Did you mention a girl called Madeleine?—No, sir.

On Boxing Day of 1964 you brought a girl to the house of Brady and Hindley, did you not?—No.

That girl was Lesley Ann Downey?—No, sir.

Do you have a friend called Keith?—I know a boy called Keith. He's not exactly a friend. I know of him.

Did you tell Brady on Boxing Day, 1964, that the girl had been brought by a man in a van and his name was Keith?—No.

Was not that girl brought to the house in a dark van?—I don't know, sir. I don't know how she got to the house.

I suggest that there was a conversation between you, when Brady said that the girl you had brought was too young for the photographs?—No.

Then you said that there was a market for that kind of stuff?—I don't know anything about markets for pornographic film.

I suggest you stayed in that house while photographs were taken of the girl upstairs. You were downstairs and you went later on the landing. And at 7.30 you left with that girl in the van?—I was in Manchester. I spent an hour in a public house called the Three Arrows.

What time do you say you were there?—From about nine-ish.

What day of the week was it?—I don't know, sir.

How do you remember it clearly, then?—I have had it almost drummed into me by the police and it is very hard to forget.

What do you mean, you have 'had it almost drummed into you by the police'?—They have asked questions about it, and things.

What do you mean, 'and things'?—More questions.

How do you remember where you were that night?—Because it was Boxing Night.

You had a small child then?—That is correct.

And your mother-in-law had not got that child that night?—My mother-in-law is a liar.

When did you decide that?—She is a liar if she said that. My father saw us walking round from my mother-in-law's with the baby on Boxing Night.

Now I want you to go to the discussions you say you had with Brady about robbing a bank. They were never in Hindley's presence?—That is correct.

You were very anxious to make money without working?— I should imagine I would have kept on working after the robbery.

What? As before?—When I was employed, yes, sir.

Do you remember having a discussion with Brady once about this at a public house called the Wagon and Horses?—Yes.

And you told Brady that you would be prepared to kill for money?—No, sir.

Do you remember after your baby died—that was in April 1965?—Yes.

One Saturday night you went round, I think, with your wife to see Brady and Hindley and then you all drove up late at night on to the moors?—Yes.

And you had had a very great deal to drink? I am not criticising you for this. I am simply putting it as a fact.—I had a great deal to drink, but I wasn't drunk.

I think the position was that you drove up and stopped for a very short time so that you and Brady could relieve yourselves, did you not?—No, sir.

You both went to look at the moon shining on the reservoir?— That is correct.

This discussion about robbing a bank, was it over many months?—Over a long period of time. I couldn't exactly say how long.

I suggest to you that never at any time was there a mention of using live bullets in a raid on a bank?—That is not true.

And never at any time was there any mention by Brady of having killed three or four people?—He did say that.

There was a discussion at the end of September about the bank. You had had too much to drink and you were sick in the toilet.—I was sick, yes.

Do you remember speaking to Brady when you were lying on the bed getting over your sickness?—That is correct, sir, yes. I had got drunk that night because I had a dog which had been destroyed and I mentioned it to Ian and they came round, Myra and Ian came round, that night. Ian walked into the bedroom and he asked me if I was all right. Then he turned round and he said: 'It's that bleeder who should have got the needle and not the dog.'

You were angry with your father over something?—I wasn't

angry with him—not that I can remember. I was upset about the dog.

Who had done away with the dog? Your father?—He hadn't done away with it: he had had it humanely destroyed.

What had led to the destruction of the dog? Was it something your father had done?—Not that he had done. He was, unfortunately, out of work—working in London.

Did you say out of work?—It was a slip of the tongue. I am positive he was working in London.

Before he went to London, was he out of work?—Yes.

Did he have to give up the tenancy of the house in Manchester because he was evicted for non-payment of rent because he was out of work?—I don't think he was evicted. I think he left.

How long had he been out of work? Was it for a period of months?—It might have been a week, days, months. I couldn't say.

He certainly was not in a position to provide you with money, was he?—He didn't provide me with money every week.

You were very angry with him for taking the dog to be destroyed?—I was upset about it.

And when you were lying on that bed, you told Brady that you were going to do your old man in?—No, sir. I don't recollect saying anything, except I was upset.

That is all?—That is all. Myra went out of her way to try and save the dog. She drove all the way down to the dogs' home to—

—try and stop it?—Yes. She was just too late.

Was the dog with your father at that time?—The dog was in the house on its own because my father was working in London.

Was the dog at that time living, as it were, with your father?—Yes.

Well, it could not have been in London, could it?—The dog was living at the house.

Where your father lived?—Where he was a tenant.

What day of the week was it when your father took the dog to the vet?—(*No answer*.)

I suggest that nothing was said to you by Brady about having photographs of graves, either.—Pardon? He didn't say he had photographs of graves: he said he had photographic proof.

I want to go now to the conversation of 2 October. By this

time, were you and Brady discussing breaking into the offices of the Electricity Board?—That was mentioned. It was used as an example of the kind of job.

Did not Brady tell you on 2 October that if you were going to do it, both of you would have to take anything incriminating away and put it in a suitcase?—I haven't a very good head for dates, but he did say that—that we would have to when we did a bank job.

It was in relation to the Electricity Board, was it not?—No, a bank.

On that night there was no suggestion by Brady that he had killed other people or that he was not due for another one for another three months, as you have suggested he said.—He did say that.

Do you remember, that night you played a tape recording to Brady, reciting something from a book on Goering, I think?—Yes, it was one of his favourite subjects.

Did you take round a cosh on the Tuesday, 5 October, and ask him to put that in the suitcase? That is yours, is it not? (*Exhibit produced to the witness.*)—No. It was mine at one time, but it's not mine now. It belongs to Myra Hindley, it doesn't belong to me. I gave it to Myra Hindley.

Who put that lashing of string on it?—I wrapped it up, yes, with string.

In exactly the same way as you would put lashing on a stick?—There is no special way. You just wrap it round.

I want to ask you about Wednesday, 6 October. Had you got another dog by then?—Yes.

Look at the note from the rent collector. (*Exhibit produced to the witness.*) Was it on the Wednesday that you took it round to see Brady?—Yes.

You were desperately anxious for money at that time?—Not really, no.

Well, how were you going to pay the rent?—I wasn't worried about it. I could have got the money within three or four days.

From whom?—My father.

We have heard that he had just moved to London.—That is correct. He was a maintenance fitter.

At the end of September, when your first dog died, he was

still in Manchester, was he not?—He worked in London for quite a time.

If your father would provide the money just like that, why had you not paid the rent earlier?—Because I had not asked him earlier.

So you were not worried about the rent?—Not unduly.

I suggest that that is absolutely untrue.—I am never worried about money troubles.

Why?—I just don't think it's worth worrying about. You grow old that way.

For what purpose did you want to rob a bank?—For money.

Why did you want money if you had no worries about money? —When I say I had no worries about it, I love having money, of course, but I don't worry about owing money.

You were being threatened in this letter with legal proceedings, and you knew you might lose the tenancy because of it?—Not really. They usually issue about eight or nine of those before they do anything.

On the Wednesday evening you went round to see Brady, first of all, at 6.30—you were anxious to raise some money from Mrs Maybury, the grandmother?—No.

You had borrowed money from her before—at least, your wife has?—The fantastic amount of two shillings for the electric meter, yes.

And you were hoping to get some money from her to meet this? —What, fourteen pounds? No, sir.

You asked Hindley if gran was home and she told you that she was out?—She was out visiting.

You then went home and you came round again at eight. You showed the note to Brady, did you not?—That is correct. The reason I showed him the note had nothing to do with the rent. I have already said the rent money didn't have me worried: it was the bit about the dog I was worried about.

Did you not suggest to Brady that you might get that money by, to use your own words, 'rolling a queer'?—No, sir. No.

Did Brady tell you that he was going out?—He didn't say he was going out, no.

I want to ask you now about the later events of that evening. Mr Smith, you said yesterday that you had some arrangement.

Hindley was going to flick lights. Three lights were going to be flicked to you.—They were going to be flicked three times.

You see, in the previous evidence about this, she told you they were going to be flicked twice, and they were flicked twice.— Three times, she said.

Have you been trying to learn a statement off by heart?— No.

Brady opened the front door—at least we are agreed about that—but as soon as the door was opened, Brady nodded at the living room to indicate there was someone in there?—No, sir.

And you nodded back?—No, sir.

And you tapped the stick that you carried in the palm of your hand?—No, sir.

Then you went into the kitchen?—That is correct.

Was Hindley in the kitchen?—No, me and Brady.

I suggest that the first thing you heard from the living room was some shouting, not screaming?—No, some screaming.

As if there was a scuffle there?—No, sir.

And Hindley opened the door and shouted 'Dave'?—'Dave, help me.'

And you rushed into the sitting room with your stick?—That is correct—in my hand.

Why did you take a stick?—It's a usual habit with me. It's purely nerves.

I suggest that you rushed in and you hit Evans on the head with the stick first of all?—No, sir.

And at that stage Brady had not hit him with a hatchet at all.— No, sir, that is wrong.

Then it is not disputed that Brady picked up the hatchet and hit Evans with the hatchet?—That is wrong, that, sir. He already had it in his hand. He was already striking him when I went into the room.

The truth is that you were hitting Evans and kicking him.— The truth is that Brady was hitting Evans with the axe.

You know that on that stick were found a lot of blood and hairs from Evans's head?—I have been told this.

You certainly did not see Brady ever use that stick, did you?— No, sir. Nobody used that stick.

What did you do with the stick?—I dropped it. It just dropped. I must have opened my hand.

You carried that stick looped so (*demonstrating*) over your arm?—No.

What was the point of having a loop?—If I ever went into the valley. It's very hilly. You can open your hand and don't lose your stick.

I suggest that you had the stick in your hand, that it was looped over, and you were using it.—No.

Hindley, as far as you know—and I am suggesting to you that this is absolutely right—was not in the room?—I can't swear she was in the room. That is correct.

Did you say to Brady, brandishing your stick, 'Imagine trying to hit him with this'?—No, sir.

What did you say to Brady?—I didn't say anything.

Not a word?—Not a word.

Not a single comment?—Not a single comment.

Did you not say to him: 'I kept calling him a bastard. I don't know why I called him that'?—No, sir.

Did you put a newspaper under Evans's head?—No.

Did you then see Brady put a cushion cover under his head?—Under his head?

He put it round the back of Evans's head and you used the flex to tie the cushion cover on.—I saw him use the flex to strangle him.

I am suggesting that you put the flex round the neck to tie the cushion cover on.—No.

By that time, it appeared the body was dead, but you actually used the flex?—No.

Did you not take Edward Evans's wallet out of his pocket and open it and say: 'Christ, it's empty'?—No, sir.

Did you take a green card from that wallet and say: 'He's only earning £4 a week. He's an apprentice'?—No.

Up to this point, what had you said?—Nothing.

I suggest that after Brady cut the string off the stick, he wiped the stick and you said: 'I don't want that. We had better destroy it'?—No.

You helped to clean up at the house. What did you say when you were cleaning up?—Nothing. I just cleaned up.

I suggest that this is quite untrue—that you in fact were discussing with them cleaning it up. There was a discussion, 'What on earth would we do with a body?', and there was a discussion about how to tie the body, all of which you took part in with Brady. —No, sir.

Did you have a graze somewhere on your leg?—Yes.

Did you tell Brady about it?—No. I was rubbing it and he asked me.

What did you say?—I said: 'My leg's cut.'

That is the first bit of conversation we have had, then, that you took part in. What was said about how you got your leg cut? —Nothing, sir. There was no discussion about it.

How did you get it cut?—I felt something hit my leg and, later on, realised it was the axe.

Then you and Brady wrapped up the body?—Yes.

It was you who said, going up the stairs, 'This is what you would call a dead weight'?—No, sir.

Was there any discussion as to what to do with the body?— No.

I suggest to you that Brady wrote a list in your presence.— No. He wrote nothing at all when I was in the house.

Did you have no comment to make at all about what had happened?—No, sir. I wanted to get out of the house.

What did they say to you when they said you had to leave?— I had to leave? It wasn't them that said I had to leave. I said that. Ian said: 'All right.' He opened the door for me.

No concern as to whether you would say anything to anybody? —No.

Did you not suggest that you might use a wheelbarrow to move the body rather than the pram, because of the blood?—No.

Are you really telling my Lord and the members of the jury that you had seen what happened, on either version of what is said to have happened, and you did not have any comment of any kind to make?—That is right, yes.

I asked you at the commencement about your arrangement with the newspaper. Do you mind telling us what sum you are going to have?

MR JUSTICE FENTON ATKINSON: Are you passing away now from 6 October?

MR HOOSON: Yes, I am.

MR JUSTICE FENTON ATKINSON: Can I be quite clear what you are suggesting. Are you suggesting that this killing of Evans arose out of a plot between him and Brady to roll a queer?

MR HOOSON: No, my Lord. I have put my exact instructions.

MR JUSTICE FENTON ATKINSON: Then they have left it a little vague exactly what you are suggesting to this witness.

MR HOOSON: The conversations I am suggesting, that I am instructed on, have been put exactly to this witness.

MR JUSTICE FENTON ATKINSON: Very well.

MR HOOSON: Were you expecting, as a result of your conversation with Ian earlier that evening, that there was a possibility that he might bring somebody back to the flat whom you could take money from—rob?—No.

I was going to ask you about the sum you are going to have from the newspaper. If two people are convicted partly on your evidence, you get a very large sum?—I don't know that, sir.

If they are acquitted, then you might get a very small sum. Have you and your wife been staying in a hotel in Chester during this trial?—Yes.

Has it all been paid for by a newspaper?—Yes.

MR JUSTICE FENTON ATKINSON: The same newspaper or another one has been generous in this respect? Is that the same paper again?—Yes.

MR HOOSON: Did you have any discussion about your evidence last night?—No.

Have you and your wife been to Spain and France since the committal proceedings?—To France, yes. Not Spain.

Who paid for it?—The newspaper.

Have you ever told somebody you are getting £20 to £25 a week, that you sometimes used to ask for more, but you were afraid of taking too much?—No, sir.

Now do you mind telling us which newspaper that was? Was it the *News of the World*?—I refuse to answer the question. It could have been the *Daily Mirror*.

I am not asking you which it could have been. I am asking you which it was. Are you denying that it was the newspaper I am suggesting to you?—I am not denying it and I am not confirming it, sir.

MR JUSTICE FENTON ATKINSON: You will appreciate, members of the jury, Mr Heilpern, for other important reasons, is unavoidably absent.

Cross-examined by MR CURTIS (*for Hindley*):

You are very firm in your refusal to disclose the name of the newspaper. Has that matter been discussed with you before the questions were put to you?—No, sir, not at all.

Well, why are you refusing?—I didn't like to get them involved.

Do you think there is something improper in the arrangement you have made with that newspaper?—No, sir.

If there is not, how can you get them involved?—Well, I would like that to be confirmed by the newspaper.

I see. Will you be in contact with them over the luncheon adjournment?

MR JUSTICE FENTON ATKINSON: They are probably standing him lunch!

THE WITNESS: I will try to, yes, sir.

MR CURTIS: You will try to? It would be more difficult not to, would it not?—Yes, sir.

Take your mind back to November of last year. How do you say contact was made between you and this newspaper?—There were many reporters round where we live, at the flats, and all of them paid me.

Paid you? What for?—That is what I would like to know. Usually nothing. Usually they just left their cards and there would be a £5 note or something just tucked underneath it. This happened on a number of occasions, but not with the newspaper I am dealing with.

Were you really holding a kind of auction for your services in this matter?—No.

What made you decide to make an arrangement with the particular paper?—They offered me a great deal of money.

You appreciate that if either of these two accused people were acquitted here, that would make it very difficult for the paper to implement the agreement?—Yes, now that you point it out.

I leave that now. I want to ask you one or two questions about your notebook. Will you look at page 24? 'Murder is a hobby and a supreme pleasure.' That, you say, is not your view; that is something you picked out of a book?—That is right, yes.

Now will you read on from the word 'God'? Just read it out so that the jury can hear.—I prefer you to read it, sir.

MR JUSTICE FENTON ATKINSON: I have no doubt you do. Will you please read it?—It will take rather a long time.

MR CURTIS: It will take longer if you do not begin.

MR JUSTICE FENTON ATKINSON: You are ashamed to read it out in court now, are you not?—No, sir. 'God is a disease, a plague, a weight around a man's neck, a disease which eats away his instincts. God is a superstition, a cancer, a man-made cancer, which is injected into the brain in the form of religion.' Shall I go on?

MR CURTIS: Yes.—'An infant is taken from its parents and for the first time in its life it is forcibly introduced to the cancer. From the age of five to sixteen its mind is forcibly fed—'

MR JUSTICE FENTON ATKINSON: Do you want much more of this?

MR CURTIS: That is as far as I want. What I want to put to you is this: that, to put it mildly, you have no religious belief?—That is correct.

The oath which you took yesterday, so far as you are concerned, is completely meaningless?—Yes.

I want to go to the beginning of your story. I gather you exchanged books with Brady? You lent him some of yours and vice versa?—That is correct.

Mein Kampf, I think, was one of them, was it not?—Yes.

The Last Days of Goering?—Yes.

Those were books rather glorifying the nazi ideal, were they not?—I believe so.

And books on sexual perversion of various kinds?—Yes.

About a girl being flogged, and that sort of thing. Now, you took pleasure in writing this down, did you not?—I took pleasure in trying to understand why the author had written it.

You say, 'Copied for further enjoyment.' Does that not mean you had enjoyment in copying it?—I enjoyed them in trying to find out what the author was getting at.

You were really curious. You were studying the matter?—Studying the matter.

You are a man of somewhat violent disposition, are you not?—If provoked, yes. If not provoked, very calm.

Is the position this: that being of rather a violent disposition (you say when provoked), you also had a rather unhealthy interest in the matters which appear in these books and parts of which you copied?—I had an unhealthy interest, as it happens.

You were quite prepared to take part in a bank robbery where guns were to be used?—Yes.

I want to ask you quite shortly about Boxing Day, 1964. The truth is this, is it not: that you took that little girl Downey with another man to the premises of Hindley and Brady at Hattersley?—No, that is a lie.

And took her away after the photographs had been taken?—No, that is a lie.

I must put it to you that that is what happened and, so far as they are concerned, that is the last that was seen of them.—No, sir.

The persons who know what happened after that are you and your friend.—The only lad I know called Keith is a lad I know called Keith Blimstone, but he is not a friend.

Now I want to ask you about your visit to the moors on 26 April. You went up somewhere near a reservoir, did you?—That is right. That is correct.

Was that near where the graves of these two children were later found?—It was pointed out to me.

Your baby had died on 24 April?—Yes.

Did Myra Hindley and Ian Brady invite you to spend the weekend with them because of Maureen's upset condition?—Yes.

On Saturday evening, did you all have a fair amount to drink, apart from Hindley?—And Hindley. We all had a substantial amount to drink.

At about 11.30 somebody suggested, 'What about going for a run?'—Brady suggested it.

I must put it to you that it was you.—No, sir.

You say that you got out of the car and went for a walk because Brady wanted to show you the reservoir?—Yes.

Did that strike you as curious at that time of night?—Not for Ian Brady, no. He liked walking.

Coming to the events of 6 October, are you quite sure it was Maureen and not you who answered the bell late that night?—Yes, quite sure.

Why are you so sure?—She usually answers the buzzer.

Of course, if in fact you were not in bed, but dressed, you might very well answer the buzzer, might you not?—If I wasn't in bed.

Did you meet Myra as she came in?—No.

When she first saw you, did she not say: 'Ian wants you'?—No.

As I understand your evidence, you say that she came with some message for Maureen. Did you hear what the message was?—Only vaguely.

I must put it to you that she told you that Ian wanted you.—No, that is not true.

If she had given you that message, would you have gone?—Not at that time of night, no.

You were simply going to see her to a point at which you could be satisfied she would get in the house?—That is correct, yes.

Are there some desperate customers around the Hattersley estate?—I would not know, sir.

I must put it to you that you went to the front door with Myra.—No, sir.

That she knocked and you were both there when Brady answered the door.—No.

Are you telling my Lord and the jury that when the buzzer rang at a quarter to midnight, you had no reason to know who the caller was or what the purpose of the call was?—That is correct, yes.

I do not understand. If your sister-in-law called and you knew it was your sister-in-law, probably to see her sister, and you are in bed, why bother to get out of bed, get dressed, and go into the living room?—Just an act of friendliness.

I must put it to you that the reason why you came out was because you were going back to that house with Myra.—No.

You have told my Lord and the jury that outside the house Myra said something to you about miniature bottles.—Wine bottles, yes.

Are you saying that you would not have gone into the house had it not been for the invitation to take the wine bottles away?—Yes.

No question of your being concerned jointly with Brady in anything that was going to go on?—That is correct.

When you got in, did you eventually hear or see something?—I heard a scream from the living room.

Did you approach the door to the living room?—Yes.

Is it then you say you saw what you thought was a rag doll?—That is correct, yes. It was just the impression I got.

When did you get that impression?—Now that I think about it.

You never said anything about this impression at the committal proceedings, very much nearer the time of these matters.—That is correct.

Again, your description of Brady using the axe: you said yesterday that he had about as much emotion—I am quoting from memory—'as a butcher cutting up a sheep,' I think you said.—A sheet of ribs.

You never said anything as colourful as that when you first gave evidence in December?—Not as colourful as that, no.

Is it that you have been associating with rather colourful people in the meantime? People with a dramatic turn of phrase?—No, sir.

You told my Lord and the jury that after having entered that house for the purpose of taking away some miniature wine bottles, then to go back to the bed you say you had just left, you saw this scene of a youth being savagely attacked with an axe, and you said nothing and you did nothing?—That is correct.

Did you move into the room or away from it?—Into the room.

What was your purpose of moving into the room?—I don't know. I just moved.

Try and think. Had somebody put a bolt on the front door?—Not that I know of.

There was nobody between you and the front door to bar your progress if you had run out?—If I had thought of it, no.

But you did not think of it?—I am sorry to say, no, sir.

Tell me, were you frightfully upset by this sight?—I was scared stiff.

Do you think your fright might possibly make your recollection of what happened afterwards not quite as reliable as otherwise it might be?—No, sir.

I think you agree that you assisted Brady to tie the body up?—Yes.

Were you still very frightened?—Yes.

Did you at one stage hold your hand out and say: 'Look at that'?—No.

'No trembling.'—No, sir.

Did you not say, referring to what appeared on the carpet as a result of this attack, 'Eddie's a brainy swine'?—No.

Did you not say that he was a bleeder, referring to the blood?—No, sir.

I must put it to you that the cut on your leg was caused when you were kicking this unfortunate boy's head, and the axe wielded by Brady struck you.—No, I didn't strike the lad at all.

After you and Brady had trussed the body up, you then had a pot of tea?—That is correct.

You say it was at that time Myra Hindley said something about burying a body on the moors?—Yes.

I suggest that what she said was that when she and Brady were up on the moors and Brady was practising with his pistols, and she was waiting in the car, a policeman came up.—No, sir.

And that she was hoping that Ian would not come up with his guns while the policeman was there.—She said she was praying Ian would not walk over the top. She didn't say anything about guns.

I must put it to you that you were completely calm and self-possessed the whole of the time.—I had one intention in my mind and that was to leave in one piece.

Of course, you had had a cosh for self-protection, had you not?—Not for self-protection. I had a cosh for ornamental reasons. I had it on the sideboard.

You did not mean as an ornament on your person?—No.

Why was it necessary to put that with the other embarrassing and incriminating objects in the Central Railway Station left-luggage office?—I wouldn't know, sir. It wasn't my cosh at this time. I gave it to Myra Hindley when I was living in Gorton quite a long time ago.

The truth is this, is it not: that you were well indoctrinated? Although the views on murder in your notebook may not be your views, you were affected by them.—No, sir.

And when you saw violence committed, were you not so much affected that you had to join in?—No.

Nobody put any pressure on you not to leave the house until you did leave?—No.

That is all.

MR JUSTICE FENTON ATKINSON: Mr Curtis, there was one piece of evidence about Myra Hindley. Her alleged remark: 'You should have seen the look on his face. The blow registered in his eyes.' I assume you want to deal with that?

MR CURTIS: I am very much obliged.

When do you say this remark was made?—Afterwards, when we were having the cup of tea.

Do you remember the precise words?—No, those are not the exact words, but it was the same sound. You couldn't mistake what she meant.

In other words, you say she used words to say that Evans looked astonished?—Yes.

But you cannot honestly tell my Lord and the jury that Myra Hindley was ever in that room while that youth was being killed?—Well, she was in the room because she shouted me.

I must put it to you that you have not said that before today. When she shouted 'Dave, Dave,' she was in fact in the kitchen and you were in the lobby.—No, sir, I was in the kitchen.

Where do you say she was in the living room?—When I caught a glimpse of her, she was just to the right as I went through.

Of course, your attention then, I presume, was riveted on the rag doll waving its arms about?—That is correct.

Do you think that in those circumstances you might conceivably be mistaken as to where Myra Hindley was?—Possibly, sir.

MR CURTIS: Thank you.

MR JUSTICE FENTON ATKINSON: Mr Curtis, you said a moment ago that this was the first time he had mentioned Myra being in the room at the relevant time. Have you looked at the deposition, page 16?

MR CURTIS: No, I meant today. The first time in his evidence today. I quite agree. I meant, of course, the first time in your evidence in this case.

THE ATTORNEY-GENERAL: Before the re-examination begins, there is a matter of law upon which I desire the ruling of your Lordship, and it may be desirable that it should be given in the absence of the jury. It may be as well for the witness, also, to retire at this stage, my Lord.

(*The jury and the witness left the court.*)

THE ATTORNEY-GENERAL: I apply to put in a statement made by Smith within a few hours of the events that occurred (this is, on the morning of 7 October, finishing in the afternoon of 7 October).

MR JUSTICE FENTON ATKINSON: In reply to the suggestion that pressure has been brought to bear and a lot of people have suggested things to him, and so on and so forth?

THE ATTORNEY-GENERAL: Yes. I do not know if your Lordship needs any authority on this. It is pretty clear, but it may be helpful for me to read a passage by the learned author of Cross *Evidence* [Cross, R., *Evidence*. London: Butterworth] at page 206. Has your Lordship a copy?

MR JUSTICE FENTON ATKINSON: I carry it round with me.

(*The passage, headed 'Previous Consistent Statements Admitted to Rebut Afterthought,' quotes the judgment by Holmes, J., in R v. Coll*: '. . . If it is alleged that a prisoner's story is a recent concoction, a previous statement concerning the nature of his defence becomes admissible. . . . The question whether a situation has arisen in which a previous statement may be proved under this head is, both in civil and criminal cases, largely a matter for the judge's discretion. . . .')

MR JUSTICE FENTON ATKINSON (*after reading David Smith's statement*): One of the troubles here is this: he is saying in the statement that Myra arrived on the spot so near that she was nearly hit with the hatchet herself, whereas in the evidence today he has come very near to saying that she was not there at all or he was not really quite sure whether she was in the room or not. . . . This goes much further than anything he has said in the witness box as regards her participation or presence. . . . I think it would be much fairer not to have this put in, Mr Attorney. . . . Mr Hooson and Mr Curtis have already seen what he did say to the police before this press business began.

(*The jury and the witness returned to court.*)

DAVID SMITH *re-examined by* MR MARS-JONES:

Why did you go to the police?—Well, I had to. I couldn't hardly keep it to myself.

The expressions have been referred to in your notes, 'morons', 'cabbages', 'fish bait', and so on, in referring to human beings. When did you first hear these words used?—'Morons', that was a regular expression of Myra's and Ian's—and 'cabbages'. The other one was my own.

Coming to the incident of March of this year when you agree you struck one of a number of boys, ten in number, with a chain. You said that you were extremely provoked. What was the provocation?—I was in a friend's flat on the Hattersley estate and there was this crowd of boys and girls in the street. My friend and I were on the balcony. One of the lads, the tallest of the bunch, shouted up to the balcony: 'You're no bleeding good without the axe, Smith,' and I went downstairs.

DETECTIVE SERGEANT ALEXANDER CARR *of the Cheshire Constabulary, stationed at Hyde*: At 8.20 am on Thursday, 7 October 1965, I accompanied Superintendent Talbot and other officers to the vicinity of 16 Wardle Brook Avenue. As soon as the superintendent had obtained entry into the kitchen I joined him. [*The witness confirmed Police Superintendent Robert Talbot's evidence of conversations with the two accused; see page 69.*] I noticed that when Brady got out of bed there was a cloth round his left ankle. He removed this on getting dressed. I did not notice any injury to his ankle but he limped.

I then accompanied him to Hyde Police Station. I took Brady into the CID office and said to him: 'Would you care to tell me what happened in the house last night?' He said: 'There was an argument.' I interrupted him: 'Do I understand you wish to make a statement?' He said: 'Yes.' I took down his statement at his dictation:

'Last night I met Eddie in Manchester. We were drinking and then went home to Hattersley. We had an argument and we came to blows. After the first few blows the situation was out of control. When the argument started, Dave Smith was at the front door and Myra called him in. Eddie was on the floor near the living room door. David hit him with the stick and kicked him about three times. Eddie kicked me at the beginning on my ankle. There was a hatchet on the floor and I hit Eddie with it. After that the only noise Eddie made was gurgling. When Dave and I began cleaning up the floor the gurgling stopped. Then we tied up the body—Dave and I. Nobody else helped. Dave and I carried it upstairs. Then we sat in the house until three or four in the morning. Then we decided to get rid of the body in the morning early next day or next night.'

At 8.20 pm I formally cautioned and charged Brady with the offence of murder of Edward Evans. He replied: 'I stand on statement made this morning.' He wrote this reply on the charge form himself and signed it.

At three o'clock in the afternoon on 11 October I saw Myra Hindley at Hyde Police Station. I cautioned and charged her with the offence of accessory after the fact to the murder of Edward Evans, and she replied: 'Nothing to say until I see Mr Fitzpatrick.' Mr Fitzpatrick is the solicitor instructed on her behalf.

DETECTIVE POLICEWOMAN MARGARET CAMPION *of the Cheshire Constabulary, stationed at Hyde*: At two o'clock in the afternoon of Thursday, 7 October 1965, I saw Myra Hindley at Hyde Police Station. I said to her: 'This morning the body of a man was found at your house. Who is that person?' She replied: 'I don't know and am not saying anything. Ask Ian. My story is the same as Ian's.' I said to her: 'What is the story of last night?' She replied: 'We came home from work about six o'clock, then went out about eight o'clock and then went to the outdoor in Stockport Road, Longsight, for some wine. We often go there. Then we went up to Glossop near the moors and sat talking for ages. It was just a normal evening out before all this happened. It was the same as hundreds of other evenings out.' I said to her: 'Would you care to tell me what happened at your house last night?' She replied: 'All I am saying is that I didn't do it, and Ian didn't do it. We are involved in something we did not do. We never left each other. We never do. What happened last night was an accident. It should never have happened.' I said to her: 'If what you say is true, it is in your interests to tell the truth of what did happen.' She replied: 'No. Ask Ian. His story is the same as mine. We never left each other. Ian can't drive, and that's that. What are they going to do with Ian, because what he has done I have done.' I said to her: 'Do you realise how serious this matter is?' She said: 'Yes, and I also know that David Smith told you this, and he is a liar.' I said: 'David Smith alleges that you cleared the mess up in the living room after the murder of this man.' She replied: 'Yes, and I suppose he told you that he sat on the chair benevolently looking on whilst I cleaned up.' I said to her: 'Is it true that you went to David Smith's house last night and he walked home with you?' She replied: 'Yes.' I said: 'What time did you go there?' She said: 'I am not saying. All this happened because there was an argument, and that's that.' I said to her: 'How did this man get to your house, and who brought him there?' She said: 'I am not saying how he got there or when. I have told you before, I'm not saying anything.'

DETECTIVE SERGEANT ROY DEAN *of the Cheshire Constabulary testified as to sketch plans he had made of the living room, kitchen and back bedroom at 16 Wardle Brook Avenue on 7 October 1965, and gave details of articles he had removed from the house.* 'I found an exercise book bearing the name and address of Ian Brady. On one of the pages, amongst other things, there appears the name "John Kilbride".'

FIFTH DAY   *Monday, 25 April*

DR HERBERT ELLIS, *in general practice at Hyde, said that on Thursday evening, 7 October 1965, he was called to Hyde Police Station. With the agreement of the two accused, he took samples of their hair, nail clippings, saliva and blood. (Evidence read.)*

DR JOHN BENNETT, *in general practice at Hyde, said that at 2.30 pm on 8 October 1965, he examined Ian Brady.* 'I found a small, superficial abrasion on the dorsal of the foot just in front of the lateral malleolus. I would describe the injury as trivial.' (*Evidence read.*)

DR CHARLES ST HILL, *Home Office Pathologist for the Liverpool area*: At about 1.15 pm on 7 October 1965 I was shown a large bundle beneath the window in an upstairs bedroom at 16 Wardle Brook Avenue. I opened the bundle and saw inside the body of a man later identified to me as Edward Evans. The body was bent up with the legs brought up to the chest and the arms folded across the body. The legs and arms were kept in position by two cords. It was further secured by two loops of cord which kept the neck bent forward towards the knees; these cords passed round the neck and were attached to the other two cords which bound the legs and arms. I found a blood-stained cloth wrapped round the head and neck, and a piece of electric light cable was around the neck but not tied. The body was enclosed in a white cotton blanket which had been knotted. A polythene sheet lay outside this, and was itself covered by a grey blanket.

I carried out a preliminary examination on the spot. Later that day I carried out a post-mortem examination at Hyde Mortuary. I found that the body was that of a fairly slim youth, 5ft 6in tall and of about 9–10 stone. It was fully dressed but there were no shoes on the feet.

There were fourteen irregular lacerations distributed over the scalp, right cheek and ear, with surrounding bruising. These lacerations measured from 1–5in in length. Around the neck was a slightly depressed white band in the flesh, corresponding in position and width to the electric light flex. There was a little reddening of the skin in one or two places along the edge of this band. There was widespread bruising of the back of the neck and over the back of the tops of the shoulders and upper back. There was a 1in bruise in the small of the back. There was extensive lacerating and bruising of the backs of both hands, the left forearm and the right upper arm; these wounds are accurately described as 'defence wounds'. I found the greater part of the right side of the skull was fragmented and a somewhat rounded depressed fracture was present on the right frontal region.

I came to the conclusion that the injuries to the skull could have been produced by the axe found in the house; I think probably by both the blade side and the back of the axe.

There was much blood on the surface of the brain with extensive bruising on both sides. The mouth and pharynx were normal. The trachea contained a little frothy fluid. The lungs were congested with a few small haemorrhages on their surfaces. The right side of the heart was dilated and there were numerous haemorrhages on this surface. The coronary arteries and great vessels were normal. In the abdomen the stomach contained a little turbid fluid only. I came to the conclusion that the cause of death was cerebral contusion and haemorrhage due to fractures of the skull due to blows to the head, accelerated by strangulation by ligature.

I removed hair from the head, eyebrows, pubis and around the anus. I found two loose fibres around the anus; also numerous fibres on both hands. I also took a swab from the mouth and the anus of the deceased; two swabs were taken from the skin of the penis.

Spots of blood found on Hindley's shoes were consistent with blood falling on them; spots of blood on David Smith's shoes could have been obtained in the same way. Smith's shoes are soft-toed, and I do not think they could have caused the lacerations.

Cross-examined by MR HOOSON:

Dr St Hill, am I right in thinking that the signs that you found to suggest strangulation by a ligature were minimal?—They were very small.

Very, very small?—Yes.

And you have also described that at the time you found this electric flex, at the back it was anchoring a cushion cover?—That is correct.

So if the purpose of the flex had been to anchor the cushion cover, that is exactly the position you would expect to find it?—That is correct.

When you have gross injury to the head, as you clearly had here, respiration can cease before the heart ceases to beat? The heart is still beating, but breathing appears to have stopped and the man appears to be dead?—Quite correct.

The signs that you normally find following upon a strangulation are haemorrhages in the scalp and on the face, forehead, eyelids, and so on?—Yes.

None of these signs were present in this case?—No.

So that this ligature could certainly have been applied after the body appeared to be dead?—It could have been applied when respiration had ceased. Yes.

With regard to the injury to the head, the fourteen lacerations you have described: could one or two have been caused by the heel of shoes of the kind worn by Smith?—If you used a stamping action. I think some of these small lacerations could have been caused by that.

You have described the haemorrhages of the heart and pleura. Whenever you have a lack of oxygen you can have haemorrhages, whether it is caused by strangulation or head injury, so those haemorrhages do not assist you one way or the other?—That is quite right.

Cross-examined by MR HEILPERN:

I want you to look at Miss Hindley's shoes. Dealing with the large patches of blood, two of them, they are consistent with stepping into blood?—Yes.

By no stretch of the imagination could you call the spots of blood splashes, could you? They are tiny spots?—They are small splashes. The same thing. About one eighth of an inch across.

COLIN BANCROFT, *a biologist, identified more than fifty exhibits— chiefly clothing and personal belongings of the two accused, David Smith, and Edward Evans, and articles removed from 16 Wardle Brook Avenue, which the witness had examined for blood, saliva, semen, hairs, etc.*

At the witness was describing systems of grouping human blood, MR JUSTICE FENTON ATKINSON *interrupted to ask* MR HOOSON *and* MR HEILPERN: 'Is there going to be any controversy about his evidence as to whose blood was found where?' *Both defence counsel replied that there was not, and* MR MARS-JONES, *examining for the Crown, said that he would shorten the evidence.*

THE WITNESS: All the blood which was found in the living room was of the same blood group as that of Edward Evans. I examined two fibres taken from the anus of Edward Evans. I would say they were animal hairs. The stick belonging to David Smith was very heavily bloodstained for almost the whole of its length; there were also head hairs similar to those of Edward Evans generally distributed over the surface together with animal hairs. On the three carpets from the living room I found numerous animal hairs but no bloodstaining.

Cross-examined by MR HOOSON:

Mr Bancroft, am I right in thinking that, broadly speaking, you have similar dispositions of blood on the clothing of David Smith as you have on the clothing of Ian Brady?—Yes.

I want you now to deal with the stick. It is right to say from your examination there was far more blood on the lower two-thirds of that stick?—Yes.

Would it be right to say that most of the hairs from Evans's head were almost certainly on the lower part of the stick?—I cannot say this.

You cannot say that they were evenly distributed, as you replied to Mr Mars-Jones?—Yes, I can. There were only a few hairs on the stick. I can say that the impression I have at this time is from over a wide area rather than located as a clump of hairs in one locality.

You have just told us you could not say whether most were on the lower part of that stick. This is vitally important evidence, Mr Bancroft. You cannot remember whether they were evenly distributed or not, can you?—If they were located in one definite area I should say this.

I am not suggesting they were in one clump. If they had been spread out over the lower part of the stick you would have made no particular note?—That is true.

Because you said today, for example, the blood was evenly distributed over the stick. Now you have agreed that most of it was on the lower two-thirds.—I said blood was contained over the whole length of the stick.

You agree now that most of it was on the lower two-thirds?—Yes.

Did you find any on the upper part of the stick? (*Exhibit produced to the witness.*)—There is blood in *this* area.

The highest point on that stick which you have pointed out would not be the area in which a man's hand would hold, would it? Put your hand around the top of that stick. Above the bottom of your hand there are no blood spots at all?—Holding it in this manner, there is a blood smear next to my thumb.

Just below your thumb?—Yes.

But where your hand is there are no blood spots at all? There is a blood smear just *there*. This is from visual examination. I would have to confirm this by microscopic tests.

Cross-examined by MR HEILPERN:

I want to ask you a few questions about Myra Hindley's clothing. You have spoken broadly of three things—a black and white coat, faint blood smears on the right cuff on the outside. A brown skirt, a small blood smear on the left centre of the front. —That is correct.

I suppose both those smears are consistent with her having brushed against something that had blood upon it?—This could be so.

Now we come to the shoes. The marks on the left-hand side of the left shoe—the comparatively large patches—are blood smears, are they not?—They are.

Consistent with somebody stepping into a pool or patch of blood?—Not stepping into it: brushing against it.

No matter; one or other of those. And would you agree that the other spots would add up to an extremely minute quantity of blood?—Yes.

Re-examined by MR MARS-JONES:

Would you look at the stick? (*Exhibit produced to the witness.*) Would you put it on the flat surface in front of you? Does all or only part of the stick come in contact with the ground, or with that straight surface?—Only parts of the stick. There are lumps on this stick, which are knots in the original wood.

It depends which way it falls which part of the stick comes in contact with the surface?—Yes.

DAVID NOEL JONES, *Director of the Home Office Forensic Science Laboratory at Preston*: I have compared two fibres taken from the anus of Edward Evans with hairs taken from the deceased's home, and can find no adequate agreement between them. I have also compared the fibres taken from the anus with samples of hair taken from 16 Wardle Brook Avenue; the latter are largely animal hairs which have the appearance of dog hairs. The majority of these hairs show no agreement with the two hairs taken from the anus, but I was able to find some hairs which showed complete microscopic agreement with the two hairs.

I have examined the spots of blood on the two shoes of the accused Hindley. These would be quite consistent with spattering from a wound or a series of wounds such as were present on the head of Edward Evans. As to the suggestion that these spots of blood may have fallen from the head of the deceased while the body was being carried after death, I would think that it is unlikely but not impossible. The spots are small and I would expect blood dropping from a bloodstained head to be somewhat larger than these spots.

Cross-examined by MR HEILPERN:

You say that you would expect the blood spots to be larger if they had dropped from the body while it was being carried?—Yes.

Would not you expect them to be larger if they had been caused when blood was spurting from the head of the man when he was being hit with an axe?—No. The size of these spots is typical of the type of splashing one gets in woundings of this nature. I have seen many, many examples of this type of splashing and spurting, and this size spotting is the type of thing one expects to find. This or slightly smaller.

Why?—It is because it is spread by the spurting into a number of very small droplets.

ALFRED WEBB, *employed by the Cheshire County Council local taxation department, testified that his records showed a change of ownership of a surf-blue Austin Mini Countryman, CNC 153C, to Myra Hindley on 27 April 1965. The witness also produced an application, signed by Hindley, for the renewal of an excise licence in respect of this vehicle; the application was dated 12 August 1965, and was for a licence for four months commencing on 1 August 1965. (Evidence read.)*

THOMAS CRAIG, *director of Millwards Merchandise Ltd*: On 16 February 1959 the accused Brady commenced work for my company as a stock clerk. I am familiar with the handwriting of Brady; the letter found at 16 Wardle Brook Avenue on 7 October 1965 addressed to 'Tom' is in the accused's handwriting.

On 16 January 1961 Myra Hindley joined the company as a shorthand-typist and was so employed up to the date of her arrest.

JOHN BOLAND: I am a member of the Cheadle Rifle Club. I remember a day in midsummer 1963 when I sold a 0·45 Webley revolver to Myra Hindley, who was also a member of the club. There was some ammunition sold with it; about twenty-odd rounds, as near as I could say.

ALAN COTTAM: In 1963 I became a member of the Cheadle Rifle Club. (*Exhibit produced to the witness.*) I recognise this pistol, which is a Smith & Wesson 0·38, as one that I bought from John Boland. I was approached by a girl, Myra Hindley, who asked me did I want to sell the Smith & Wesson. I wasn't sure at the time. Then I said I would sell, and she came down to my home to pick it up. I think it was for about £5. I did not sell her

7/10/65.

Jim,

Sorry I could not phone yesterday, my family are at. Glasgow this week. I was crossing road in town last night when someone on a bike came around the corner and knocked me down, except for a few bruises. I was alright until I got up this morning, my ankle would not take my weight. I must have weak ankles or something, if its no better tomorrow, I'll have to see doctor.

Jim

Brady's letter to his employer

any ammunition. I think it was September or October 1963 when I sold the gun, certainly before Christmas. I did not ask her if she had a firearm certificate.

FRANK HOUGH, *Clerk of Works for Manchester Corporation Housing Department*: It is part of my job to examine each house on the Hattersley Overspill when it is completed. On 3 November 1965 I went to 16 Wardle Brook Avenue. I examined the door of the small bedroom. Fitted to this door was a dead lock. This had not been there when I made my first inspection. (*Evidence read.*)

DETECTIVE CHIEF SUPERINTENDENT ARTHUR BENFIELD, *Head of Cheshire CID*, *examined by* THE ATTORNEY-GENERAL:

On 7 October 1965 did you see the accused Brady at Hyde Police Station at about eight o'clock in the evening?—I did.

What did you say to him?—I said: 'I have discovered a wallet in Myra's car.' I showed him the wallet, and he said: 'Yes, it's mine.' I then said: 'Inside the wallet are several pieces of paper on which are written certain words and abbreviations. Would you care to tell me what they mean?' Brady then said: 'Yes. That was the plan for the disposal of Eddie. We planned that after it had happened. We sat up doing it.'

Yes?—The first page is divided into five columns. The letters 'OB' appear in the first column. I said to Brady: 'What does "OB" mean?' He said: 'Object.' I asked him what 'DET' in the second column meant, and he said: 'Details.' 'CARR' appears in the third column. I said to him: 'What does "CARR" mean?' and he said: 'Car.' The fourth column, 'Stn'. Brady said: 'Stationery, paper.' 'End' appears in the last column, and he said: 'End, finish.' Under the first column the word 'Hat' appears. He said this meant 'Hatchet'. 'GN' appears in the third place in that first column. He said: ' "GN" means gun.' I then said: 'What part does the gun play in this?' and he said: 'If anybody had seen us burying the body—for self-protection.' He then went on: ' "REC" means reconnaissance.' ' "PRO-P" means Pro Plus, a stimulant.' I went on to the second sheet, and he said: ' "ALI" means alibi.' The next item down, 'METH', meant method. The next but one item, 'CLOTH', meant clothing. The word 'BULLS' appears in the column opposite 'GN' on the first page. I asked him what that meant, and he said: 'Bullets.' 'P/B' meant Penistone Burn.

Do you know of any such place as Penistone Burn?—No. There is a place called Penistone, and I am aware that Burn is used in Scotland, but I know of no such place known as Penistone Burn in this district. Penistone is a town just off the moors, on the eastern side of the Pennines in the Sheffield area.

MR JUSTICE FENTON ATKINSON: How far roughly from the Downey-Kilbride graves?—I would estimate about eight miles, my Lord.

Replying to further questions in examination-in-chief, the witness said: On 11 October I told Hindley that she was to be charged with being an accessory after the fact to the murder of Evans. I cautioned her, and she said: 'I'm saying nothing.' On 2 December Hindley was charged with the murder of Evans, and she said: 'It's not true.'

Cross-examined by MR HOOSON:

Were David Smith's fingerprints taken?—I do not think so.

As far as you are aware, no systematic check was made to see whether Smith handled certain objects as opposed to Brady?—No.

I want to ask you about the interview with Brady at eight o'clock in the evening of 7 October 1965. He had been cautioned earlier, but you did not caution him?—I did.

Who else was present during this interview?—No one. I was on my own.

How long did this interview take?—Not much longer than ten minutes, I would think.

How much later was it that you wrote up the account?—Somewhere, I would think, about half-past nine.

Why did you not write your notes up straight away?—There were so many things going on during this day and evening. I did not find time to write them up right away.

On the conversation you had, interrogating Brady on the contents of the papers in the wallet, my instructions are that Brady said to you: ' "Stationery" means stationary.' This is, not paper but stationary.—No. There are two meanings obviously, and he then clarified it by saying 'paper'—not something standing still.

Another thing which I dispute is that 'CARR'—he said to you that this meant carriage.—He never mentioned carriage to me.

He said 'car', and it did not seem to make sense to me, but he did say 'car'.

Up to the time of this interview he had not been charged with the murder?—That is so.

Although you had had the statement from him—the one that he had given to the sergeant—from the morning?—Nine o'clock in the morning, yes.

THE ATTORNEY-GENERAL *said that he would now turn to the Downey case.*

GERTRUDE DOWNEY: In 1964 I and my four children were living at Ancoats with a man named Alan West. One of those four children was Lesley Ann. On Saturday, 26 December 1964, Lesley Ann was ten. I last saw her on that day about four in the afternoon. She left my house alone to go to a fair which was 200 yards away. When she had not returned by eight o'clock I went with Alan West to look for her. Just after 10 pm I went to the police.

On 17 October 1965 I went to the mortuary at Uppermill and identified the clothing which Lesley Ann was wearing when I last saw her. On the same occasion I identified the body of my daughter.

I remember on 29 October 1965 being shown by Detective Inspector Rimmer photographs of a little girl in the nude. These were photographs of Lesley Ann.

On 6 December 1965 I listened to part of a tape recording. I heard the voices of a man, a woman and a little girl. I recognised the voice of the little girl as that of Lesley Ann. (*Evidence read.*)

LINDA CLARKE: I am nine. I live at Ancoats. Lesley Ann Downey was a friend of mine. I remember Boxing Day, 1964. Lesley Ann came down to our house, this was in the afternoon, and we went to the fair. I had some money. I think it was 1s 1d. Lesley Ann had sixpence. We went on a roundabout like and then the machines. I last saw Lesley Ann on the fair. I decided to go home about 5.30 pm. (*Evidence read.*)

BERNARD KING: I am eleven years old and I live at Miles Platting. Lesley Ann Downey went to the same school as me, but she was one class above me. I visited the fair at Hulme Hall Lane on Boxing Day, 1964, at about 5.30 pm. I saw Lesley Ann Downey. She was standing by the dodgems when I was standing by the waltzer. There was no one with her when I saw her. I walked past her to the cyclone. After I passed her near the dodgems I did not see her again. (*Evidence read.*)

PATRICIA ANN HODGES: I am twelve. It was in September 1964 that I came to live at 12 Wardle Brook Avenue with my family. I found there was a man and woman living at No 16. The gran also lived at No 16; she was called Mrs Maybury. It was three or four weeks before I got to know Ian and Myra. I went to Myra's house to see if my mother was there. Myra asked me into the house and I stayed about twenty minutes. When I went to the house I think there were two dogs. They were called Puppet and Lassie. Myra suggested I should go with her down Longsight. She said she was going to pick Ian up. I went with her in a little grey minivan. We both stayed in the car after it had stopped, and eventually Ian joined us. Myra said she didn't go to his house because his mother kept her talking. I used to go with Myra every night to the same place; this carried on until about February 1965.

About two or three weeks after I started going with Myra to collect Brady, Myra suggested, I think, that I should go with them on the moors; she said it was just for a run out. I have shown the police where we went. It was through Greenfield. When we got there on the first occasion, we just sat in the van; it was light, and we just sat there talking. We went up on the moors about once or twice a week. They took wine with them nearly every time. We went to the same spot except for a couple of times when we went further down the road. There were occasions when they brought soil back from the moors. They put the soil on the back garden. This happened about ten times, sometimes in the day and sometimes at night. I had some of the wine. It was given to me sometimes by Myra and sometimes by Brady. I had it from the bottle.

I used to go to the house very regularly after I got to know them. I would have about four glasses of wine on a visit to the house.

On two occasions I went for walks on the moor with Ian and Myra. Both times we started off from the same place as I showed the police where Myra used to stop the van.

I saw a tape recorder in the house. On one occasion I think

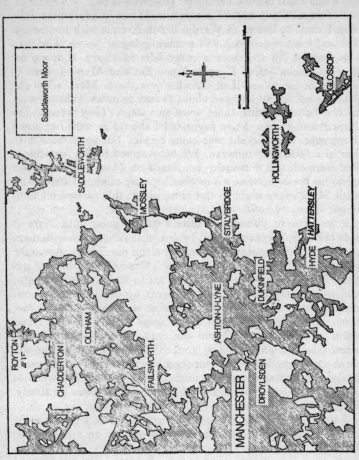

Map showing Saddleworth in relation to Manchester and Hattersley

Myra operated the tape recorder while I was there. It was played back to me what had been recorded. I did not know that the conversation was being recorded at the time. I remember that the time they made the recording I was reading from the *Gorton and Openshaw Reporter* of 1 January 1965; it was an account of a little girl who was missing. I read it out to Myra. I recognised the voices on the tape that was played to me at the magistrates' court as those of myself, Myra and Ian Brady.

I remember Christmas Eve, 1964. I was at 16 Wardle Brook Avenue that evening. My mother was there too, then my mother and I went home. Before my mother came to 16 Wardle Brook Avenue that evening I had been there with Myra and Ian alone. I had some whisky, some gin and some wine. I had no drink after my mother came to the house. It was about 11.30 pm when Myra called to ask if I could go out on to the moors. My mother let me go, with it being Christmas Eve. We went in the white minivan to the usual place on the moors. We sat in the van when we got there. Myra took some sandwiches. I might have had a little bit of wine. We stayed there until about 12.30 am. Myra said: 'Shall we go home and get some blankets and come back for the night?' Ian said: 'All right.' Myra then drove me back home. It was about 1.30 am when I got in. Shortly after I got in the house I heard the van drive off.

I did not see either Ian or Myra on Boxing Day. I kept on going out with Ian and Myra after Boxing Day, both to the moors and to Manchester to collect Ian. This stopped in February 1965 because two girls—they were twins—came to live near us, and I started going around with them. About three weeks after I had stopped going around with Ian and Myra I climbed over a wall at the side of their house—a lot of people do that. I remember meeting Ian. He said that Myra's gran had said that me and my friend Margaret had been in the garden. I said: 'We weren't in the garden.' He said: 'You were.' I said: 'Only over the wall.' He said: 'Don't let me cop you in the garden again.' He was telling me off. He said: 'I'll break your back if I cop you in there again.' I never spoke to Myra and Ian again after that.

Cross-examined by MR HEILPERN:

It is not easy to remember the number of times you went out

on the moors. How many times a week did you go on the moors?
—Only once or twice.

Are you really saying it was as much as once or twice a week?—
Yes.

Just to show you how difficult it is to remember, you said that
the first time you went up, it was light. Before the magistrates
you said it was dark when you went up. I am sure you are doing
your best, but you don't know whether it was dark or light?—
I am sure it was light.

You often went at night?—Yes.

How could you tell where you went?—We went in between
two signposts.

Nearly all the roads that go over the moors, and indeed all
roads in the country, have signs upon them. In fact, you went
to many places on those moors, didn't you?—Once we came
round the moors.

You remember Christmas Eve, 1964? In fact, you went to quite
a different part of the moors on that occasion, I suggest to you.—
We always went between road signs on the road.

It would be pitch black, and I suggest the place you stopped
at was not the same place you talked about. It was farther on?—
No.

Was the position this when you were taken to the moors in a
police car: that when the police car got to a particular place,
the car was pulled up? Were you asked by a police constable:
'Is this the place?'—No. I showed them.

Are you telling us that you stopped the car?—Yes.

I suggest that it was the police constable driving the car who
stopped without your saying anything to him.—I cannot remember.

Re-examined by THE ATTORNEY-GENERAL:

Do you remember what the two signs were on the road?—I
think one of them showed where to turn a bend. I cannot remember what the other was.

SIXTH DAY

Tuesday, 26 April

DETECTIVE INSPECTOR GEOFFREY RIMMER *of the Manchester City Police described the police search and the publicity campaign following the disappearance of Lesley Ann Downey on 26 December 1964. The witness testified that on 29 October 1965 he took two photographs of a naked child to Mrs Gertrude Downey, and that she identified the child as her daughter. (Evidence read.)*

JAMES BURNS: I live at Dukinfield. I am Myra Hindley's uncle. In 1964 it was Myra's practice to visit me at my home about once a fortnight. She would bring her grandmother with her and leave her to spend half a day at my house. She used to bring her about 2 pm. She would go away and come back about 9.30 pm to collect her grandmother. She used to bring her in a little minivan.

I remember Boxing Day, 1964. It was my birthday. Myra brought her grandmother down to see me. She did not come back at the usual time. She came about 11.10 pm. She came into the house and said: 'I'm sorry, gran, I can't take you back. The roads are too bad.' I started to have an argument with Myra. As a result of going out frequently to see whether Myra had come, I knew what the roads were like. It had been snowing, but there was only a light sprinkling of snow in the street where I lived. The argument went on for about a quarter of an hour and ended when Myra said: 'I can't take gran, and that's that.' Then she walked out. As a result, gran stayed at my house on a bed made of cushions on the floor in the living room. Myra came the next day, the Sunday, about 10.30 am and took gran home in the van.

Cross-examined by MR HEILPERN, *the witness agreed that snow had fallen during the Saturday afternoon and evening; it was very cold. He did not remember if Hindley had mentioned that she had left Brady in the van. He agreed that there was an unoccupied bedroom in the house; asked if there was any difficulty about Mrs Maybury's staying the night, the witness said that his son, who had slept in that bedroom, had died six months before on his twentieth birthday and since then the bed had not been used: 'It was a sentimental reason.'*

GEOFFREY MARTLETON, *a leading porter in the left-luggage office at Manchester Central Station, testified that a ticket relating to two suitcases alleged to have been deposited by the accused was issued between 5 pm on 5 October 1965 and 12.30 the following morning. (Evidence read.)*

DETECTIVE CONSTABLE DENNIS BARROW *of the British Transport Police identified two suitcases, one blue and one brown, which he had found in the left-luggage office at Manchester Central Station on 15 October 1965; the ticket identified by the previous witness related to these suitcases.*

POLICE SUPERINTENDENT ROBERT TALBOT (*recalled*) *testified that on 7 October 1965 he took possession of 149 photographic negatives, 170 photographic prints, a tartan-covered photograph album, a number of recording tapes and two tape recorders from 16 Wardle Brook Avenue.*

Among the contents of the brown suitcase found in the left-luggage office were nine photographs of a nude child in various poses; the child was wearing socks and shoes and had a scarf tied round her mouth. Two magnetic recording tapes were found in the brown suitcase. On one tape were two identical tracks of the voices of a man, a woman and a child. At the end of each of these tracks was a recording of two songs, 'Jolly St Nicholas' and 'The Little Drummer Boy', which the witness recognised as being from a long-playing record by the Ray Conniff Singers, entitled We Wish You a Merry Christmas. *The other tape contained four tracks: (a) a recording of music, (b) a* Goon Show *recording, (c) a recording of a commentary by Freddie Grisewood, (d) a recording of the voices of a man, a woman and a child which was identical to the two tracks on the other tape. The witness said that having spoken to Brady and Hindley on many occasions he was able to identify the voices of the man and woman on the tapes as those of the accused.*

Cross-examined by MR HOOSON, *the witness agreed that some of the photographs showing country scenes were not of Saddleworth Moor. He agreed that shadows on the bedroom wall in one of the photographs of Lesley Ann Downey suggested the use of flash photography; he had found no electrical equipment in the house that was suitable for artificial lighting for photography. (The witness later agreed that a photographic light bulb was on the list of items found in the house. Asked if that was not specifically for photography, he said: 'I wouldn't know. I am not a photographer.') Asked about plugs on the tape recorder and record player found in the house, the witness agreed that the two pieces of equipment could not have been played simultaneously unless there was a two-way adaptor; no two-way adaptor had been found in the house. He agreed that the music on the tape recordings might have been recorded from the radio:* 'I am told, however, that these two particular items of music which are coupled would not be broadcast in this country.' MR HOOSON *remarked that much recorded music was played over Radio Luxembourg.*

DETECTIVE SERGEANT RAYMOND PATON, *assistant police liaison officer on the staff of the Home Office Forensic Science Laboratory at Preston, testified that he had taken photographs of the back bedroom at 16 Wardle Brook Avenue; the bed headboard was similar to that shown in a photograph of Lesley Ann Downey in the nude.*

DAVID NOEL JONES (*recalled*): I am satisfied that the photographs of Lesley Ann Downey were made by an Ensign camera found at 16 Wardle Brook Avenue. The photograph showing the headboard was taken in the back bedroom at the house; I have drawn attention [on an enlarged print] to twenty points of similarity between the headboard and nearby wall in the photograph and the same area in the bedroom.

LEONARD MILNER, *a shorthand writer of the Supreme Court, identified a transcript which he had made of the three identical tracks on the tape recordings found in the brown suitcase.*

THE ATTORNEY-GENERAL *read from the transcript:*

MAN	This is track four.
MAN	Get out of the fucking road.
MAN	Get in the fucking basket.
	(*Sound of door banging*)
	(*Crackling noise*)
	(*Footsteps—heavy*)
	(*Steps across room and then recording noise followed by blowing sound into microphone*)
	(*Footsteps*)
WOMAN	(*Voice, quiet, unreadable*)
	(*Footsteps, light, walking across room; whispered conversation at the same time*)
	(*Footsteps*)

(Speech, distant, containing the word 'upstairs'; then footsteps, two sets)

CHILD   *(Screaming)* Don't. Mum—Ah.

WOMAN   Shut up.

CHILD   Please God, help me. Ah. Please. Oh.

WOMAN   *(Whispering)* Come on.
  (Footsteps)

WOMAN   *(Whispering)* Shut up.

CHILD   *(Pleading)* Oh, please.

CHILD   Oh. *(Then faintly:)* Help—Oh.

CHILD   I can't while you've got hold of my neck.

CHILD   Oh. *(Followed by a scream)*

CHILD   Help. *(Followed by a gurgling noise)*

CHILD   *(Heavy breathing; sounds of distress; laboured breathing)*

WOMAN   Sh. Sh.

WOMAN   Shut up. Shut up.
  (Screams and gurgles)

CHILD   Oh. Oh. Oh. *(Child crying)*

WOMAN   *(Whispering)* Keep — and you'll be all right.

WOMAN   *(Whispering)* Sit down and be quiet.

MAN   *(Whispering)* Go on.
  Quick footsteps mounting stairs, then entering room)
  (Child crying, muffled)

MAN   *(Whispering)* Here.

WOMAN   Hush, hush. Go on.
  (Woman speaking, unreadable)
  (Child crying)

WOMAN   You are all right. Hush, hush. Put it in your mouth—hush and shift that hand.
  (Child crying)

WOMAN   Put it in your mouth and keep it in and you'll be all right.

WOMAN   Put it in. Stop it.

WOMAN   If you don't—Sh.
  (Child crying)

WOMAN   In your mouth. Hush. Hush. Shut up or I'll forget myself and hit you one. Keep it in.
  (Child whimpering)

MAN   Put it in.

WOMAN   *(Spoken quickly)* Put it in.

MAN   *(Speaks, but words unreadable except for the word 'hand')*
     (Footsteps)

MAN   Put it in. Keep it in. Stop it now. Stop it now.

WOMAN   I'm only doing this and you'll be all right.

WOMAN   Put it in your mouth. Put it in—in.
     (Further words spoken by the woman which are unreadable except for 'Put it in')

WOMAN   Will you stop it. Stop it.
     (Woman's voice, unreadable)
     (Child whimpering)

WOMAN   Shut —

MAN   Quick. Put it in now.
     (Child whimpering)
     (Retching noise)

MAN   Just put it in now, love. Put it in now.
     (Retching noise)

CHILD   *(Muffled)* What's this in for?

MAN   Put it in.

CHILD   Can I just tell you summat? I must tell you summat. Please take your hands off me a minute, please. Please—mummy—please.

CHILD   I can't tell you.
     (Grunting)

CHILD   *(In quick sequence)* I can't tell you. I can't breathe. Oh.

CHILD   I can't—dad—will you take your hands off me?
     (Man whispering)

MAN   No. Tell me.

CHILD   Please God.

MAN   Tell me.

CHILD   I can't while you've got your hands on me.
     (Mumbling sound)

MAN   Why don't you keep it in?

CHILD   Why? What are you going to do with me?

MAN   I want to take some photographs, that's all.

MAN   Put it in.

CHILD   Don't undress me, will you?

WOMAN	That's right, don't —
CHILD	It hurts me. I want to see mummy, honest to God.
MAN	Put it in.
CHILD	I'll swear on the Bible.
MAN	Put it in, and hurry up now. The quicker you do this, the quicker you'll get home.
CHILD	I've got to go because I'm going out with my mamma. Leave me, please. Help me, will you?
MAN	Put it in your mouth and you'll be all right.
CHILD	Will you let me go when this is out?
MAN	Yes. The longer it takes you to do this, the longer it takes you to get home.
CHILD	What are you going to do with me first?
MAN	I'm going to take some photographs. Put it in your mouth.
CHILD	What for?
MAN	Put it in your mouth. (*Pause*) Right in.
CHILD	I'm not going to do owt.
MAN	Put it in. If you don't keep that hand down, I'll slit your neck. (*Pause*) Put it in.
CHILD	Won't you let me go? Please.
MAN	No, no. Put it in. Stop talking.
MAN	What's your name?
CHILD	Lesley.
MAN	Lesley what?
CHILD	Ann.
MAN	What's your second name?
CHILD	Westford. Westford.
MAN	Westford?
CHILD	I have to get home before eight o'clock. I got to get— (*Pause*) Or I'll get killed if I don't. Honest to God.
MAN	Yes.
	(*Quick footsteps of woman leaving room and going downstairs; then a click; then sound of door closing; then woman's footsteps coming upstairs; then eight longer strides*)
MAN	What is it?
WOMAN	I've left the light on.
MAN	You 'ave?

WOMAN   So that — (*Remainder of sentence unreadable*)
(*Child starts crying*)

CHILD   It hurts me neck.

MAN   Hush, put it in your mouth and you'll be all right.

WOMAN   Now listen, shurrup crying.

CHILD   (*Crying*) It hurts me on me —

WOMAN   (*Interrupting*) Hush. Shut up. Now put it in. Pull that hand away and don't dally and just keep your mouth shut, please.

WOMAN   Wait a bit, I'll put this on again. D'you get me?

CHILD   (*Whining*) No, I — (*remainder of sentence unreadable*)

WOMAN   Sh. Hush. Put that in your mouth. And again — packed more solid.
(*Then whispered sentences, unreadable*)

CHILD   I want to go home. Honest to God. I'll — (*Further speech muffled but uninterrupted*) — before eight o'clock.

WOMAN   No, it's all right.

MAN   Eh!
(*Music commences. Country-style tune followed by 'Jolly St Nicholas', during which various non-vocal noises can be heard; then tune 'The Little Drummer Boy', during which a voice speaks—unreadable*)
(*Three loud cracks, systematic, even-timed*)
(*Music—'The Little Drummer Boy'—goes fainter*)
(*Footsteps*)
(*Sounds on tape cease*)

THE ATTORNEY-GENERAL *referred to another tape recording. There were three voices on the tape, he said, identified as Hindley, Brady and Patricia Hodges. The tape contained the following passage:*

HINDLEY   We went to see Uncle Jim. We went up Ashton way. Do you want to read the *Reporter*? Do you ever get that?
(*Voice, unreadable*)

HINDLEY   Read all about the news.

HODGES   Is it about Gorton?

HINDLEY   All over.
(*Brady's voice was heard at this point*)
(*Hindley referred to the* Gorton and Openshaw Reporter)

HODGES   You see that little girl there at Ancoats?

HINDLEY Yes, it is near.

HODGES   She lives near my friend.

HINDLEY Did she know her?

HODGES   I don't know. There's nowt in the papers, is there?

HINDLEY No.

JOHN WEEKS, *a BBC recording engineer, said that, to achieve the two copies of the recording containing the voice of Lesley Ann Downey, two recording machines must have been used; the third copy had clearly been made from the second. A record-player found at 16 Wardle Brook Avenue was capable of playing a Ray Conniff record which contained the same music as that on the tape recording.*

Cross-examined by MR HOOSON, *the witness said that he did not think the music on the tape could have been recorded from a transistor radio, but he could not be positive. He agreed that the tape had not been stopped while it was recording, but added:* 'I think the music was played from a second tape machine. I think it had been prerecorded, probably long before this particular recording was made. I think that at the end of the first bit of music the machine stopped, the next record was put on the gramophone, and the tape was then started simultaneously with the gramophone, and therefore you have continuity.' *He agreed that there were radio programmes which played records for quite a long period, but added:* 'Between the second two of these records on the tape there is a gap where it has been run from one track on the disc to the next. I don't think a radio station would have given you that much silence.'

Re-examined by THE ATTORNEY-GENERAL:

No doubt that while whatever was being done to that child was taking place, there was background music provided?—Yes, it was being played in that room.

BRIAN SIMPSON, *manager of a photographic shop at Ashton-under-Lyne, testified that on 1 July 1965 Myra Hindley had enquired about the hire purchase of a Fujica camera. He had sold her the camera, taking as a deposit a Ross Ensign camera which he had later sold to Mr Alfred Ashton. (Evidence read.)*

ALFRED ASHTON *identified a Ross Ensign camera which he had bought from the previous witness on 3 July 1965; the camera had been in his possession until he gave it to the police on 23 October 1965. (Evidence read.)*

DETECTIVE POLICEWOMAN MARGARET CAMPION (*recalled*) gave evidence of taking a set of fingerprints of Myra Hindley on *11 October 1965.*

DETECTIVE SERGEANT ROY JARVIS *of the Fingerprint Department of the Manchester City Police testified that fingerprints on three of the negatives of Lesley Ann Downey had been made by Hindley. He had found no fingerprints of David Smith on any of the photographs and negatives he had examined.*

Cross-examined by MR HOOSON, *the witness said that he had been asked to look for David Smith's fingerprints on objects found on the moors, but not from objects recovered from 16 Wardle Brook Avenue.*

ROBERT ROGERS, *employed in the Motor Taxation Department of the Stockport County Borough Council, said that a 1961 Morris Mini-Traveller, VDB 893, was registered in the name of Myra Hindley on 6 May 1964. On 5 April 1965 Hindley sold the vehicle to a firm in Stretford.*

DETECTIVE CHIEF SUPERINTENDENT JOHN TYRRELL *of the Manchester City Police (at the time of the inquiry, Detective Chief Inspector), examined by* MR MARS-JONES:

At 12.15 pm on Monday, 11 October last year, in company with Detective Chief Inspector Mounsey, did you see the accused Brady at Hyde Police Station?—I did.

MR HOOSON: I object to the admissibility of the evidence which follows. Perhaps I should state the grounds in the absence of the jury.

(*The jury left the court.*)

MR HOOSON: The grounds of my objection are that the interview which followed, as your Lordship will see from the depositions, occupied a period of six hours twenty minutes; that the accused was being continually pressed during this period and questioned about these events; that there was no caution given at any time and that the whole interview was oppressive and rendered any answers given not of a voluntary character.

DETECTIVE CHIEF SUPERINTENDENT JOHN TYRRELL *was examined by* MR MARS-JONES *and cross-examined by* MR HOOSON *as to the conduct of the interview.* (*See this witness's evidence before the jury, page 123.*)

Similarly, DETECTIVE CHIEF INSPECTOR JOSEPH MOUNSEY *was*

examined by THE ATTORNEY-GENERAL *and cross-examined by* MR HOOSON. (*See this witness's evidence before the jury, page* 130.)

Re-examined by THE ATTORNEY-GENERAL:

What were the kind of matters that you were trying to get information on?—My particular interest was the missing boy, John Kilbride. There were other missing people, sir: a boy and a girl.

MR JUSTICE FENTON ATKINSON: Lesley Ann Downey?—Yes. And another boy as well.

THE ATTORNEY-GENERAL: Is that the sum total of the matters you were investigating?—There was one other missing person.

MR JUSTICE FENTON ATKINSON: Four missing children at that stage?—Kilbride, Downey, and two others, all of whom had vanished without trace.

THE ATTORNEY-GENERAL: Were these matters that you, as police officers, were under a duty to investigate?—Most certainly, sir.

MR JUSTICE FENTON ATKINSON: Do you wish to call evidence, Mr Hooson?

MR HOOSON: Yes, I do. I call Brady.

IAN BRADY, *sworn.*

Examined by MR HOOSON:

I want to ask you about the interview which took place on 11 October 1965. That morning you had been remanded in custody, having been charged with the murder of Edward Evans?—Yes.

From 12.15 until 8.25 approximately you were questioned at Hyde Police Station. Was there at any time any break in the questioning?—There was no break. When Mounsey and Tyrrell stopped questioning, Mattin and Leach came in. They continued to question during the meals.

We hear that there were two officers in at a time. If one was not asking questions, what was the other doing?—The last two hours there was four: Mounsey, Tyrrell, Mattin and Leach. The interview was Mounsey at one side, Tyrrell at the other, Mattin and Leach at the front. I was being asked simultaneously questions from each side. If I gave one answer to one question, I could be answering three questions at the one time. They were shouting from a foot from each ear from both sides.

Were you at any time cautioned?—I was never cautioned.

Since all this started I have only been cautioned five times. That was three times on the first day and twice on the second two charges, just before I was charged in each case.

What was your condition by the time you had had all these questions asked you?—I was feeling I had lost my temper towards the end.

Cross-examined by THE ATTORNEY-GENERAL:

At the beginning of your evidence you took the oath?—Yes. It doesn't mean anything.

Why did you take it?—Because I realise what it symbolises.

What does it mean?—It means I am telling the truth.

By Almighty God?—By what I hold.

You know you can affirm, do you not?—Affirm?

You can spare the blasphemy. You can affirm if you wish to.— I suppose there are more theatrical ways of getting round it.

There are more honest ways of getting round it.—No, more theatrical ways.

Did you hear the evidence of Superintendent Tyrrell, who said you found the interview amusing, or some of it?—At the beginning I said it was amusing.

What was amusing about it?—The fact that I was being questioned about these matters. I wasn't interested. This was the first time I had heard of it. I had been charged on the Wednesday previous with a murder. As far as I was concerned, I was finished. I wasn't interested in any more murders.

You were aware that you were being questioned about what was thought to be the murder of missing children. Did you find that amusing?—I found it amusing, yes.

Why?—Because of the way they were talking, it was serious to them. It was amusing to me.

Why?—It was amusing that they had believed Smith.

You found that amusing?—I was amused that they were taking the whole thing so seriously.

Let me ask you this. Were the answers you gave true or false?— The answers which I gave were true. The answers which he has in the notebook are false.

I put it to you, first of all, that you were cautioned.—I was not.

The two senior officers have sworn that, and they are telling the truth.—I am not worried what they say. I was not cautioned. I know the five times I have been cautioned.

You were asked by Mr Mounsey: 'I have reason to believe you have discussed the subject of doing bank jobs, killing people and burying them on the moors, with David Smith'?—I discussed bank jobs, not killing people. Killing people was discussed generally, in the event of a robbery. If they were killed accidentally. That is what I said by 'general discussion'.

Were you asked by Mr Mounsey: 'Have you discussed killing people and burying their bodies on the moors'?—I was asked if I had discussed burying bodies on the moors. I said I had discussed it on the previous Wednesday and on no other occasion.

It was all part of the fiction to impress Smith?—There was no talk about fiction to impress anyone.

Did Mr Mounsey say to you: 'David Smith has told us that on the night that Evans was killed you said it was the messiest yet. It normally takes only one hit'? Did he ask you, did you say that?—No. He asked me if I said that, and I said, something like that. I said it is a messy job, referring to the blood on the floor—wiping it up.

Perhaps what you have just said may be more significant.

MR JUSTICE FENTON ATKINSON: Brady, was there anything you said to the police that you said against your will, or under pressure?—No. Towards the end it was just —

You lost your temper but it was all quite voluntary, so far as you were concerned, or was it not?—It was, yes, but I am saying that their records of the conversation are not correct.

That is quite another matter.

THE ATTORNEY-GENERAL: It was you who lost your temper, was it not?—It was I who lost my temper? We all did towards the end, according to Mounsey.

MR JUSTICE FENTON ATKINSON: Mr Hooson, do you wish to re-examine?

MR HOOSON: No, my Lord.

MR JUSTICE FENTON ATKINSON: Do you wish to say any more?

MR HOOSON: I very much bear in mind the answer Brady has given in answer to your Lordship's question, but I ask you to find on that evidence that certainly there was a continuous questioning. The very question that your Lordship put, in my submission, is the key to this: I think your Lordship asked one of the detectives how many deaths he was investigating, virtually to say: 'Well, when police officers have the serious duty of investigating something of this kind, the implication may be that you can really stretch the rules to the limit whatever happens.' My Lord, that, in my submission, is a quite wrong approach and is the key to this case: because they were investigating matters which no doubt disturbed them—as they would disturb anyone—they were prepared to bring all the pressure they could to try and break Brady down. My Lord, when one asks: 'How many deaths were you investigating?', one is really saying that the more serious the offence, the more you can, as it were, take liberties on this matter.

MR HOOSON *amplified this submission, but* MR JUSTICE FENTON ATKINSON *ruled against him*: '. . . on the evidence I am satisfied that the evidence of this interview is admissible as being free and voluntary, and I am quite satisfied there was nothing unfair or anything relating to threats or improper inducement.'

(*The jury returned to court.*)

DETECTIVE CHIEF SUPERINTENDENT JOHN TYRRELL (*recalled*); *examination continued by* MR MARS-JONES:

How did the interview open?—Mr Mounsey introduced both of us to Brady and then he immediately cautioned him.

Did he explain the nature of the inquiries?—He did.

Did he go on and deal with other matters?—Yes.

What transpired after that?—Mr Mounsey said: 'I have reason to believe that you discussed the subject of doing bank jobs, killing people and burying them on the moors, with David Smith.' Brady replied: 'There are no others.' Mr Mounsey said: 'I believe you have also discussed with Smith which is the most satisfactory way of killing a person.' Brady said. 'I discussed many things with Smith. It's all to do with the bank jobs. I have been planning these for a long time.' Mr Mounsey said: 'Have you discussed killing people and burying their bodies on the moors?' and Brady said: 'Yes, I talked about it in a vague sort of way. It was all part of the fiction to impress him.'

Did Mr Mounsey then ask him further questions of another matter?—Yes.

And a little later did he return to what David Smith was

alleged to have said to the accused Brady?—Yes. He said: 'David Smith has told us that on the night that Evans was killed you said it was the messiest yet. It normally only takes one hit. Did you say that?' and Brady said: 'I said something like that. It was just to do with the situation we were in.' Mr Mounsey said: 'Why did you say that if there were no others?' and Brady said: 'There are no others.' Mr Mounsey said: 'You have boasted to Smith of killing three or four people.' Brady replied: 'I may have given him a vague impression but it was just part of the fiction I was promoting to impress him regarding the bank jobs.' Mr Mounsey said: 'Was that what the guns were for?' and Brady said: 'Yes.' Mr Mounsey said: 'Smith has told us that on the Saturday night before Evans was killed you were questioning whether or not he believed you capable of committing murder, and that you told him that you had and could and that the next one would not count as you were not due for another for three months yet.' Brady did not answer and Mr Mounsey repeated the question. Brady said: 'I don't remember that.' Mr Mounsey said: 'You do remember talking to Smith about killing people and burying them on the moors, don't you?' and Brady said: 'I spoke in general terms.'

Did you then question him regarding other matters?—Yes.

At 3 pm did you break off the interview?—Yes.

Did you and Mr Mounsey resume the interview at 3.30?—Yes.

And after making inquiries of Brady about other matters, what did you say?—I said: 'I think you went on the moors at night to dispose of bodies of victims you killed, just as you told Smith.' Brady said: 'That's not true. What I told Smith was only to build up an image.' I said: 'You have boasted to Smith about killing people. Was it in order to impress him should it be necessary to kill again when you did the bank jobs?' and Brady said: 'Something like that. I am only interested in profit. Killing is a last resort.'

Did Mr Mounsey then ask him questions on the same theme? —Yes. He said: 'Smith says that after Evans had been killed, Myra told him that on one occasion on the moors she was stopped at the roadside in the mini with a body in the back while you were digging a grave some distance away. A policeman came up and asked if anything was the matter, and she said she was drying her sparking plugs.' Brady replied: 'I remember something about an incident, but I wasn't burying any body. I would be practising with my revolvers.'

Did you then discuss other matters with him until 5.30 pm when the accused Brady had his tea?—Yes.

Did you and Mr Mounsey resume your interview with the accused Brady at 6.20 pm?—Yes.

Was Detective Chief Superintendent Benfield present?—Yes.

On this occasion did you ask questions about the disposal plan?—Yes.

Did Mr Mounsey refer to the entry, 'Check periodically unmoved'?—Yes. He said: 'Does that refer to the bodies you have buried on the moors and is it a reminder to check that the graves are still intact?' Brady said it was only to do with Evans.

Were other matters discussed with Brady until the interview finally ended at 8 pm?—Yes.

SEVENTH DAY *Wednesday, 27 April*

DETECTIVE CHIEF SUPERINTENDENT JOHN TYRRELL (*recalled*); *examination continued by* MR MARS-JONES:

The witness testified that he and Detective Chief Inspector Mounsey interviewed Hindley at Risley Remand Centre at 11.25 pm on 14 October 1965: After some preliminary questions, I said: 'You told David Smith that on one occasion on the moors you were stopped in the mini at the roadside with a body in the back while Brady was digging a grave some distance away.' Hindley replied: 'That's rubbish.' Mr Mounsey said: 'Brady has agreed he talked in general terms of robbing a bank, killing people and burying their bodies on the moor.' Hindley said: 'It is not true. There have been no conversations like that.' Mr Mounsey said: 'Not even about doing bank jobs?' and Hindley said: 'No. Smith's an idiotic moron.' Mr Mounsey later asked Hindley if she knew anything about the disappearance of Lesley Ann Downey. Hindley said: 'I don't know anything about her.

I have never been near the fairground.' We continued to talk to her about her association with Brady and her background. I also showed her several photographs. I left her at 2.15 pm.

The witness testified that at 3.05 pm the same day, he and Detective Chief Inspector Mounsey interviewed Brady at Risley Remand Centre. After cautioning Brady, Mounsey asked him to identify several photographs. Brady was shown a photograph of himself standing on a rock, which it was now known was taken near the A635 road on Saddleworth Moor; Brady was looking in a direction near to the place where the body of Lesley Ann Downey was found. Brady said that the location of the photograph was Whaley Bridge. The interview continued with Brady being asked further questions about his conversations with David Smith, and ended at 4.05 pm.

The witness testified that on 20 October 1965 he examined a prayer book found at 16 Wardle Brook Avenue: It bears an inscription on the fly page: 'To Myra from Auntie Kath and Uncle Bert, 16th November 1958. Souvenir of your first Holy Communion.' I examined this book carefully and found a counterfoil of a left-luggage ticket. I found this rolled very, very tightly and pushed down the spine of the prayer book. The counterfoil was for two suitcases in the left-luggage office at Manchester Central Station.

Cross-examined by MR HOOSON:

Mr Tyrrell, I want to go back to the interview of Monday, 11 October. I understand that neither you nor your colleague, Mr Mounsey, took any steps to inform Brady's solicitor that this interview was going to take place?—I personally did not.

You started the interview at 12.15 and completed it, you say, about eight. Accepting now the breaks that you say took place, during the whole of that period he was subjected to constant questioning by you and Mr Mounsey?—We were asking him questions most of the time.

Constantly, were you not? Let us not argue about the meaning of words here.—Yes.

And the aim of this questioning was to produce as much pressure as you could to try and get admissions from Brady?—The aim of the questioning was, so far as I was concerned, to establish the truth of the matter. Here was a man who we had heard had boasted about killing several people and we were inquiring about the disappearance —

MR HOOSON: I can understand your feelings.

MR JUSTICE FENTON ATKINSON: You interrupted.

MR HOOSON: I am sorry.

MR JUSTICE FENTON ATKINSON: He was in the middle of a sentence.

THE WITNESS: We were inquiring about the disappearance of several young people in the Manchester area and I was trying to establish, from my point of view, the truth.

MR HOOSON: When these interviews started you started making a note of the questions and answers?—Yes.

Am I right in saying that, after half a page, you found it impossible because the questions were coming so fast?—I would not say that was the only reason I found it impossible. I wanted to see this man's reactions.

What time did you write up your notes of the first part of this interview after giving up your attempt to record it properly?—It was about one o'clock.

Had you left the room to write up your notes?—Yes.

Your notes were your recollection of a very fast conversation?—Yes. They were read over by Mr Mounsey shortly afterwards and he agreed that this was a correct record.

They were not read over to Brady, were they?—Oh, no.

I suggest, you see, that the man Brady was never cautioned on this occasion.—He was cautioned by Mr Mounsey right at the start.

To get the picture correct, we know that he was brought in some food at 3 o'clock. You have got it recorded as a meal break between 3 and 3.30, but a senior officer stayed in with him the whole of that period?—Yes. I understand Mr Mounsey stayed in. I certainly left the room.

When you came back, certainly Brady was still being questioned?—I cannot honestly remember.

Between 5.30 and 6.20 when you were absent, Mr Mattin and Mr Leach, who are detective inspectors, were with him?—They came in to relieve us while he had some tea.

And they were still questioning him when you came back?—No. They may have been talking. I cannot remember.

Your clear impression was that when he was being questioned about what Smith said—and there must have been many questions, and you are really giving the gist of it—Brady said: 'My discussions with Smith were confined to bank jobs and to do with Evans'?—He stressed the bank jobs and mentioned Evans later on when we were discussing the disposal plan.

Your impression was that any conversation relating to the burying on the moors related to the disposal of Evans?—Yes. He did not refer to any other person.

According to your record, Mr Mounsey said: 'David Smith has told us that on the night Evans was killed you said it was the messiest yet.' That is one thing. Then: ' "It normally only takes one hit." Did you say that?' What did you understand that this question referred to? That it was the messiest yet, or it only takes one hit?—I understood it meant he was referring to the whole of the question.

You agree that might easily have been, in the fast conversation that took place, two questions?—As I recall, it was one question. Mr Mounsey asked that, and Brady replied: 'I said something like that.'

If you were asked now to give a full and accurate report of our questions and answers this morning, do you think you could?—It is a different situation when one is asking the questions and when one is answering them.

Do you think it is easier for the questioner to record this than the answerer?—I think it would be.

MR JUSTICE FENTON ATKINSON: Perhaps the judge can say: 'I have got down in my notebook the things I think are important, and not the others.'

MR HOOSON: The modern judge is normally making a note as it takes place.

Is it right that towards the end of this interview, getting on for 8 o'clock, tempers were getting rather frayed?—No. Certainly not as far as the police officers were concerned. Brady did not appear to be in any way distressed about this. He had an arrogant, contemptuous air about him.

Towards the end of the interview, was Brady saying less and less?—From about 7.30 it was more in the form of a conversation than questions and answers.

I want to move now to 14 October. In the course of that interview, Brady was shown some photographs, was he not?—I think he was shown seven altogether.

With regard to photograph 2, did not Brady say it was taken across from Crowden? [*Photographs produced to the witness.*]—Mr Mounsey wrote the replies Brady made on the back of the photographs.

The photograph with woods in the background: did Brady say that was Whaley Bridge?—He did.

I look at the back of it and see: 'Yes, Myra took this. It is across from Crowden somewhere.'—I do not know when that was written on. The writing Mr Mounsey wrote was 'Whaley Bridge' on that occasion.

Who gave the reply: 'Yes, Myra took this. It is across from Crowden somewhere'?—I have no idea.

When was that written on it? Just look at it.—I have no idea. I do not even recognise the handwriting. *That* [the words 'Whaley Bridge', also written on the back of the photograph] is certainly Mr Mounsey's handwriting.

Just hold the photographs up for the jury. You see how completely different the two places are? One is a wooded area and the other is a moorland area.—We only recorded what he said.

I suggest to you that the reply he gave when questioned about that wooded photograph was: 'It was taken by Myra across from Crowden,' and that is what is written on that photograph.—Certainly not at that stage. This is neither my handwriting nor Mr Mounsey's.

Cross-examined by MR HEILPERN:

I want to ask you about the interview which you and Mr Mounsey had with Myra Hindley on 14 October. Would there have been any difficulty in getting Mr Fitzpatrick, her solicitor, there?—I suppose not.

Did you think you stood a better chance of getting your answers if he was not there?—Possibly.

MR JUSTICE FENTON ATKINSON: Did she ask to see her solicitor?

THE WITNESS: If she had asked, we would not have questioned her at all until he was present.

MR HEILPERN: You have given evidence of the discovery of

the left-luggage ticket down the back of a prayer book. Isn't it right that the information came from Brady?—No. Brady never mentioned any prayer book to me at all.

Didn't you at Ashton-under-Lyne Police Station on 28 October say to Hindley: 'We searched very carefully indeed. We would never have found it by ourselves until Brady told us where it was'?—I certainly did not say that to her.

Re-examined by MR MARS-JONES:

It is suggested that in the interview with Brady there was a non-stop fusillade of questions. What was the tempo of that interview?—At times it was quite slow because Brady paused while he thought of answers, and on some occasions he came out with the answers immediately.

What was his reaction to the questions put to him in the early part of the interview?—He appeared to be amused about it. He was quite calm and composed.

DETECTIVE CHIEF INSPECTOR JOSEPH MOUNSEY *of the Lancashire Constabulary, stationed at Ashton-under-Lyne, testified that at 12.15 pm on 11 October 1965 he and Chief Superintendent Tyrrell interviewed Brady at Hyde Police Station; he cautioned Brady and told him that they were making inquiries about the disappearance of two boys, one of whom was John Kilbride. The witness confirmed Chief Superintendent Tyrrell's evidence relating to this interview and to the interviews with Hindley and Brady at Risley Remand Centre on 14 October; he said that, at the start of the interview with Hindley, she was cautioned and told: 'We are making inquiries regarding two missing children, one of whom is John Kilbride.'*

Cross-examined by MR HOOSON, *the witness said that he wrote his notes of the first interview with Brady from the notebook of Chief Superintendent Tyrrell; he did this after the interview, at about 9 pm.*

MR HOOSON: Your note is merely copying Mr Tyrrell's?—I agreed with what he put. The only disagreement was whether the phrase 'Killing is a last resort' was in fact 'Killing as a last resort'.

When you put to Brady the remark that Evans's death was 'the messiest yet,' did he not say that he had said it had been a messy job?—No, sir.

How can you recall hours later his exact words?—This was

the impression of an unusual situation, and the words used made a profound impression on me.

Towards the end of the interview did you say: 'Don't pull the shutters down'?—I did not.

Were you anxious to go on?—I was anxious for the truth.

Cross-examined by MR HEILPERN, *the witness said that Hindley was not denied the opportunity of having a solicitor present at the interview on 14 October:* 'It is our rule and practice that if a person asks for a solicitor, we get one. Ordinarily, we do not tell them. Admittedly, I preferred to conduct the interview without a solicitor present as long as Miss Hindley accepted that.'

MR HEILPERN: Why did you prefer that course?—It has been my experience that if a solicitor had been present we would have been less likely to get at the truth.

But one of the consequences of having a solicitor present is that there can be a separate record of what has taken place.— That might be helpful.

DETECTIVE CONSTABLE PETER CLEGG *of the Lancashire Constabulary*: On Friday, 15 October 1965, I went with Patricia Ann Hodges in a police car, and at her direction we travelled along the A635 road between Greenfield and Holmfirth. She indicated to me a spot on the roadside. The spot indicated is the area of black peat land just below the reference 'Oldham 7¾' on the map exhibit [See page 160.].

MR MARS-JONES: A suggestion has been put into terms that you took this young girl to the spot and stopped the car and asked her if certain places were familiar.—This is not correct. I have never previously travelled on that road beyond Mossley.

Cross-examined by MR HOOSON, *the witness said that it was the only time he had been with the girl in the car; before 15 October 1965 he had never seen any of the photographs in the case. He had spent about twenty-five minutes in the car with the girl:* 'We travelled rather slowly in order that she could familiarise herself with landmarks.'

Cross-examined by MR HEILPERN, *the witness said that the girl also indicated an area on the south side of the road just beyond a black and white crash barrier. The crash barrier was the only landmark which the girl had been able to remember.*

MR HEILPERN: Did you say: 'Do you recognise this part or the next part?' or words of that kind?—On one occasion I did mention something like that in relation to the black and white crash barrier.

POLICE CONSTABLE ROBERT SPIERS *of the Lancashire Constabulary*: On Saturday, 16 October 1965, I was part of the force excavating at the north side of the A635 road and working its way up towards the hill known as Hollin Brown Knoll. At 2.50 pm on that day I was searching an area on the top of that hill when I saw a depression in the peat which contained water. I also saw a piece of bone protruding out of the water, as if it was coming from the ground under the water. I called Detective Sergeant Eckersley to the scene.

DETECTIVE SERGEANT LESLIE ECKERSLEY *of the Lancashire Constabulary*: At 2.55 pm on 16 October 1965 Police Constable Spiers showed me a piece of bone sticking up from the water in a depression. I carefully removed a little soil from around the bone and I saw further bone. There was a strong smell of decomposing flesh, and I removed a little more soil and I saw flesh and a human head. I then informed Detective Chief Inspector Mounsey who came to the scene with Detective Inspector Mattin. I was present when the remains of a body I now know to be Lesley Ann Downey were recovered from the ground. The body was naked and near the body from the ground was recovered certain clothing, a pair of shoes and a string of beads.

POLICE INSPECTOR JOHN CHADDOCK, *stationed at Uppermill in the Saddleworth sub-division of the Huddersfield Division of the West Riding Constabulary*: The village of Greenfield is within the area of my supervision, as is the A635 road for a distance of three and a half miles from Greenfield. This length of road embraces the part of Saddleworth Moor known as Hollin Brown Knoll and the adjacent part known as Sail Bark Moss.

On Boxing Day, 1964, I spent the whole day knocking about in the Saddleworth area. I was there from 9 am until 11.30 pm. I recollect that it was a cold, frosty day; there had been snow the previous day, not a heavy fall but some of this remained and in the late afternoon and early evening of Boxing Day a further fall took place—this was only a moderate fall. Neither the frost nor the snow affected the A635 road. Traffic was moving along the road all day. Rock salt was applied from the early evening.

Wessenden Head is the area on the north side of the A635 road. It is the watershed where the terrain falls away towards Marsden, which is on the east side of the Pennines.

On Saturday, 16 October 1965, at 7.15 pm, as a result of what I was told I went to Hollin Brown Knoll and I there saw the remains of a body. At 10.50 pm I accompanied the body to Uppermill Mortuary, and at 5.35 pm on 17 October I was present at the mortuary when Mrs Gertrude Downey identified the body as that of her daughter. I was also present when she identified the clothing, shoes and necklace found with the body.

DETECTIVE SERGEANT THOMAS RYLATT *of the Photographic Branch of the West Riding Constabulary proved three sets of photographs which he had taken: (a) at 8.30 pm, 16 October 1965, of the position of the body of Lesley Ann Downey as it was exposed in the ground and of the clothing found in the grave; (b) on 17 October at Uppermill Mortuary of the condition of, and marks upon, the body; (c) on 17 October of the deceased's clothing. (Evidence read.)*

DETECTIVE CHIEF INSPECTOR JOSEPH MOUNSEY *(recalled) testified that he was present when the remains of Lesley Ann Downey were recovered from the ground. The witness also testified that he had enlargements made of the photographs found in the suitcases deposited at Manchester Central Station*: 'From a detailed search, I came to the conclusion that eight of the photographs had been taken in the vicinity of the place where the body of Lesley Ann Downey had been found.'

DETECTIVE CONSTABLE RAYMOND GELDER, *official photographer to the Lancashire Constabulary, identified photographs he had taken in the vicinity of Hollin Brown Knoll; these photographs matched those referred to by the previous witness.*

GEORGE BIRCH, *photographer for the* Daily Express, *identified an aerial photograph he had taken on 20 October 1965 of the A635 road where it crosses Saddleworth Moor.*

DR DAVID GEE, *Lecturer in Forensic Medicine at the University of Leeds*: On 16 October 1965 I went to a spot on the north side of the A635 road, on what is known as Saddleworth Moor. I was shown a partly excavated grave by Detective Chief Inspector Mounsey. My colleagues and I then set about exposing the remains in that grave. The body lay on its right side; the skeletal remains of the left arm were extended above the head, and the hand was missing. The right arm was beneath the body, the hand being near the right knee. Both legs were doubled up towards the abdomen, flexed at hips and knees. The head was in normal position. The body was naked. A number of articles of clothing were present in the soil near to the feet.

On Sunday, 17 October, in the presence of Professor Polson, Drs Manning and Bartley and numerous police officers, I carried out a post-mortem examination of the body at Uppermill Mortuary.

The initial impression given by the injuries, notably two eliptical injuries of the right chest, was that the child had been stabbed; the clean-cut margins of the injury in the right groin had the appearance of a long incised wound. As soon as it was possible to examine these injuries more closely under low magnification, it was apparent that all the damage done to the body was unlike that due to human interference but entirely consisted of damage by animals. Stabbing was definitely excluded by the fact that the damage in the region of these injuries was entirely superficial. The disappearance of the abdominal organs could have destroyed signs of the cause of death. The heart, lungs, air passages, gullet and brain were sufficiently preserved to permit the statement that no gross injury to which this death could be ascribed was present. Signs of asphyxia were absent and therefore proof of suffocation was lacking. In summary, the post-mortem examination established that this was the body of a female child of an age between the years of seven and thirteen. Subsequent dental examination narrowed the age limit to that of approximately ten years. The post-mortem changes in the body were consistent with its having lain in peaty soil for a prolonged period: probably several months, but not several years. It was impossible to demonstrate the cause of death. The examination excluded certain possible causes, notably injury by blunt force, calculated to fracture bones. It also excluded strangulation by a ligature. It did not exclude other forms of mechanical asphyxia, notably smothering. I cannot, of course, exclude death by natural causes.

DETECTIVE CHIEF INSPECTOR CLIFFORD HAIGH *of the Manchester City Police*: At 2.35 pm on Monday, 18 October 1965, I was present with Detective Chief Superintendent Benfield and

Superintendent Talbot in an office at Hyde Police Station when the accused Brady was brought in. I recorded the conversation in my notebook. After cautioning Brady, Mr Benfield said: 'Have you got a driving licence?' Brady said: 'Yes.' Mr Benfield said: 'What is it for?' Brady said: 'For a motor cycle.' Mr Benfield said: 'Can you drive a motor car?' Brady replied: 'Yes, but I have never driven on a road; only on private land.' Mr Benfield said: 'There are two suitcases, a blue one and a brown one, which I believe are your property.' Brady replied: 'Yes, they are.' Mr Benfield said: 'I believe these were deposited by you at Central Station, Manchester, on 5 October 1965.' Brady said: 'I can't remember the date.' Mr Benfield said: 'In these cases, there are several articles bearing your name. Do they belong to you?' Brady said: 'Part of them do.' Mr Benfield said: 'Firstly, will you look at this envelope which bears the initials "I. B." and contains photographs of a young girl with a scarf round her mouth. Did you take these?' Brady replied: 'Yes, I took them.' Mr Benfield said: 'Where?' Brady replied: 'At Hattersley, at Wardle Brook Avenue.' Mr Benfield then showed the accused a number of books on sex, sexual anomalies and perversions. Brady said that some were his, others were David Smith's. Mr Benfield then showed the accused a wooden box which contained, amongst other things, a length of rubber hose partly covered with lead; this is accurately described as a home-made cosh. Brady said: 'It's mine.' Brady also admitted ownership of five boxes of ammunition and a bandolier containing a quantity of 0·303 cartridges. Later he was shown two books wrapped in a newspaper, namely *Justine* by De Sade and *The Life and Ideas of the Marquis de Sade*; a notebook containing a list of titles of books and notes about perversions; and a handle-shaped instrument, a cosh, bearing the word 'Eureka'. Brady said that these items were Smith's.

Mr Benfield then said: 'I would like you to look at these articles of clothing and this set of beads. These garments were recovered from the moor near Greenfield late last Saturday night. This clothing has been identified as that of Lesley Ann Downey, whose body was recovered at the same time and place. I have reason to believe that the photographs of the naked girl which were found in your suitcase are of Lesley Ann Downey. Would

you like to say anything about these photographs?' Brady replied:
'Not at present.'

Mr Benfield then said: 'I would like you now to listen to a tape
recording. Two tapes were found in the blue suitcase belonging
to you.' Brady replied: 'I know the tape.' Brady sat throughout
the playing of the tape with his head bowed. Then Mr Benfield
said: 'You say you know the tape. The voices appear to be those
of yourself and Myra and of Lesley Ann Downey.' Brady said:
'She didn't give the name "Downey". It was something else.'
Mr Benfield said: 'Do you wish to say anything else about that
recording—about what took place?' Brady said: 'Not at the moment.' Mr Benfield said: 'As I have said previously, this girl's
body was recovered from the moors last Saturday evening.'
Brady said: 'There is an explanation for it. I didn't kill Lesley,
but I took those photographs.' Mr Benfield said: 'The girl was
missing from about 5 pm on Boxing Day, 1964. Where did you
meet her?' Brady said: 'I met her at the house. I don't know
how she got there.' Mr Benfield produced the shoes and socks
identified as those of Lesley Ann Downey. Mr Benfield said:
'Look at these photographs. Do you agree that the shoes and
socks on the photographs are similar to these?' Brady said:
'Yes.' Mr Benfield said: 'It is reasonable to assume that Lesley
Ann Downey died at Wardle Brook Avenue.' Brady said: 'No,
I only took the photographs.' Mr Benfield said: 'Can you tell
me how and where she met her death?' Brady said: 'I don't
know. There's only the photographs on my part.' Mr Benfield
said: 'How did she arrive at the house?' Brady replied: 'She
came in either a car or a van.' Mr Benfield said: 'Who brought
her?' Brady replied: 'Two men. One stayed outside—I don't
know him—the other man I do know but I am not prepared to
tell you at present.' Mr Benfield said: 'It appears that the photographs were taken in a bedroom. Who was present when they
were taken?' Brady said: 'Only Myra, myself, and the little girl.'
Mr Benfield said: 'Where was the man during this time?' Brady
said: 'Downstairs.' Mr Benfield said: 'When the man arrived
at the house with the little girl, what did he say about her?'
Brady said: 'He didn't need to say anything. I knew why he had
brought her.' Mr Benfield said: 'During the recording of the tape,
it appears that you are trying to get the girl to put something in

her mouth. What was it?' Brady replied: 'The scarf.' Mr Benfield then said: 'After the photographs had been taken, what happened to the little girl?' Brady said: 'She left the house with the man who brought her.' Mr Benfield said: 'Was she alive when she left?' Brady said: 'Yes. I was told later that she had been dropped off at Belle Vue.' Mr Benfield said: 'If you say the girl left Wardle Brook Avenue alive, surely you are prepared to tell us the name of the man who brought her and took her away.' After some hesitation, Brady said: 'No.' Mr Benfield said: 'Don't you think that in your own interests and in order that necessary inquiries may be made immediately, if there is such a man you should tell us now?' Brady remained silent for a short time, then he said: 'No, I'm not saying who it is. I've met him in Manchester and he goes in Liston's Bar.' Mr Benfield said: 'Do you know his name?' Brady said: 'Yes, but I am not going to say who at present, until I have had advice. I will mention this to Mr Fitzgerald on Thursday and I will take his advice. When I saw him this morning, he told me not to make any statement.' Mr Benfield showed Brady a photograph of Brady standing on a rock against a moorland background. Mr Benfield said: 'This appears to be the site where the body of Lesley Ann Downey was found.' Brady said: 'I don't know the place. I have been all over the moors.' Mr Benfield said: 'Last week you said to other police officers, in my presence, that you had told David Smith that you had buried a body on the moors, but that you had said that only to impress him. We have now found the body of Lesley Ann Downey whose last known whereabouts was in the house at Wardle Brook Avenue with you and Myra.' Brady said: 'I never said anything like that to Smith, and I deny what you say about telling other police officers that I had said it to Smith. I mean that I said I had buried a body.'

Mr Benfield concluded the interview by saying to Brady: 'You may sign the note taken by Mr Haigh.' Brady replied: 'Not at this stage.' The interview ended at 8.05 pm.

On the same day I attended an interview with Myra Hindley at Hyde Police Station. After administering the caution, Mr Benfield showed the accused the two suitcases and the photographs of Lesley Ann Downey. Mr Benfield said: 'I have reason to believe that these photographs were taken in your bedroom by

Ian Brady in your presence.' Hindley held her head in her hands; she made no reply. She was sitting with her head down and had her handkerchief across her mouth with the knuckles of both hands against her cheeks. Mr Benfield then told her of the discovery of the body of Lesley Ann Downey, showed her the child's clothing, and said that he believed the photographs were taken on Boxing Day, 1964. Hindley still did not speak or change her position. Mr Benfield then said: 'Brady has told me that the little girl was brought to your home by two men. One of the men came into the house and remained downstairs whilst Brady was taking the photographs in your presence.' Hindley said: 'I'm saying nothing.' Mr Benfield then played the tape recording of the voices of the two accused and Lesley Ann Downey. Hindley was sitting with her head bowed, and she started sobbing and a pulse at the left side of her throat was pulsating rapidly. When the recording was finished, Mr Benfield said: 'Did you hear that recording?' She nodded her head and in a very quiet voice said: 'I'm ashamed.' She then commenced to cry. This lasted a very short time and then she said: 'I'm saying nothing.' The interview terminated at 9.45 pm.

Cross-examined by MR HOOSON, *who did not dispute any of the answers given by Brady during the interview on 18 October, the witness testified that at no time did Brady ask to see his solicitor, and that Brady was cautioned immediately the interview started.*

Cross-examined by MR HEILPERN, *the witness gave similar testimony regarding the interview with Hindley on 18 October.*

DETECTIVE CHIEF SUPERINTENDENT ARTHUR BENFIELD (*recalled*) *confirmed the accounts given by the previous witness of the interviews with the two accused on 18 October.*

Cross-examined by MR HOOSON:

You thought it essential to have somebody present to record the questions and answers?—Indeed, sir. That is why I had Mr Haigh taking the notes.

At some stage of this interview—let us forget when it was— Brady told you he had been advised by his solicitor not to make any statement?—He did.

Nevertheless, having been told that, you continued to question him.—And he continued to answer.

Are you saying that at no time did Brady ask for his solicitor?—

I am, sir. There have been other occasions when the accused Hindley has asked for her solicitor and I have called him. There was no reason for me not to do it, had Brady requested me.

POLICE SUPERINTENDENT ROBERT TALBOT (*recalled*) *confirmed the accounts given by Detective Chief Inspector Clifford Haigh of the interviews with the two accused on 18 October.*

DETECTIVE INSPECTOR NORMAN MATTIN *of the Manchester City Police*: On Thursday, 28 October 1965, I was present at an interview conducted by Detective Chief Inspector Tyrrell when Hindley was asked about matters other than the Downey case. She said: 'As far as Lesley Ann Downey is concerned, Ian didn't kill her, I didn't kill her. I suggest you see Smith.' Mr Tyrrell said: 'If you have any evidence against anybody else, it is in your interests to tell me now, and I plead with you to do so.' Hindley replied: 'You know Lesley Ann Downey was at the house. She was brought there by Smith and taken away by Smith.' Mr Tyrrell said: 'How can you prove that?' She replied: 'I can't say.' Mr Tyrrell then said: 'When we saw you previously, you said you didn't know Downey.' Hindley made no reply. Mr Tyrrell went on: 'I think you know about this unfortunate child being killed and buried on the moors.' Hindley said: 'As far as I know, there was nobody killed, nobody buried, and as far as Lesley Ann Downey is concerned, Smith took her out of the house and I haven't the slightest idea who did them.'

KEITH BLIMSTONE, *aged seventeen, living in Gorton, testified that he went to the police after seeing his name in a newspaper report of the trial. He said that he knew David Smith at school. In 1964 he had no van and no driving licence. He had never been to Wardle Brook Avenue and had never seen or heard anything of Lesley Ann Downey.*

MR HOOSON: As far as the defence is concerned, no implication is made against this man.

EIGHTH DAY *Thursday, 28 April*

DETECTIVE CHIEF SUPERINTENDENT ARTHUR BENFIELD (*recalled*) *testified that at 9.40 am on 31 October 1965 he cautioned and charged Hindley with the murder of Lesley Ann Downey, and she replied: 'It is not true.' At 9.55 am on the same day he cautioned and charged Brady with this murder, and Brady replied: 'Not guilty.'*

THE ATTORNEY-GENERAL *said that that concluded the prosecution evidence in the Downey case. The prosecution would now turn to the Kilbride case.*

DETECTIVE CONSTABLE PETER MASHEDER, *official photographer to the Lancashire Constabulary*: On 21 October 1965 I went to a point on the south side of the A635 road. At the request of Detective Chief Inspector Mounsey, I studied the landscape, looking in a northerly direction, and was satisfied that I had found the place where one of the photographs found in a suitcase at Manchester Central Station was taken; the photograph showed Hindley squatting and looking down at the ground. I took a photograph of the same view. Preparations were then made to dig the area shown at the bottom of the photograph. Inspector Chaddock pushed a stick into the ground. When he removed the stick there was a strong smell of decomposing flesh. I was present when human remains were exposed in the ground at that point.

SHEILA KILBRIDE: I live at Ashton-under-Lyne. I last saw my son John at 1 pm on 23 November 1963 at my home. He had always enjoyed very good health. He had a marked gap between his upper middle front teeth; his upper front teeth were large and square. On 22 October 1965 I was taken to the mortuary at Uppermill where I saw the clothes my son was wearing when I last saw him that Saturday. The grey check jacket has plastic buttons in the appearance of a football. I sewed those buttons on myself and I had one left over; I handed this button to Mr Mounsey. I had turned the hem of the jacket up and I recognised this when I saw the jacket. This jacket was part of a suit that had been given to me by Mrs Thornton. John was not wearing the trousers of this suit that Saturday. Mrs Thornton had not given me the trousers. I recognised the vest as one of John's father's. I had taken it in at the sides in order to make it fit John. The pullover and underpants were similar to those John was wearing when he disappeared. The trousers were also similar, and I recognised some odd-coloured buttons which I had stitched on myself. I recognised a shoe as one of a pair of shoes which John was wearing; I had recently had them mended at the Co-op and they were 'Supaduke' make. (*Evidence read.*)

NELLIE HAGUE, *living at Audenshaw, testified that in June 1963 her son had outgrown a grey check suit; she had kept the trousers but given the jacket to her mother, Mrs Annie Thornton. This was the jacket found with the body of John Kilbride. On 3 December 1963, after the disappearance of John Kilbride, she had handed the trousers to the police, and recognised them now. (*Evidence read.*)*

ANNIE THORNTON, *living at Ashton-under-Lyne, testified that the grey check jacket shown to her had been given to her by her daughter in June 1963; within a few days of receiving the jacket, she had given it to Mrs Doran, her next-door neighbour, who was Sheila Kilbride's mother. (*Evidence read.*)*

MARGARET DORAN, *living at Ashton-under-Lyne*: I remember, in June 1963, Mrs Thornton sent her husband in with a grey check jacket. I folded it and put it on a chair until John Kilbride, my grandson, came. John tried the jacket on and it fitted him. His mother came later and took it away with her. (*Evidence read.*)

JOHN RYAN: I am fourteen. I knew John Kilbride well. I used to see him at the morning matinée at the Odeon. On Saturday afternoon, 23 November 1963, I saw John outside the Pavilion picture house in Ashton. We went into the pictures together. The picture ended about 5 pm. Then we went on to the market to make some money by doing errands for the market people. We went and fetched a trolley from the station for a man on the market. I earned sixpence for this. John got about threepence or sixpence, I'm not sure exactly. Then we went to a man who sells carpets in the open market. There were two lads there, one from the same class as me. After I had had some talk with them I decided to go home. When I set off to catch the bus, John Kilbride was not with me. I last saw him beside one of the big salvage bins on the open market near the carpet dealer's stall. There was no one with him. It was about 5.25 pm when I last saw him. I never saw him after that.

PETER CANTWELL: I am the foreman at Warren's Autos, Manchester. I produce a car hire agreement. The hirer was the accused woman in the dock. This agreement is dated 16 November 1963 but the hire period is from 23 November to 24 November

23 DEC   23 DEC   169.

WARREN'S AUTOS
63/67, LONDON ROAD, MANCHESTER 1.   № 1168
Telephone: ARDwick 2017

Hirer's Name **Miss Myra Hindley** .... Date **16/11/63**

Address **7 Bannock St Gorton m/c 18** . Time out **10 A/h**

Hirer's Tel. Nos. Private .... Business .... Time due in **10 A/h**

Reg. Car No. **9275 ND** .... Driving Licence No. .... Expiry

Endorsements

Hire Periods from **23/11/62** To .... Date due in **24/11/63**

HIRE	Anglia	21/—	10/—	£2.10–0
PETROL		10/3	2/—	2/—
INSURANCE	White	10/—		
DEPOSIT		Paid a/c £2.0.0		10/—
				£ 14/10/–

1. The Hirer will bear the first £10 of any claim on the Insurance Company or any damage to car or tyres whilst on Hire.

2. The Hirer will limit the use of car to tariff as agreed.
(a) Use the Car in proper manner, and carry the number of passengers as the vehicle is specified.
(b) The Hirer will bear the cost of any small incidental running repairs including punctures.
(c) Should serious mechanical trouble occur Hirer will notify the Owner by wire or telephone and the Owner will advise what to do.
(d) When the car is Hired out on Period, Hirer will have Car greased every 500 miles.

3. The Owner accepts no responsibility for any delays which may occur through breakdown or any other cause.

4. EXCESS HIRE.
All cars are booked strictly to time.
The Hirer will notify the Owner, at the earliest possible moment if through any circumstances beyond his control the Car is not returned at the specified time, If not returned within 2 hours of the agreed time, it will become uninsured and reported to the Police as such.
It is clearly understood that only the Hirer can drive car, after completing insurance form. If the Hirer allows anybody else to drive car, the car is automatically uninsured and Hirer makes himself liable for any damage. Driver will also be liable to prosecution under the Road Traffic Act.
No Hire Cars are insured against Passenger Risk.
I understand and agree that in the event of my returning the car at a later time than that stated above I am liable to the charge of 10/- per hour or part of per hour overdue, and that I may not be insured to drive the car during this time if I fail previously to obtain permission in writing to extend my Hire.
Deposit returnable 24 hours after completion of Hire.

SIGNATURE FOR & ON BEHALF OF OWNER ....

SIGNATURE OF HIRER **M. Hindley** ....

To be signed after reading agreement.

Printed by A. F. Elmer & Son Ltd., Waterloo Rd., Stockport.

CAR HIRED FOR DAY KILBRIDE DISAPPEARED

**Agreement for hire of the car on the day of
John Kilbride's disappearance**

1963. The car in question was a light-coloured Ford Anglia, and the period of hire was from 10 am to 10 am. Hindley was wearing a pair of black trews, a leather jacket, a high-necked sweater and, I would say, black shoes. I think it was in the morning when she called for the car. She was alone. I remember the car being returned between 10 am and 11 am the following day. She returned the car on her own. It was extremely dirty; it looked as if it had been through a ploughed field. She also hired a car on 27 November and 21 December, both times for 24-hour periods.

Cross-examined by MR HEILPERN, *the witness said that there was nothing unusual in booking a week in advance; there was no record of the mileage covered by the car while it was in Hindley's possession.*

JOHN DOWN: Between April 1959 and July 1964 I was a detective chief inspector in charge of the CID for the Ashton-under-Lyne Division. I took charge of the search and inquiries to trace John Kilbride. Market traders were interviewed and vehicles and skips were searched at Ashton market. A thorough search of the area was made, and there was a house-to-house inquiry in the area where John Kilbride lived. The press, radio and television gave extensive publicity to the missing boy. 500 posters were distributed. Over 700 statements were taken from members of the public and on 1 December 1963 over 2,000 people took part in a detailed search of the Ashton-under-Lyne district. (*Evidence read.*)

DETECTIVE CHIEF SUPERINTENDENT JOHN TYRRELL (*recalled*): At 12.15 pm on Monday, 11 October 1965, in company with Detective Chief Inspector Mounsey, I saw the accused Brady at Hyde Police Station. [MR JUSTICE FENTON ATKINSON *reminded the jury that they had already heard some evidence from this interview*.] Mr Mounsey cautioned Brady, then told him that he was making inquiries regarding the disappearance of John Kilbride. The accused said words to this effect: 'I have read about him, I think, but I don't know anything of him.' Later, the accused was asked about an exercise book found at 16 Wardle Brook Avenue. He said that it was his and that he had written certain names in the book. Mr Mounsey said: 'Amongst these names is the name "John Kilbride". Can you tell me why you have written it in this book?' Brady said: 'I don't know.' The accused went on to say that the name in the book referred, not to John Kilbride of Ashton-under-Lyne, but to a lad he had known at Hull Borstal.

After there had been a break for a meal between 3 pm and 3.30 pm, a photograph of John Kilbride was shown to Brady. Mr Mounsey said: 'John Kilbride was last seen on Ashton Market at 5.30 pm on Saturday, 23 November 1963. Where were you then?' Brady said: 'I don't know.' He said that he hardly knew Ashton Market and that he had not been there more than once or twice. Mr Mounsey said: 'Did you and Myra do any shopping there?' Brady replied: 'No. We used to go to Hyde Market more often than not.'

On Thursday, 14 October 1965, in company with Mr Mounsey, I saw Hindley at the Risley Remand Centre at 11.25 am. After cautioning Hindley, Mr Mounsey told her that he was making inquiries regarding John Kilbride. Mr Mounsey said: 'I have been told that you visited Ashton Market regularly for over two years, particularly on Saturday afternoons, and it was there that John Kilbride was last seen.' Myra Hindley replied: 'I have never been to Ashton Market.' Mr Mounsey said: 'I have been told by your sister that you visited Ashton Market regularly.' Myra Hindley replied: 'It's not true.' A little later Mr Mounsey asked her: 'Where were you on 23 November 1963?' Hindley replied: 'I don't know.'

On 20 October 1965, in the course of a search of 16 Wardle Brook Avenue, I discovered seven lady's stockings; four of them were diamond-patterned.

Cross-examined by MR HOOSON, *the witness agreed that a poster showing a photograph of John Kilbride was put on a table and shown to Brady at the interview on 11 October.*

MR HOOSON: Wasn't it referred to quite a lot in the course of that interview?—No. As I remember, it was only referred to when Mr Mounsey actually pointed it out to Brady.

I am suggesting that it was not once he was asked about Kilbride's death. He was asked several times?—The questions that were put to him were as I repeated this morning.

Why did an officer not take notes as the interview was going on, in the way Mr Benfield has described was done at another interview?—I did not think it was necessary at the time.

MR JUSTICE FENTON ATKINSON: Is any of what the witness has got down challenged as being inaccurate?

MR HOOSON: One or two points. I suggest he selected these questions and answers, and that on the subject of John Kilbride there were many questions repeated a great deal to Brady.

MR JUSTICE FENTON ATKINSON: He has answered that question.

MR HOOSON: The exercise book is occupied mainly with what appear to be bookkeeping exercises?—Yes, there are quite a number.

On the page we have copied there are the names of a number of people, some of whom are well-known film-stars?—Yes.

Then there appears the name, for instance, of John Birch. Wasn't there quite lengthy questioning about the John Birch Society of the United States?—Mr Mounsey did ask him about that.

I suggest Brady was asked why he made those entries and he said: 'I don't know. It looks as if I had been testing a pen,' and both of you said: 'Oh, come on.'—I don't recollect that at all, sir.

Cross-examined by MR HEILPERN:

I suggest that Hindley's answer, in relation to the question about Ashton Market, was: 'I have never been to Ashton Market except on two occasions,' and she thereupon told you when the two occasions were.—She mentioned two occasions at a later interview—not at this stage.

DETECTIVE CHIEF INSPECTOR JOSEPH MOUNSEY (*recalled*) *confirmed the previous witness's accounts of the interview with Brady on 11 October and with Hindley on 14 October.*

Cross-examined by MR HOOSON, *the witness agreed that his notes of the interview with Brady were a copy of those made by Detective Chief Superintendent Tyrrell.*

MR HOOSON: You had been questioning for over six hours on that day?—It was not all taken up by questioning.

However experienced, however good you are, at the end of the day you could remember all the questions and answers and their accuracy or otherwise?—Yes, sir.

If you were sitting in this court for five hours without taking notes, you could remember all the questions and answers?—I wouldn't say that, sir.

No one could do it, Mr Mounsey.—What I have in my note-book is true, sir.

DETECTIVE SERGEANT ROY DEAN (*recalled*) *testified that on 7 October 1965 at 16 Wardle Brook Avenue he found an exercise book bearing the name and address, 'Ian Brady, 18 Westmorland Street, Longsight, Manchester 12'. On one of the pages of the book, among other things, there appeared the name 'John Kilbride'.*

POLICE INSPECTOR JOHN CHADDOCK (*recalled*): At 11.45 am on Thursday, 21 October 1965, I went to Sail Bark Moss on Saddleworth Moor. Detective Chief Inspector Mounsey showed me a photograph of the accused Hindley squatting down, holding a little dog, apparently looking at the ground. I was able to identify Hollin Brown Knoll and the A635 road in the background and some stones in the foreground. I and others prepared to dig the ground shown in the foreground of that photograph at the spot where the accused is apparently looking. Before we did so I pushed my stick a short distance into the ground at that spot. Upon withdrawing my stick, there was a strong smell of putrefaction on the end of it. We removed the top soil to a depth of about nine inches and uncovered a boy's left black shoe. Underneath the shoe I saw some socks and what appeared to be part of the heel of a body. At this stage digging operations were suspended and I cleared a little more soil and exposed the right lower leg. I was present at 3.30 pm when Professor Polson and Dr Gee arrived, and I was present when they carried on the process of excavation by hand until some human remains were removed from the earth.

On 22 October I was present when Sheila Kilbride identified the clothing as that of her son.

DETECTIVE SERGEANT THOMAS RYLATT, *stationed in the photographic branch of the West Riding Constabulary CID at Wakefield, proved photographs he had taken of the body and clothing of John Kilbride, both on Saddleworth Moor and later at Uppermill Mortuary.*

ABDUL LETIF CHAUDHRI: I am a trader at Ashton-under-Lyne Market. I sell, amongst other things, nylon stockings. I have been shown a bundle of stockings, four diamond pattern, three micromesh. I sell similar diamond-patterned stockings at my stall. Since three or four years ago, I and everybody have been selling similar diamond stockings.

Cross-examined by MR HEILPERN, *the witness agreed that diamond-patterned stockings were very popular, especially with young girls. Such stockings were sold in many stores and markets.*

DR CYRIL POLSON, *Professor of Forensic Medicine at the University of Leeds*: At 3.30 pm on Thursday, 21 October 1965, I and Dr David Gee arrived at Saddleworth Moor at a spot which had been surrounded by screens on the south side of the A635 road. In the ground in this area where superficial excavation had been carried out was a black shoe, approximately size 6 with a rubber sole that was worn relatively slightly; also visible in the excavation was part of a shirt. Dr Gee and I then began to excavate with hand tools. We soon came upon two rounded objects covered with cloth, later shown to be socks; the rounded objects were the heels of the deceased. By careful hand digging we traced the lower limbs, then the trunk and head, and finally exposed the body and undercut it so that it could be removed intact. The orientation of the body was approximately at right angles to the main road; he had his feet towards the road, head away from the road and facing towards Holmfirth. The body lay at a depth of approximately twelve to eighteen inches. The soil in the region was apparently more sandy than in the grave on the opposite side of the road already investigated. The body I was exposing on this day was fully extended with the front of the lower limbs and toes facing downwards. The upper part of the trunk was twisted somewhat to the left. The head also faced to the left. The right forearm was folded across the chest and was under the body. The left arm was straight and lay against the left side of the body. The features were now obscured by post-mortem change. Short brown hair was still present. The small bones of the feet and hands had separated. Those of the feet were still held within the socks. After the body had been exposed and all appropriate photographs taken, it was carefully lifted from the grave, rolled on to a sheet of galvanised iron, and transported to the post-mortem room.

On 22 October 1965 I carried out a post-mortem examination of the remains at Uppermill Mortuary.

The body was still clothed, and the following garments were

removed by me: a jacket of greyish blue bearing a football type of button on the cuff; a woollen pullover in royal blue; a shirt; a woollen vest; trousers of jean type; underpants; socks—these I had to cut to effect removal.

The trousers were pulled down to about mid-thigh position. They were nearer to the knee than to the top of the thigh. The underpants were also rolled down in a band about $1\frac{1}{2}$in broad at about mid-thigh level, and appeared to be knotted at the back. The coiled underpants were removed so as to leave them in the form found on the body.

The principal feature of the unclothed body was a general transformation of the body fat into adipocere—that is a white, soft, soapy material. No obvious injury was found. Loss of surface tissue was minimal and entirely consisted of the disintegration and loss during burial and recovery of the body. The skin of the neck was intact; no ligature was round the neck nor were there any marks to indicate strangulation or throttling. There were no signs of asphyxia visible, and these, if present, would have been completely obscured by advanced post-mortem changes. Extensive search failed to detect any fracture of long bones or the skull.

The brain was shrunken and now a semi-liquid tissue. No trace of bleeding was found inside the skull, nor was there any obvious damage to the brain. The neck structure showed advanced post-mortem change; no obvious signs of bruising were present. The pleura, lungs and wind pipe showed severe post-mortem change; there was no obvious disease or injury. The heart showed severe post-mortem change; there was no obvious disease or injury, and no congenital malformation. The liver and kidneys showed severe post-mortem change. The stomach and intestines showed post-mortem change but were still identifiable, especially the appendix. The anus was patent but I found no obvious injury to the passage; the expression 'patent' means that it was open. The external genitalia were now of indefinite shape owing to severe post-mortem change; the skin between the front of the body and the back passage was intact; there was no vaginal orifice, nor did I find any female genitalia inside the pelvis, where preservation was relatively good.

In the presence of this severe post-mortem change, it was not possible to ascertain the cause of death. It was possible to exclude certain causes of death. First of all, there was no gross injury of a kind which would lead to the breakage of bones, and there was no major wounding. There was no gross disease. If the death had been due to suffocation, no proof of this was obtained, but it was not excluded as a possible cause of death. The position of the trousers—more particularly, the position and arrangement of the underpants—appeared to be unusual and was not consistent with the lowering of the garments on a visit to the toilet.

The stature during life was approximately 4ft 9in. It appeared to be the body of a boy of between ten and fourteen years. The extent of the post-mortem change indicated that burial was of several months rather than several weeks.

Cross-examined by MR HOOSON:

Many causes of death, both natural or otherwise, cannot be excluded?—Yes. A virus, for example.

MAXWELL SAUNDERS, *Lecturer in Conservative Dentistry at the University of Leeds Dental School:* I received from Professor Polson a specimen of upper and lower jaws bearing teeth, and made an examination of them on the same day. The middle teeth in the upper jaw had a space between them. These teeth were squarish in shape. Having examined all the teeth I came to the conclusion that the age of the body was between twelve and fourteen years.

DETECTIVE POLICEWOMAN MARGARET CAMPION (*recalled*): When Myra Hindley was interviewed on 7 October 1965 she had a dog with her. On 1 November I identified that same dog to James Gourley, a veterinary surgeon. The accused called the dog 'Puppet' during the interview.

JAMES GOURLEY, *a veterinary surgeon practising in Ashton-under-Lyne:* On 1 November 1965 I was shown a dog by Detective Policewoman Campion at my surgery. It had tan colouring in addition to black and white. I examined this dog to arrive at an estimation of its age, then it was suggested to me that confirmatory evidence should be obtained by X-rays of its teeth. I estimated its age, from my examination, to be between one and a half and three years old. To X-ray a dog's teeth, the dog must be absolutely still; X-ray plates must be placed in the dog's mouth. To achieve the required stillness I administered general anaesthesia. While I was carrying out these X-rays I noticed that the dog was not breathing as it should be; in fact, it was not breathing at all. Immediate steps were taken to apply artificial respiration, and this was continued for about three-quarters of an hour. The dog failed to revive. (*Evidence read.*)

DETECTIVE CHIEF INSPECTOR JOSEPH MOUNSEY (*recalled*) *testified that at 1.30 pm on Thursday, 28 October 1965, with Detective Inspector Leach, he saw the accused Brady at Ashton-under-Lyne Police Station.*

MR HOOSON: I take formal objection to the admissibility of the evidence that follows.

(*The jury left the court.*)

MR JUSTICE FENTON ATKINSON: Mr Hooson, the objection here, I take it, is how the questions were asked and the matter of whether the solicitor was asked for, and so on? It is not turning on the actual terms of the questions and answers?

MR HOOSON: Yes, there are certain inaccuracies, but that is a different issue altogether.

DETECTIVE CHIEF INSPECTOR JOSEPH MOUNSEY *was examined by* THE ATTORNEY-GENERAL *and cross-examined by* MR HOOSON *as to the conduct of the interview.* (*See this witness's evidence before the jury, page* 155.)

Similarly, DETECTIVE INSPECTOR JEFFREY LEACH *was examined by* THE ATTORNEY-GENERAL *and cross-examined by* MR HOOSON. (*See this witness's evidence before the jury, page* 158.)

MR HOOSON: I will call the accused Brady.

MR JUSTICE FENTON ATKINSON: Does he wish to affirm?

MR HOOSON: Yes, he does.

IAN BRADY, *affirmed.*

Examined by MR HOOSON:

Following upon your remand at the Hyde Magistrates' Court at ten o'clock in the morning of 28 October, did you see your solicitor?—Yes. For I should say half an hour.

Just answer this question 'yes' or 'no'. Had you received advice?—I had received advice after 11 October.

At what time did you arrive at Ashton-under-Lyne Police Station?—At 12.30.

Were you taken up a back entrance staircase where Inspector Mounsey was waiting for you?—Yes, with three other detectives. There was about a dozen detectives in plain clothes with those in the van.

Were you taken into a room and left there?—Yes, with three detectives.

For how long were you there while Mr Mounsey was out?—Approximately fifteen minutes.

What happened while he was out?—I was sitting on a bench with my back to the wall. There was a detective standing on one side of me, one on the other, and one at the front, and the three of them stood cracking their knuckles and there was no word spoken and I sat watching the detective in front.

When Mr Mounsey came back in, did he say something to you?—He said: 'Right,' and nodded his head at the three detectives. I then says: 'I want to see a solicitor. I am not making any statements until I see a solicitor.' He said: 'That's all right. All I want is for you to look at some photographs.'

Did he ask you questions about the photographs?—I refused to answer any questions unless in the presence of my solicitor. Eventually, I agreed to tell them where some of the photographs were taken.

Were you ever cautioned?—I was never cautioned.

Did you mention your solicitor again?—I mentioned him all through the interview. Every time they brought up the subject of Kilbride I said: 'I am making no statements unless in the presence of my solicitor,' and he kept saying: 'You will be charged with the murder,' and I says: 'Am I being cautioned?' as I was instructed to do.

What did he say?—He says: 'You will be charged.' He just ignored the question. He just kept saying: 'You will be charged with the murder,' and continued questioning and I gave him the same answers.

For how long were you questioned in all by Mr Mounsey?—From 12.45. He went out a few times during the afternoon. Most of the afternoon was taken up by talking about religion and politics. About six o'clock he came out with a copy of the *Manchester Evening News*. He showed me a photograph —

We need not go into this now.

Cross-examined by THE ATTORNEY-GENERAL:

You are a man who takes a pride in not being frightened of anybody or anything, are you not?—No.

Are you an intelligent man in your view?—I haven't the slightest. I don't know.

You knew that you could have refused to answer any of these questions?—Yes, I could have refused.

But you chose, in fact, to answer them?—I did not answer any. I answered some—all negative. I denied all knowledge of Kilbride and all knowledge that that photograph was one of the grave.

So that what you are saying is that what Mr Mounsey says is wrong?—I saying that Mr Mounsey's whole statement is lies from beginning to end. Every answer—he's not just changed it, he's manufactured it. Except for a few little pieces of truth at the beginning of the statement.

You see, you have mentioned the cracking of knuckles by the police. Is it right that not a finger was laid on you?—That is correct.

At any time during this — (*Witness interrupts:*) Yes, yes.

— long and painful searching for the truth that the police were engaged upon?—Yes, yes.

At no time were you threatened with violence?—No. I was threatened when they brought in the *Evening News*. He says: 'How would you like having to get hold of him?' That was a photograph of Downey's uncle struggling with two policemen. He said: 'We could arrange it.'

That did not affect your answers to these questions, did it?—I was calm throughout the interview because I had no intention of answering any questions.

Not only were you calm, but you were a willing participant, were you not?—I was willing because I could not leave the room.

You were a very willing participant because you were willing to talk to — (*Witness interrupts:*) I was not going to talk.

— and deal with these matters, and you knew perfectly well that you could refuse if you wanted to do so.—I refused repeatedly.

I suggest that it is entirely untrue that you ever asked for your solicitor to be present.—I started the interview. Except for the word 'Right', I started the interview.

You were a man who thought himself well capable of dealing with the situation yourself?—After the experience I had had of police interviews at that date, yes.

MR JUSTICE FENTON ATKINSON *listened to legal argument by* MR HOOSON, *then ruled against the defence submission*: 'On the evidence that I have heard, I am quite satisfied that these answers, whatever they may have been, were free and voluntary and are admissible, and I do not believe that the solicitor was asked for and refused. But it is a matter, of course, for the jury ultimately to decide what weight they give to it.'

(*The jury returned to court.*)

DETECTIVE CHIEF INSPECTOR JOSEPH MOUNSEY (*recalled*); *examination continued*: At the start of the interview with Brady on 28 October 1965, I cautioned him. I then showed him a number of photographs, including that of Myra Hindley squatting down, holding a little dog, apparently looking at the ground. I said: 'Did you take this one, and where is it?' Brady said: 'It's the moors somewhere. I took it about eighteen months ago.' I said: 'How do you know it was taken then?' Brady said: 'The reason I said eighteen months ago is the age of the dog. It's approximately eighteen months old.' I said: 'On Thursday last, I recovered the body of John Kilbride from the piece of ground shown at the bottom of the photograph.' Brady said nothing. I then showed him three other photographs taken in the vicinity of the A635 road where the graves of Lesley Ann Downey and John Kilbride were found. Brady said nothing. I then showed him some other photographs and said: 'Did you and Myra kill Kilbride?' Brady said: 'I don't know anything about John Kilbride.' I said: 'In addition to taking the photograph of his grave, you wrote his name in an exercise book found at your home. I don't believe you when you say you don't know anything about his death.' Brady said: 'I don't know anything about anything.'

I again showed him the photograph of Hindley. I said: 'This photograph was taken by you showing your girl friend crouching over John Kilbride's grave. How could you possibly say you know nothing about his death?' Brady said: 'I've only got your word that it is a grave.' I said: 'Do you imagine for one moment I would tell you lies about a matter as serious as this?' He said: 'If my solicitor gets another photograph from somewhere —' and paused. I said: 'What do you mean?' He did not reply.

At 2.05 pm I left the accused with Detective Inspector Leach while I completed my notes of the interview so far. At 6.35 I resumed the relevant part of the interview. I said: 'What is

Page containing the name 'John Kilbride' from Brady's exercise book

your explanation for taking this photograph of Myra Hindley crouching over the grave of John Kilbride?' Brady said: 'There is no explanation.' He said: 'If that grave is near the other grave there is an explanation. It can be covered by the explanation I made in the statement I gave to my solicitor.' I said: 'What do you mean by explanation? Did you kill John Kilbride?' Brady said: 'No.'

I said: 'Did Myra Hindley kill John Kilbride?' and he said: 'No.' I said: 'You took a photograph of his grave. You must know who killed John Kilbride. Do you know?' He said: 'Yes.

It's one of two men. I have given their names to my solicitor.'
I said: 'If neither you nor Myra killed John Kilbride and you
know the name of the man who did it, it is surely your duty and
to your advantage to tell us his name.' Brady said: 'It will come
out at the trial.'

I said: 'You say you know who killed him. You must have
known that the photograph of Myra showed John Kilbride's
grave,' and I showed him the photograph again. I said: 'You
knew that when you took it, you knew it was John Kilbride's
grave, didn't you?' He said: 'Yes.'

At 6.55 pm the interview with the accused Brady was concluded.

At 7.50 pm, with Detective Inspector Leach, I saw the accused
Myra Hindley at Ashton-under-Lyne Police Station. After
cautioning her, I asked her to look at some photographs—the
same photographs that had been shown to Brady. She refused
to look at them.

I told her of the discovery of the body of John Kilbride. I
said: 'He disappeared from Ashton Market on 23 November
1963. I have been told you used to frequent Ashton Market on
Saturday afternoons. This photograph shows you looking down
on the ground at John Kilbride's grave.' She refused to look at
the photograph and made no reply.

I said: 'I have reason to believe that you and Ian Brady killed
John Kilbride.' She said: 'It's not true.' I said: 'I do not believe
you.' Hindley then said: 'I refuse to answer any questions.' I
then asked her about other matters and at 8.10 pm I left her
with Detective Inspector Leach.

Cross-examined by MR HOOSON:

Brady said, immediately the interview started, that he wanted
to see Mr Fitzgerald, his solicitor?—No.

Did he tell you that Mr Fitzgerald had told him not to say
anything?—He told me that later in the interview.

I suggest this request to see a solicitor came immediately.—No.

Cross-examined by MR HEILPERN:

At no time, despite the many hours of interviewing, did Myra
Hindley make any admission of being implicated in any way in
the murder of John Kilbride?—That is true.

Re-examined by THE ATTORNEY-GENERAL:

Why is it that these interviews took place at Ashton and not at Hyde?—Because there was an irate crowd at Hyde.

It was for reasons of security?—Yes, sir.

DETECTIVE INSPECTOR JEFFREY LEACH *of the Lancashire Constabulary confirmed the previous witness's accounts of the interviews with the two accused on 28 October 1965.*

Cross-examined by MR HOOSON:

Are you saying that during the whole of this interview, Brady never once mentioned his solicitor until towards the conclusion? —That is perfectly true. He never once asked for his solicitor. Never once.

DETECTIVE INSPECTOR NORMAN MATTIN (*recalled*): At 2 pm on Thursday, 28 October 1965, in company with Detective Chief Inspector Tyrrell, I saw the accused Hindley at Ashton-under-Lyne Police Station. Mr Tyrrell cautioned her, then asked her a number of questions about her parents and where she was brought up.

Mr Tyrrell said: 'How long have you known David Smith?' Hindley said: 'He lived in the same neighbourhood since he was about six years of age.' Mr Tyrrell said: 'Have you known him personally since then?' Hindley said: 'No, only since he started going out with Maureen.'

Later, Mr Tyrrell showed Hindley the photograph of herself crouching and apparently looking at the ground. Mr Tyrrell said: 'Where was it taken?' Hindley said: 'I don't know.' Mr Tyrrell said: 'When was it taken?' Hindley said: 'I don't know.' Mr Tyrrell said: 'Who took it?' Hindley said: 'Ian, I suppose.' Mr Tyrrell said: 'How old was the dog then?' Hindley said: 'He was only a pup. He's two years old in January. That will make him twenty months old now. It's my other dog's pup.' Mr Tyrrell said: 'What are you looking at there on the photograph?' Hindley said: 'The dog.' Mr Tyrrell said: 'You are looking at the ground.' Hindley made no reply. Mr Tyrrell said: 'According to the photograph, it appears to have been snowing.' Hindley said: 'It looks like it.' Mr Tyrrell said: 'Who chose the place where you would kneel?' Hindley said: 'No one. We just took a photograph where we felt like it.'

Mr Tyrrell said: 'Did Ian take all the photographs of you?' Hindley said: 'Not all, but quite a lot.' Mr Tyrrell said: 'Who else would take photographs of you?' Hindley said: 'Just depends who I was with.' Mr Tyrrell said: 'Who else has taken a photograph of you on the moors?' Hindley said: 'What do you mean?' Mr Tyrrell said: 'Who has taken a photograph of you on the moors other than Brady?' Hindley said: 'What do you mean?' Mr Tyrrell said: 'It's quite simple. Who else has taken a photograph of you on the moors?' Hindley said: 'You say these are on the moors, do you?' Mr Tyrrell said: 'Yes, they were taken on Saddleworth Moor above Greenfield.' Hindley said: 'Possible.' Mr Tyrrell said: 'Who else took photographs of you on the moor?' Hindley said: 'Well, Smith could have taken this. I can't remember.'

Mr Tyrrell indicated a photograph taken very close to the grave of Lesley Ann Downey and the photograph of Hindley crouching. He pointed out that the first photograph was taken close to where the body of Lesley Ann Downey was found. He said: 'The ground in the area of both photographs was dug up, and immediately beneath where you are crouching the body of John Kilbride was found.' Hindley said: 'So there could be bodies all over where I have stood, then.'

Mr Tyrrell said: 'Both photographs were taken within a few hundred yards of each other, and as a result of examining them, coupled with other evidence, two bodies have been found—first that of Lesley Ann Downey and now that of John Kilbride who disappeared from Ashton Market on Saturday, 23 November 1963.' Hindley said: 'I told you before that I don't frequent Ashton Market.' Mr Tyrrell said: 'Do you go to Ashton to do any shopping?' Hindley said: 'I have been to Ashton to buy two fireside chairs.' Mr Tyrrell said: 'When I last saw you, with Chief Inspector Mounsey, you told us you had never been to Ashton.' Hindley said: 'I said I had never been to Ashton Market.' Mr Tyrrell said: 'Do you frequent Ashton, then?' Hindley said: 'I don't. I pay my accounts by postal order. I have bought a camera from Marksons, the photographers.'

Mr Tyrrell said: 'I suggest to you that the purpose of these photographs was to locate the graves again and satisfy yourselves that the ground had not been disturbed.' Hindley said: 'They have no significance for me.' Mr Tyrrell said: 'Are you suggesting —' and at that point Hindley interrupted: 'I am not suggesting anything. I can't remember when it was taken. We've taken photographs all over the place.'

At 4.30 pm Hindley was provided with tea. She had two or three cups. Mr Tyrrell left at this stage but I remained. I spoke to her about her life before meeting Brady and the apparent change in her make-up since knowing him, and that he had apparently changed her. Hindley said: 'I made all my own decisions. People go through several stages in their life. After discussions they change their mind. Ian never made me do anything I didn't want to do. All that about killing is bloody rubbish. What time did Smith say he left our house that night?' I said: 'I don't know, but it was very late.' Hindley said: 'It was about 3 am or just after. And what time did he go to the police? They tell me it was some time after he left the house. Well, obviously he was getting his story straight.'

I said: 'If you say he is responsible for these deaths, let's be knowing just what it is that you know.' Hindley said: 'I'm not saying any more, except that he brought her to the house with another man and Smith took her away with the other man.' She then said words to the effect that she didn't know anything about Kilbride, and neither did Ian.

At 6.20 pm Hindley was provided with tea, bread and butter and ham. At 7.20 pm Detective Chief Inspector Tyrrell resumed the interview with her.

Mr Tyrrell said: 'I must ask you again, have you ever been to Ashton Market?' Hindley said: 'I've only been twice in my life. The last time was a month before I moved to Hattersley. I went with two girls to buy a tea set. The other was when I was working at Lawrence Scott's, when I was fifteen. I went with three or four other girls to buy an outfit.'

Mr Tyrrell then said: 'When did you first know that John Kilbride was missing?' Hindley said: 'I don't know anything about John Kilbride.' Mr Tyrrell said: 'I must tell you that Brady has told the other officers who are interviewing him that he didn't kill Kilbride but that he knows it was one of two men who did, and that he has told his solicitor who they are. Would you —' Hindley interrupted and said: 'He didn't kill Kilbride and I didn't kill Kilbride. I've never set eyes on Kilbride before.'

Mr Tyrrell said: 'Since you and Brady have been associating

together, has he, so far as you know, ever been out on his own?' Hindley said: 'Never. Wherever he has gone, I have gone.'

Hindley refused to answer further questions, and the interview concluded at 7.30 pm.

At about 7.50 pm on the same evening, in company with Mr Tyrrell, I saw the accused Brady at Ashton-under-Lyne Police Station. After cautioning Brady, Mr Tyrrell asked him if he remembered hiring an Anglia car on 23 November 1963. Brady said that he and Hindley had hired a few cars, but he could not remember hiring one on that date. Mr Tyrrell said: 'What did you do with the cars?' Brady said: 'Go for a run.' Mr Tyrrell said: 'Where?' Brady said: 'Leek—yes, Leek.'

Mr Tyrrell said: 'How many times have you been over the A635 Greenfield to Holmfirth road?' Brady said: 'I have been shown photographs of Myra with the dog.' Mr Tyrrell said: 'Were they taken near that road?' Brady said: 'Yes. We've been over there several times. I like it up there.'

Mr Tyrrell then said: 'You have taken a young girl called Pat Hodges on to the moors at night.' Brady said: 'I know a girl called Pat Hodges. She's got black hair and a fringe. She lives near Myra.' Mr Tyrrell said: 'This girl says that she used to come to pick you up with Myra in the car when you lived in Westmorland Street, Longsight, and that they used to wait in the street until you came out, sometimes for an hour. Why didn't Myra come to the house for you?' Brady said: 'I told her never to come to the house. I like to keep the two environments separate. Relax at home and drink at Myra's. It's just a question of keeping things separate.'

Mr Tyrrell said: 'Did your mother know Myra?' Brady said: 'Yes, I eventually introduced her to my mother over a year ago.'

Mr Tyrrell said: 'Are you fond of children?' Brady said: 'I like children. I never thought of it.'

Mr Tyrrell said: 'Do you know the stretch of road you took Pat Hodges to? One spot she has pointed out is on the A635 from Greenfield to Homfirth.' Brady said: 'Yes, it would be. If it's the road where you can hear the shots from the Crowden rifle range.' Mr Tyrrell said: 'What attraction has this place for you?' Brady said: 'No attraction as far as I'm concerned. We used to go to Glossop as well.'

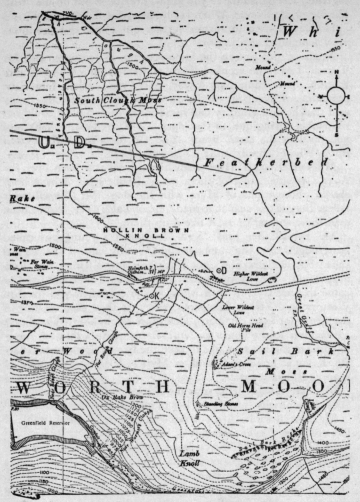

Large-scale map of vicinity of Hollin Brown Knoll

Mr Tyrrell then said: 'Is it a coincidence, do you think, that this spot should be where the bodies of two young children have been recovered?' Brady said: 'I don't know. It's just fantastic. I've made a statement about that to my solicitors and also answered a few questions from Mr Benfield. I'm not going to discuss these matters any more now.' The time was then 8.30 pm and there was a break of fifteen minutes. At 8.45 pm the interview was resumed concerning matters not connected with this case. At 9.30 pm the interview was concluded.

DETECTIVE CHIEF SUPERINTENDENT JOHN TYRRELL (*recalled*) *confirmed the previous witness's accounts of the interviews that he (Mr Tyrrell) had conducted with the two accused on 28 October 1965.*

EDWARD BROADHEAD, *a surveyor employed by the West Riding County Council*: On Monday, 8 November 1965, I went along the A635 on Saddleworth Moor, to an area approximately seven miles from Oldham. There Mr Mounsey indicated to me two places where excavation had been carried out. One of those excavations was 71yd on the northern side of the A635 and another 88yd on the southern side of that road. The direct measured distance between those two points was 373yd. I have had an enlargement made of part of the Ordnance sheet for this area. On this enlargement I have added certain features in the area of Hollin Brown Knoll. I added by drawing in the rocks on the north side of the A635 to the east of the mile-post showing 'Holmfirth 7 miles, Oldham 7¾ miles'. I then added two road signs on the southern side of the A635 in the near vicinity of that mile-post. I have also indicated three areas where it was possible to park on the side of the road.

NINTH DAY   *Friday, 29 April*

In the absence of the jury, MR HEILPERN *submitted that there was no case for Myra Hindley to answer on counts 3 and 4 of the indictment (the murder of John Kilbride and the alternative count of accessory after the fact), but* MR JUSTICE FENTON ATKINSON *ruled that there was matter proper for the jury's consideration on these counts.*

The jury was brought into court.

MR HOOSON, *opening the case for the defence on behalf of the accused Ian Brady, told the jury*:

'It is terribly, terribly important that you dispose from your minds all the natural revulsion one has in reading or hearing evidence connected with the death of children.' *The systematic killing of children was very difficult for the normal mind to comprehend. Nevertheless, the jury had to decide fairly, on the evidence, whether the prosecution had proved all or any of the charges against the accused. Probably no case in modern history had aroused such feelings or been so widely reported.* 'The very least or the meanest person of this country is entitled to a fair and dispassionate trial and a proper assessment of the evidence for and against. It is important not to yield to the temptation of bending the standards to accommodate one's preconceptions of the case.'

Referring to Brady's alleged conversations with David Smith and to what Brady was alleged to have said in interviews with police officers, MR HOOSON *said that the prosecution relied strongly on* 'alleged incriminating answers given by Brady'. *Apart from one or two minor disagreements, the defence did not challenge police evidence of interviews at which a careful note was taken; but at two interviews notes had been written up later, and it was alleged that at these interviews incriminating answers had been given.* MR HOOSON *went on:* 'According to our rules, a person at any stage of an investigation should be able to communicate with his solicitor.' *When a man had been charged, except in exceptional circumstances, he should no longer be asked questions. The jury might think that if questioning went on and on, evidence of what was said was not good evidence.* 'In this case one can understand the feelings of the police officers being inflamed, especially if they subscribe to what the prosecution has put forward. . . . You may think the average mind would boggle at the thought that Brady at no time asked to see his solicitor during this period. I say there was a changing of standards, of the rules, and it is vital that you should bear this in mind.'

MR HOOSON *reminded the jury that there were three separate charges against Brady and that they must consider each one separately. There was a great deal of difference between the evidence in the Evans case on the one hand and the Downey and Kilbride cases on the other:* 'Much of the prosecution case is founded on theories—dangerous ones so far as the second and third counts are concerned.

'Don't let the length of the case and the number of exhibits hide from you the fact that much of the theory, the very rock on which it is founded, is the evidence of Smith. You may think that he is a crumbling rock on which to found anything.' MR HOOSON *suggested that the jury should regard Smith as* 'a man without principle, without scruple, without mercy'. *He was also a man of considerable intelligence:* 'Hardly a man who would have been dominated intellectually by Brady. The Attorney-General has suggested that Smith was developed by Brady as a sorcerer's apprentice or a devil's disciple. You may think that this may well have been a profound misreading of this case.' *Brady's statement regarding the killing of Evans contained no suggestion that anyone but himself had wielded the hatchet:* 'This does not fit the Machiavellian, completely unprincipled character presented by the prosecution. Wouldn't it have been the easiest thing for him to say: "It wasn't me"?' MR HOOSON *said that, having seen Smith, the jury might think that he was far more involved in the Evans case than he admitted.*

MR HOOSON *pointed out that Brady had always been ready to make admissions on things such as the ownership of items found in the suitcases and the photographing of Lesley Ann Downey*—'but he has always been adamant that, though he used the hatchet which killed Evans, he has no responsibility for the death of Downey or Kilbride.'

EVIDENCE FOR THE DEFENCE

IAN BRADY, *affirmed.*

Examined by MR HOOSON: I am twenty-eight. I lived in Glasgow until 1953, when I moved to Manchester. Since the age of twenty-one I have been employed as a clerk at the Levenshulme Road Works at Gorton. I had some trouble with the police in my teens, but have never been convicted of any offence of violence. I started going out with Myra Hindley at the end of 1961. I'd first seen Smith in October or November 1963, when he called at the offices at Millwards. He called there because there had been some trouble between his wife and him—he hadn't married her then.

Did you see Smith often or seldom after that?—I seen him off and on until April 1964 and then I had some conversation with him. I didn't see much more of him until August 1964. In April he told me details of his criminal record.

Were there any conversations between you about making money or getting money?—After August, yes. The conversations started in the car coming back from the Lake District. Then the subject was raised in October 1964. This was when we got down to brass tacks.

I want to come straight away now to Wednesday, 6 October 1965. When did you first see Smith that evening?—He came round to the house at 6.15 approximately. He didn't appear to come round for anything special. Myra and I were having tea. He said Maureen was reading *Fanny Hill*. That is the only thing I remember.

Anyhow, did he leave and come along later?—He came back at 7.15 approximately. He showed me a letter. The relevant part which he was worried about was the amount of rent—£14-something—short. He didn't have the money.

Was Myra Hindley there or not?—She was in the kitchen getting ready to go out.

Where were you?—In the living room.

What was the conversation about?—He was agitated regarding the money. He was asking about the job which we had been talking about on the Saturday previous. The Electricity and Gas Board on Hyde Road.

What had been planned as far as that was concerned?—Smith and I found that on the Saturday there was only two men in the shop. We intended to do the job on the Saturday. At one point there's only one man left in the shop.

Was anything else said in the conversation that night?—He asked if the job would take place on the Saturday and I said there was nothing certain. It could be that Saturday or the Saturday afterwards. It just depended on how I felt.

Was there any other conversation about how Smith could get the money?—He was talking about screwing—that is, housebreaking—and one of the suggestions was that we should roll a queer. This was discussed for a bit. I told him the point was that if anything went wrong, this person would be unlikely to complain to the police, so that there was no real risk.

Was anything decided about this suggestion of rolling a queer, as you say?—Yes. Smith told me it would be practice or a hotting-up session for the Saturday or the Saturday afterwards. I told him that Myra and I were going to Glossop and to be prepared, anyway, for that night. There was later discussion after we left the house to go to the car. He left with Myra and I. Myra entered the car and switched the engine on. I was stood outside the car with Smith and I didn't shut the door of the car—I held it to, closed, but not completely shut. Smith and I continued to talk about whether, if something did take place, when it did take place, we would come back to Hattersley. Myra interrupted by tooting her horn. I asked her what was wrong and she said she was cold. As soon as I got in the car, I bawled Myra out for interrupting the conversation, and we went towards Glossop, about one or two miles.

Then where did you go to?—Then I told Myra to go back into Gorton. I wanted some wine and Myra wanted to buy the wine at Hyde, but I said I wanted the Gorton brand.

Will you tell my Lord and the members of the jury how Evans came back to your house that night?—When we got to Glossop, Myra went to the wine shop. Then we drove up Stockport Road and ended up on Ashton Road. There was a young couple in the middle of the road with a dog, standing between the two lines of traffic. As we passed, the dog broke away from its lead, there was a scream, and Myra stopped the car.

You need not worry about the dog.—I am telling you the events of that night.

All I asked you was how Evans came back to the house.—Then I told Myra to go down to the city centre. When we got to the city centre I told her to go to Central Station to see if the buffet was open. When we got to the buffet it was about two minutes off half-past ten. I said to Myra the buffet would probably be closed, but I would go and see if I could get some bottled beer.

Did you meet someone there?—Yes. Evans was standing at a

milk vending machine. I knew Evans; I had met him on several occasions previously. As I went to try the door, he said it was closed, but I tried the door anyway. Then we got into conversation. He kept saying there was no place to get a drink. I knew Evans was a homosexual because he went to one club especially, called the Rembrandt, in Manchester, which is a homosexual hang-out. I invited him back to the house.

Did you take him to the car?—Before I got to the car, I had decided he would do for what Smith and I had been talking about earlier on that night. I told Evans that my sister was meeting me in the car. We got to the car and I told Myra this was a friend who was coming back to Hattersley. She was surprised at first, then annoyed afterwards, because she would not take part in the conversation. We arrived at Hattersley at approximately 11.30. Evans went in the living room and I switched the television on. Myra let the dogs out in the garden for a few minutes. When she came back in, she began making tea. I went to the scullery and told her to go round and get Smith. She said, couldn't it wait till morning. I said I wanted him now. While she was gone, Evans was talking mostly about clothes. I wasn't taking an interest; I wasn't listening.

Where were you and Evans?—In the living room. The only time he left, he went upstairs to the toilet. I told him to be quiet, there was somebody sleeping up there. He came back before Smith arrived.

What was the next thing that happened?—The next thing, I answered the door. Smith and I stood on the doorstep. The dogs had followed me out into the hall. Myra ushered them into the kitchen and shut the door. I said to Smith in a loud voice: 'So you've come round for the miniatures?' I could have said anything. This was in a loud voice for Evan's benefit, nobody else—or perhaps Myra's. He stood there with his mouth open: he didn't know what I was talking about.

Did Smith say anything?—He just went like this (*demonstrated*). You know—'What's going on?' He was carrying his stick. I then said to him in a low voice: 'There's a queer in the living room. I'll ask him for the cash. If he tries to leave, you stop him.'

Just carry on in your own words.—When I said that, Smith

nodded and slapped his hand with the stick. I then asked him to say something loud for Evans's benefit in another voice and he said: 'Just the job. Just the job,' twice. I then went into the living room and Evans was sitting in Myra's grandmother's chair with his back towards the door. I went round the front of the chair at the fireplace, stood by the fireplace and said to Evans: 'There's another bloke at the door who doesn't like queers. All you have to do is put your cash and valuables on the table. Then you can get going.' Evans was surprised and then he started swearing loud. As he was getting up from the chair, he kicked at me. I grabbed him by the lapels to butt him, pulled him towards me; there was again a kick or a stamp. Myra shouted: 'Dave, Dave.' Myra wasn't in the room. Then almost simultaneously there was two thuds or vibrations passed through Evans into my head. Perhaps I had my head against him. Evans was swinging round; his hands were flailing all over the place. He was shouting at the top of his voice. Smith was hitting him—I won't say hard— he was hitting him. It was just a struggle. I was shouting Evans, or telling Evans, to shut up—I was probably whispering it. He kept shouting. I picked up the axe from the side of the fireplace and I hit Evans with the blunt side of the axe. The axe just bounced off his head. It didn't seem to have any effect—it just bounced. Then he kept shouting. I hit him again. The shouting continued, only louder. Smith was in the general struggle hitting Evans and then —

Do you know how many times you hit him?—No. The point was, when I had hit him, I thought he would shut up. I hit him again and it wasn't having any effect. There was blood appearing. Then, after that, it was just a question of—I don't know how many times I hit him. I just kept hitting him until he shut up.

Did you see Smith do anything when Evans fell?—Smith hit him a couple of times with the stick as he was on the floor. Smith was contributing to this all the way through with kicks and with the stick, but this specific part, he hit him two or three times with the stick and as he was going under the table and as he was under the table, he was kicking him about the head and shoulders. Evans ended up under the table lying face downwards.

What appeared to you to be Evan's condition then?—Well, there was blood all over the place at that time—on the walls, and there was pools of it on the floor. He was gurgling. Myra was in the room then.

Had she been in the room at all when you attacked him?—I didn't notice. I didn't notice anything. But she was in the room at the end, by the door—by the open door.

At this stage, did Evans appear to you to be alive or dead?— Evans was alive. He was gurgling—blood, I suppose. He was lying face downwards, and Myra kept asking: 'What's happened? What did he do? What did he do?' I told her there was an argument. 'Get out. Keep out.' Then Smith dragged Evans out and turned him on to his back parallel with the table. He took out Evans's wallet. He was standing over Evans as he was rifling through the wallet; the contents were falling out. He says: 'I don't know why I called him a bastard. I don't even know him.' I didn't actually hear Smith call Evans anything during this. He then showed me a card—a green card. He said: 'He isn't anyone. He's only an F-ing apprentice.' I didn't touch the card.

Was Evans by this time dead or alive?—He was still alive. I was sitting rubbing my ankle and I made some comment regarding the blood. Smith picked up either a magazine or a newspaper and shoved it under Evans's head. Then shortly— within half a minute, I suppose, if that—Evans stopped gurgling and Smith was at the boy. I was almost two foot away. Smith felt the pulse. He says: 'He's a goner,' or 'He's gone.' I got up from the couch and looked at Evans. He wasn't breathing— completely still. There was no gurgling. I then said we would have to get him out of the house.

Did you say something else?—I think the next thing I said, I told Myra—I think she was at the door when that happened— that Evans was dead, and she became overwrought, hysterical, whatever you want to —

Just have a look at this piece of flex, will you, please? (*Exhibit produced to the witness.*) How did that come into the case?— Before this, I wanted to take Evans out as a drunk. Take him out as a drunk between us—an arm each.

Just explain how *that* came into it.—Yes. And Smith said we would leave a blood trail along the way. He suggested tying him up into a wrapping of some sort. He then asked Myra for string; she brought back *this*. He took it, picked up Evans's legs and folded them towards his chest. He then lay on top of Evans's legs and put *this* round the back of Evans's head—I don't know how he put it round—and began to pull it up. I then came over to the side of Evans and started pressing down his legs to get this flex round them.

How did the cushion cover come into it?—This flex was too short to tie. Smith made a joke then. He said: 'He's got no control.' This was referring to the fact that there was a smell. Evans had soiled himself. I then suggested getting the place cleaned up. The blood was being walked in all over the floor.

I was asking about the cushion cover.—I asked Smith to get some mops and buckets. He went for them. I picked up the cushion cover and wrapped it round Evans's head, partly to hide his features, partly to soak up the blood. There was no string in the house. The stick was lying on the floor. He says: 'This'll do,' and picked it up, tried to undo the knots, he couldn't, and handed it to me. He said: 'I bite my fingernails. Can you do any better?' I cut the string with a knife. As I rolled it off, I handed it to Smith; he tied it together into different lengths.

Where had the stick been?—Lying on the floor.

We have heard that a polythene sheet or a blanket was used. Who provided these?—I asked Myra for something—a blanket— and she looked out a white sheet. After we put the white sheet on, the blood was coming through, soaking through, from Evans's head. I asked her for some rag. I think she went upstairs and got a blanket and a piece of polythene, which we spread out on the floor. Smith and I put it over a second time and tied it up exactly the same way as we did the sheet.

Was Evans taken upstairs?—Yes.

At whose suggestion?—At my suggestion because I couldn't put my weight on my ankle. Myra was again going off her head because of the fact that the body was left in the house. Smith and I carried the body upstairs. I told Myra to go upstairs and hold grandma's door shut so she wouldn't come out.

Was anything said as the body was being carried upstairs?— As Smith picked it up—this was in the living room—he said: 'He's a dead weight.'

What was Smith's demeanour during this time?—Theatrical, jocular. He was going out of his way to crack jokes. I don't know if he was trying to prove something, but he was just reeling off different jokes at all stages.

Who cleaned up downstairs?—Smith and I. Myra cleaned up a few spots.

When you invited Evans to the house, had you any intention of killing him?—No, it was just a question—to me, it was a hotting-up—a bit of practice—for the following Saturday and the Saturday afterwards.

Yes, but what did you intend to do, if anything, to Evans?—Nothing. I didn't think there would be any violence at all. That was why I kept Smith interested—because if there were two people present, a person would be less inclined to make a show. If he did have an audience, he could stand a lot of humiliation. He would give over the cash easily, whereas if there wasn't two, he would put up some sort of show, some sort of resistance.

Who began to discuss where to get rid of Evans?—Smith and I. I suggested the road which leads from Hattersley to Stockport: it's a rural road. I suggested stripping Evans completely at the spot.

Why were you going to do that?—To take traces of dog hairs, fingerprints, everything, off Evans.

Why did you want to dispose of the body?—To get away with it. Smith suggested taking him up on to the moors where we shoot. We had been up dozens of times shooting, not once or twice. Then Myra came in with the tea. Just before that, when the question of tea—Myra said she could do with some whisky because she was feeling faint, and she had been sick earlier on. Just before that, Smith said: 'I don't need anything,' and he held out his hand to show how steady it was. The discussion started just after that.

You have seen this plan, which has been described as the 'disposal plan'?—Yes. I wrote it.

Will you tell my Lord and the members of the jury when you wrote it?—I should say it was just after two—round about—after two I started to write it. It wasn't finished till about quarter to four.

Was there any further discussion as to how the body was to be taken to wherever it was to go?—Yes. Myra, she came in with the tea, and Smith said: 'Take him up where we shoot.' Myra said: 'People use up there.' It was me that suggested the Penistone moors—the Penistone Burn.

Was anything said about a pram?—There was a prayer book. This was later on —

No, a pram.—Oh, a pram. That was for the transport. This was, again, later on. Smith wanted to use a wheelbarrow; he didn't want a pram used because it may leave traces of blood on it. I said it was ludicrous to steal a wheelbarrow to transport the body.

What was his condition when he left?—Casual.

Was anything said about the stick?—Yes. Well, this was when we were cleaning up. I picked up the stick and I handed it to him. He said: 'No, destroy it,' which was the jargon we used on the list—anything to be obliterated, destroyed.

Did Myra know anything about the wallet containing the plan going in the car?—No, I didn't put it in the car deliberately. I went down to lock up the car. I put it on the dashboard to chain the steering wheel.

The following morning the police arrived. We have heard that you were taken to Hyde Police Station and that there you made a statement under caution admitting that you hit Evans with a hatchet. Was that statement true?—The statement was basically true. I left out the sordid details, but the statement itself contained the salient facts. I didn't mention about robbery or anything of that sort, except where he put in the part about drink. I pointed out to Carr twice—he said when he was writing the statement, he said Evans and I had been drinking; I said I offered Evans wine in the car, I offered him some in the house, but he refused, he wanted beer.

Why did you take the suitcases down to the left-luggage place on the previous Tuesday?—To clear the house for the job. For the board—the Electricity Board.

With regard to the books that Smith owned, did you give these to Smith?—He bought them himself. I didn't know he was even interested in this sort of thing until—it was nearly in 1965 I seen one book which he had, called *Kiss of the Whip*. He had this lying in his living room.

You said you had discussions with Smith about a bank job?—There was never a discussion about a bank job: it was payrolls being taken from the bank. There were discussions about if a person's hit too hard or where to hit them to get them to drop the bag; discussions about the bullets. There was never any discussion about using blank bullets: there was always going to be live ammunition in the guns. The guns weren't to be brandished —it just depended on what type of job it was—they weren't to be shown at any time because armed robbery was—if the gun was shown, armed robbery would entail a much larger sentence.

Had you at any time told Smith that you had killed anyone?— No.

Did you at any time suggest to Smith that you had buried somebody on the moors?—No. The only discussion I had about burying bodies on the moors was the night Evans died. It was a concentrated discussion on how to go about getting—the list is based—Smith and I have made dozens of these lists in the past, between us, all based on jobs, the principle being that no trace of the starting point was left at the destination and no trace of the destination was taken back to the starting point. He's seen these lists dozens of times.

Was the conversation about burying a body on the moors in relation to Evans only?—On Evans.

MR JUSTICE FENTON ATKINSON: Do I understand you right? You say Smith had seen dozens of lists?—We worked on the lists together.

Wait a minute. Of the same general type as this?—Yes, exactly the same.

Which were made, so to speak, before the possible event?— Not these lists. This was a practice of the method, the theory, that no trace was left; everything was accounted for which was taken—worn.

MR HOOSON: In relation to what had you prepared these lists before?—In relation to payroll jobs. How to cut out all possible risk.

Was there any discussion about moving books and photographs and tape recordings before killing anybody?—No, it was removing anything which was off-beat in the house, not just books.

I want to move now to the case of Lesley Ann Downey. Did you have anything to do with her death?—No.

I want you to tell my Lord and the jury how Lesley Ann Downey came to your house.—The discussion started on either 23 or 24 December between Smith and I. Myra and I went to Myra's mother's house at Gorton. I was sitting in the van—I never go into the house—and Myra went into the house. Smith then entered the van after a couple of minutes. He asked me was I willing to take some pornographic photographs. He said he had a friend who could distribute them. We discussed the matter and I asked him about the financial aspect. I asked him who would pose for the photographs. He says he could get a girl called Madeleine. I asked him who she was and he said it was a girl he knew in Ashton.

Did he bring a girl round to 16 Wardle Brook Avenue on the Saturday, about 6.15?—Myra and I were having tea. There was a knock on the door. There was a lot of arrangements before this Saturday. I answered the door and it was Smith with a young girl.

Did Myra have any knowledge that you had entered into this arrangement with Smith?—No.

Did you make any comment to Smith about the girl?—No. He said could he have a word with me and we entered the kitchen. He explained that he could not get the girl Madeleine to pose and that this girl had agreed to pose for 10s. I said the girl was too young. He said: 'There is a market for that sort of thing.'

Was that conversation a loud one?—Whispers. Hushed.

Could you see how the girl had been brought into the house?—No. Myra came into the kitchen and I told her to go back into the house. It was then he made a reference about Keith in the van. I asked him who Keith was and he said he was the person who would take the photographs. He then went out. We had an argument regarding the fact that he had brought Keith up because I told him never to mention our association and criminal activities to anyone. He then went out to the van and I followed him to the door. He walked along to the end of the path and shouted to the street below. I seen a van or car and it was dark-coloured. As he shouted, I could see the person's legs and as he shouted the person's hand as he moved across to open the window to shout back.

Did you go upstairs?—I shouted Smith back into the hall and

told him I was going to take the photographs and that Myra would be present. I prepared the bedroom and got a camera out and a tripod and flood-lamps. I then put a white sheet over the bed. At the bottom of the bed there was a tape recorder plug socket.

How many tape recorders did you use?—One.

There is one socket in that bedroom?—Yes, except for the light.

Where were the flood-lights connected to?—The same plug as the tape recorder eventually, but not by the same plug. One is taken out and the other put in. There is no two-way plug.

Why did you have the tape recorder there?—I wanted to make a record of what took place in case anything happened afterwards. If either Smith or Keith interfered with the girl or she made a complaint. I would have a record of what took place while she was in the house.

Who brought the girl upstairs?—Myra.

Had the girl said anything to you up to that time?—After the conversation in the kitchen she had been listening to this. I asked her if she was all right, or words to that effect, and she kept repeating the phrase that she had to be home at eight o'clock.

MR JUSTICE FENTON ATKINSON: Am I to understand she was not willing to pose?—No. I am not saying that at that stage. I found this out later on.

MR HOOSON: When Myra brought the girl upstairs, what happened on the landing—anything?—That was after I switched the tape on. I went out to call Smith up. I had left him on the landing. He wasn't there. I'd told him I would shout down: 'Ready.' I looked out of the stairhead window and he was down talking at the fence, and it was snowing slightly at that time. I shouted down —

What happened about the girl?—I shouted down: 'Ready,' and the girl was brought up by Myra. After I shouted down: 'Ready,' I went into the bedroom and switched on the tape— the current on the tape.

Did the girl scream at all?—Myra left her in the bedroom. I went into the grandmother's bedroom next door. I think it was for a reflector. I then came out. Myra went downstairs. I then entered the bedroom. I asked the girl was she ready. The words are on the tape. She said something in reply. I then reached out to take her coat. She stiffened and jerked back and then began to shout. I put my hands over her mouth. She kept trying to shout. Finally Myra came upstairs. She saw what was happening and tried to placate the girl, telling her to be quiet and shut up.

We have seen in the photographs a handkerchief and a scarf. How did the handkerchief come into this matter?—The handkerchief was the girl's. I put it in her mouth to keep her quiet. The scarf was put on at a later stage. I think it was while the music was on. Just before the end.

MR JUSTICE FENTON ATKINSON: 'Just before the end'—what do you mean by 'the end'?—The end of—just before the—or it could be just after the tripod being opened.

MR HOOSON: How did the music come to be on that tape?—Myra switched on a small brown transistor radio that she had received from her uncle Bert as a present, to ease the situation—to ease the tension.

You heard the suggestion that the music came from another tape recorder. What do you say about that? What about the opinion of the expert?—The music was played over that radio.

We heard in the tape recording, almost at the end, three metallic clicks.—That is the tripod being opened.

Why was the tape recorder switched off then?—To plug in the flood lamp.

What happened after you completed taking the photographs?—After completion we all got dressed and went downstairs. There was conversation in the hall.

Before that, where was Smith while you were taking the photographs?—He was on the stairs. There is two poses on the photographs which were suggested by Smith.

How was the girl undressed?—I went downstairs for Smith. Told him what had been happening. Went back upstairs. In the presence of the girl when she was in the room and we were standing at the hall door, I said: 'Doesn't she know what she is here for?' He said: 'Of course she does. Get undressed.' And she got undressed.

What happened to the girl after the completion of the photographs?—The four of us went downstairs. The girl dressed herself. I asked the girl if she was going to complain and she said: 'No.' I asked if she knew who I was, if she knew where this place was, and she said: 'No.' I asked her if she had the money. Smith said he hadn't any change and would give it to her on the way back.

What time was it when she left?—About 7.30.

MR JUSTICE FENTON ATKINSON: She left quite happily, did she?—No, tense all the time.

MR HOOSON: Do you know what happened after she left your house?—The next discussion I had with Smith was on New Year's Eve.

Did he tell you where he brought —

THE ATTORNEY-GENERAL: Do not lead, please.

THE WITNESS: The discussion was after—there was another person sleeping in the same room—there was two persons sleeping in the same room, and the discussion was what had happened when he left on the Saturday. He said that he dropped her off at Belle Vue. I asked him who the girl was and he said Keith knew her. There was further discussion about the fellow.

MR HOOSON: Did you know a girl called Patricia Ann Hodges? —Yes.

Has she been up on the moors with you and Myra?—Yes.

What moors?—All over. Glossop, Leek, Whaley Bridge, Crowden.

Do you know that spot? (*Photograph of vicinity of Hollin Brown Knoll produced to the witness.*)—Yes.

Did you take her up there at Christmas Eve, 1964?—No.

Where did you go that night?—Glossop. First of all we stopped at a building site.

We have heard that there were copies of the tape found in the suitcase. Why were copies taken?—The tape was played to Smith about February. He asked for a copy. I said I would give him a copy, but I would block out parts of the tape.

MR JUSTICE FENTON ATKINSON: Was it put to Smith at any stage that he had been given or asked for a copy of this tape?

MR HOOSON: No, my Lord.

To go back to the night of Boxing Day, after the girl had left where did you and Myra go, or did you stay in the house?—

Towards 9.30 we were going to collect Myra's grandmother. I didn't want to go because of the weather conditions, but Myra insisted. The side roads were bad, but when we got to the main road, there is a hill running down. On the way down there was cars slewing from one side of the road to the other and cars stopped on the hill with their wheels spinning. At the bottom of the hill we meant to turn right and had to turn back on to the main road because we couldn't get up that hill. About a mile or three-quarters of a mile from Dukinfield, Myra had trouble controlling the skids on the road. She eventually stopped the car because I said she couldn't go any further. She went to her uncle's house and I sat in the car. She was gone about three-quarters of an hour. When she came back I said to keep her mouth shut and we started off as slow as she wanted to drive. We got down one hill by using a zig-zag, but we couldn't get up the other hill. The car was abandoned and we walked the rest of the way.

I want to ask you now about certain photographs which were found at Wardle Brook Avenue, and others found in the suit-case. (*Photographs of moorland scenes, some featuring Myra Hindley, produced to the witness.*) Was there any significance at all to these photographs?—No.

How many photographs had you got in the house of views of this kind on the moors?—I couldn't say. The album is full of them. There is Leek, Whaley Bridge, Glossop, Crowden.

How many photographs are there that you have taken of Myra Hindley in different parts of the moors?—I don't know the exact number. Dozens.

(MR HOOSON *then examined the witness regarding his interviews by the police. Brady's answers were similar to those he had given in evidence-in-chief in the absence of the jury; see pages* 120–2 *and* 150–3.)

MR HOOSON: I am going to move on now to the Kilbride case. Do you know anything of the circumstances surrounding the death of John Kilbride?—No.

It is said that he disappeared on 23 November 1963, and that Myra Hindley had hired a car on that day. Do you know exactly where you had been that day or not?—Leek.

Would you kindly look at the exercise book? (*Exhibit produced to the witness*.) What is that book basically?—It was exercises I was doing when I applied for a job at Millwards on book-keeping.

You see a page there with some names on it, and some drawings. Do you remember when you wrote those names there?—No. I never used this book after I got the job at Millwards. That is seven years ago.

There are many names on that page—why did you write them there?—I said to Mounsey that I didn't know. There is doodles all over the page. He said: 'Come off it.' He says: 'Do you know John Kilbride?' I said: 'I knew somebody called Kilbride or McBride at Hull or Salford.' I met the same person afterwards. It is Paddy—an Irish person.

Do you know now whether his name is Kilbride or McBride?—I know it is not Kilbride.

According to Mr Mounsey, he said you took a photograph of the grave, you must know who killed John Kilbride, and you were asked: 'Do you know?' You said: 'Yes, it is one of two men.'—No.

You were asked later: 'If you did not kill John Kilbride and Myra did not kill John Kilbride and you know the name of the man who did it, surely it is your duty and to your advantage to tell us his name?' You are alleged to have said: 'It will come out at the trial.' Did you say that?—I could have done.

Why did you say that?—That rings a bell.

Why did you say that?—I said it, as a fact. I was saying that a few times.

Did you know the name of the man who killed John Kilbride?—No. He kept saying: 'You killed Downey, you are charged with Evans,' and he said: 'The graves are near each other.' I said: 'If you are working on that assumption, the statement I have given to my solicitor will also cover Kilbride, and Benfield has part of that statement.'

According to Mounsey, he said to you: 'You knew when you took it, this was John Kilbride's grave,' in relation to the photograph of Myra Hindley crouching and looking at the ground, and you said: 'Yes.'—No.

Did you ever say that?—No. Every answer I gave was a negative.

Just tell the members of the jury, in what kind of atmosphere was this interview taking place? Was Mr Mounsey the whole time speaking in a normal voice to you?—No. It began with his preparations. The general tone set by the fact that we were taken in a Black Maria with a dozen plain-clothes people and taken up the iron staircase with police all down below. There was no public about, so I didn't need to be protected from any-one. I was then taken into this gymnasium with these three and didn't say anything, and when Mounsey came in and he saw my attitude, that was it. We got on to a political—after the photographs, a political discussion and religion, and from six to eight, that is when the shouting started with Leach and Mounsey.

Shouting?—One each side again. One in each ear. Shouting the question simultaneously.

Did you get up at one stage?—In the afternoon when we were talking about politics, I walked about and Mounsey walked about with me.

How did the interview end at eight?—It ended with Mounsey grabbing hold of the door and saying 'Bastard' and banging the door shut, and then I was left for about ten minutes until Mattin took over.

Cross-examined by MR HEILPERN:

Just a few matters I would like you to help my Lord and the jury about. You and Myra Hindley were living together at 16 Wardle Brook Avenue?—From February 1965.

And though it might appear fairly obvious, I would like you to tell us, if you would, what were her feelings for you?—Well, the same as man and wife.

Was she in love with you?—Yes.

And in general, Mr Brady, supposing that you and she were having a discussion about going anywhere or doing anything, and you had different views about it, whose view would prevail? —Mine.

Why?—Because she was my typist in the office. I dictated to her in the office and this tended to wrap over.

I think you gave us an illustration of it when you said that you on the night of 6 October told her to go and fetch Dave Smith?—Yes.

She said: 'Can't it wait until the morning?'—Yes.

And you then said: 'No, I want him here now'?—Yes.

And she went?—Yes.

No other argument?—No.

Would that be a fair sample of your relationship?—Yes. When I argued with her, when she did, it just made me worse. She argued so little—I had to tell her to argue at times. When she did, it had the opposite effect—it was worse.

Just a word or two about the events of October 6. You and Smith had an arrangement for that night?—Not an arrangement. It was tentative.

Myra knew nothing about that tentative arrangement for that night?—No.

Is it not right, not only had she no part in the arrangements—or tentative arrangements—but she was not in a position to overhear you and Smith talking about it when she was in the car and you and Smith were standing outside?—No. The door was not closed entirely. It was not shut, locked, but the engine was on.

You then went into Manchester and met this young man Evans?—Yes.

Myra remaining in the car?—Yes.

When you got back into the car with him, I think you said to Myra: 'This is Eddie'?—As far as I know, I said: 'This is a friend.' I don't refer to them by their first names.

You then drove back to the house. She did not want to go and get Smith, but you told her to do it and she went. When she came back with Smith, did you open the door?—Yes.

She walked past you into the kitchen whilst you stood and spoke to Smith on the doorstep?—Yes. The dogs followed me out, and she took the dogs back into the kitchen and shut the door.

I just want to ask you one or two things about the actual struggle that went on between you and Evans. Is it not right, Mr Brady, that in fact Myra shouted 'Dave' from the kitchen?—I couldn't rightly say.

Is is not right that throughout the struggle, Myra was not in fact in the living room?—No, she wasn't.

I think we heard from Smith that he assisted in dressing up the body. Myra had no part in that, had she?—No, nothing.

I think you have told us, Mr Brady, about her condition. You used two words, if I remember rightly. One was 'overwrought' and the other was 'hysterical'?—Yes. At certain times. And sick.

I am obliged. Was Smith overwrought and hysterical, or sick in your presence?—No.

Do you remember something being said to show that people knew you went up on the moors? About a policeman seeing her? —That was in reference to Penistone. When I mentioned Penistone she said something about police patrols up there, and went on to say about the time I was practising with the pistol.

Smith gave in evidence that she said something to this effect: 'You should have seen the expression. The blow registered in his eyes.' Did she say that or anything like that?—No.

Did Myra have any part in what we have been calling the 'disposal plan'?—No.

Just a question or two about the Downey matter. You have told us that the suggestion of taking pornographic photographs came from Smith. I think you have told us that Myra knew nothing about this arrangement at all?—No. Myra—I told Myra small details but I never gave—not about photographs. I am saying this is an overall picture. I gave her a small hint if there was something in the wind, but I never gave anyone any details.

I think you have already told us that there was an argument between you and Myra. She was against taking photographs of the girl?—Yes.

You told her that you wanted it to be done?—Yes.

For money?—Yes.

And you wanted her to help?—I wanted her to —

To assist. You have told us why, but this is the fact. It was you who wanted her to help?—To help, yes. I wanted her to be there.

I think you used the words 'as a witness'?—As a witness, and for the girl's sake. To keep the girl at ease.

MR JUSTICE FENTON ATKINSON: To keep her what?

MR HEILPERN: 'At ease' were the words he used.

And because you wanted this done, and because you wanted her to be present, she agreed?—Yes.

That is the situation, is it not, Brady?—Yes.

I think that is all I have to ask this witness.

MR JUSTICE FENTON ATKINSON: Mr Attorney, would you rather start on Monday morning?

THE ATTORNEY-GENERAL: I am at your Lordship's disposal. Perhaps Brady has had rather a long day, but I am quite happy to begin to cross-examine.

MR JUSTICE FENTON ATKINSON: I do not see much point, really. Monday morning.

TENTH DAY

Monday, 2 May

IAN BRADY, *recalled.*

Before THE ATTORNEY-GENERAL *commenced cross-examining,* MR HEILPERN *questioned the witness regarding the photographs taken in the vicinity of Hollin Brown Knoll, and the witness agreed that it was he who had chosen the places to be photographed.*

Cross-examined by THE ATTORNEY-GENERAL:

Am I to understand from your evidence that you admit killing Edward Evans?—Yes.

And that you are not suggesting that Smith either caused his death or contributed to it?—Smith took part in it. I am not suggesting anything regarding what happened. I told you what happened—it is up to you.

You admit it was you who killed Evans?—I admit that I hit Evans with the axe.

Are you suggesting that that did not kill him?—No. Somebody else has.

Who?—The pathologist said it was accelerated by strangulation.

The questioning of the pathologist by your own counsel was to the effect that Evans was dead or dying when the ligature was applied, was it not?—Yes.

And that was the conclusion of the pathologist?—Yes, eventually.

You killed Evans. There is no qualifying that, is there?—I hit Evans with the axe. If he died from axe blows, I killed him.

Very well. Do I gather that you deny being in any way concerned with the death of Lesley Ann Downey?—Yes.

Do you know who killed Lesley Ann Downey, if you did not?—No.

Any idea?—No.

Do I understand that you also deny being in any way concerned with the death of John Kilbride?—Yes.

It is the case, is it not, however, that in a notebook in your house you wrote the name of John Kilbride?—Yes, amongst others.

A name that you had apparently never heard before?—I never said that I had never heard the name 'Kilbride' before. I said I knew somebody called McBride or Kilbride.

It was not 'McBride' that you wrote in the book, you know. It was Kilbride, the name of the dead boy, was it not?—I also wrote Jimmy Idiot, who is nobody, and a lot of other names as well, doodles. There was another two pages in that book which have been torn out, which contained other names.

John Kilbride was not nobody, was he?—He was nobody, yes.

He was one of your victims, was he not?—No.

Do you know, if you deny killing John Kilbride, who did kill Kilbride?—No.

You told Chief Inspector Mounsey when he asked you that question: 'It is one of two men. I have given their names to my solicitor.'—I did not tell him that.

You do not like being landed with that answer now, do you?—I did not tell him that. I know what I told him.

Because it is very difficult to blame Smith for Kilbride. Smith was about fourteen or fifteen when Kilbride was murdered.—I haven't the slightest.

Do you deduce any similarities between the case of Downey and the case of Kilbride?—From what I have heard, yes.

Would you agree from what you have heard that whoever the killer was, he committed his crimes without leaving a clue to his identity?—I don't know. The police know that.

And that was precisely what you sought to achieve in regard to the disposal of Edward Evans, was it not?—Yes.

And that is what the so-called body disposal plan is all about, is it not?—Yes.

You were seeking a repeat performance of the Kilbride and Downey murders, were you not?—No.

It is the case, is it not, that you had taken photographs of the graves of Kilbride and Downey?—No.

Had you not? Do you say that in the face of the evidence the jury has seen of those photographs?—I had taken photographs, yes. Snap shots.

Just look at photograph thirteen. You know it was a deliberately taken photograph of the grave of Lesley Ann Downey, do you not?—No.

And a number of photographs similarly taken. Those are photographs of this cemetery of your making on that moorland, are they not?—Those photographs are snap shots.

That photograph has no merit whatsoever as a snap shot, has it?—No, but there are plenty more without merit in the album.

I ask you again, why did you take it?—It is probably to use up a spool of film.

Why did you not point the camera in the direction of this (*indicating another photograph*)? It is a lovely moorland place for those who go there to enjoy it.—I don't know. The camera does not always catch what you can see.

The camera here caught precisely what you wanted it to catch, namely the grave of Lesley Ann Downey, did it not?—No.

And you took that photograph so that it would be available to you to know where you had buried her for your future reconnaissance?—No.

That was the purpose of it?—No.

Or one purpose of it. Could the other have been some morbid enjoyment of the trophies of your murders?—No.

You see, not only do I suggest to you that you had taken these photographs of the graves with deliberation, but you actually told Smith that you had photographic proof of your killings, did you not?—No.

If what I am submitting to you is true, you did have photographic proof of your killings, did you not?—No.

The graves. Very vivid. Especially for you, who knew what lay beneath the ground, as you did. Very vivid, were they not?—No.

I shall come back to that in a moment. Will you look at this photograph of the man you said in your evidence on Friday you were proposing to take out of the house as if he were a drunk. With battered, bleeding face and head. Is that right?—There was a further suggestion about a coat over his head.

I know about further suggestions. What I am suggesting to you is that you had planned all the time to give Evans the same burial as the other two—to bury him on the moors?—No.

You had killed him. The court has been told there were—how many blows did you say you struck?—I don't know. I know from what the doctors have said.

Fourteen, were there not?—I don't know. I didn't count them.

You would not like me to take you over the wounds on the photographs to prove the fourteen, would you, Brady?—No. I will take your word that there were fourteen.

This boy was a helpless target at your hands, was he not?—I suppose so, yes.

And every blow you struck was struck by you with the maximum force, was it not?—No. The first two blows were not hard. Then after that it was—they were hard.

A controlled, calculated killing, was it not?—No.

You see, undoubtedly they were hard—the greater part of the right side of the boy's skull was smashed to pieces, was it not?—I don't know. I haven't looked at the photographs in detail.

Look at them.—I don't want to look at them.

I am sure you do not, but I want you to because you did this, you see. Look at the photographs, if you can bring yourself to do it. There is a smashing in of the skull. Some of the lad's brains were on the floor, were they not?—I don't know.

You don't? Don't you?—No. I know that there was a remark by Smith that he was a brainy swine.

If that is true—and I am not accepting it for a moment—why did he say that?—Because of the blood on the floor.

Blood has got nothing to do with brains. Why did he say he was a brainy swine?—I wouldn't know his sense of humour.

He could only have said that because there were bits of the boy's brains splattered on the floor. That is the reason, is it not?—I wouldn't know. The police would know that.

But you had engaged in an extensive mopping-up operation after this killing, had you not?—Yes.

Part of the body disposal plan—the non-detection plan?—No, it was just that the blood was being tramped in.

Are you saying that you only engaged in an attempt to eliminate traces of this killing because the blood was making rather a nasty mess for the housekeeping?—It would have had to be cleaned up.

What I am submitting to you about the way you killed this boy is this, that you could not have achieved the degree of force and accuracy you did with your blows unless the level of this boy's head was well below yours. That is right, is it not?—I wouldn't know. He was up and down and all over the place.

The truth is, Brady, that you hit that youth the first blow with the axe when he was sitting on the settee and you struck him from behind. That is how this murder started, was it not?—No.

And after that initial blow, although he obviously struggled for his life, he never got on his feet again, did he?—He was on his feet the whole time, falling on to the couch and up again. Shouting at the top of his voice. All I was worried about was the noise.

You were hitting to stop the noise. But can you account for the area of twelve inches square of bloodstaining on the top edge of the back of the settee?—When he fell on the settee.

That is where you struck the initial blow?—No.

And from that position he slid down to the floor?—No.

That accounts for the blood staining on the front edge of the settee cushions, does it not?—I wouldn't know.

And it happens to fit in precisely with Smith's account of what you did, does it not? Let me put this to you: you did wield that axe like a butcher cutting up meat, did you not?—No. I wielded it to stop the noise. I don't know how I wielded it.

Of course, that was something you were accustomed to, was it not?—No.

Had you not been a butcher's assistant at one stage in your career?—Yes.

What were your feelings when you were striking this boy on the head with this axe?—All I remember was this hitting, how to stop the noise. I just kept hitting him. It was just panic.

Panic. You claim to have a very clear idea of everything that was going on in that room. You say Hindley was not there, you say Smith was there, and you claim to have given the court a detailed account of what Smith was doing?—That was after. I cannot say about during the assault. The only thing I had in my mind during it was the noise.

Do I understand that you may not be very clear in your recollection as to who was and who was not there during the assault? Is that what you are saying now?—I know who was there.

The fact is, Hindley was there the whole time, was she not, or most of the time?—The only time I seen Myra was when I sat on the couch—in the doorway. After Evans was lying on the floor.

Did it surprise you that it took so many blows of this axe to kill the boy?—Yes.

Indeed, you were so surprised that when it was over you handed this axe to Smith and said: 'Feel that. How could he take it'?—No.

You were amazed?—All I can say about that is the police must have seen Smith's fingerprints on it and he had to say something. I didn't know he had touched the axe.

That is a very interesting answer. You are suggesting now that the police have conspired with Smith?—Yes.

Are you suggesting that the police concocted a story and put it into Smith's mind in order to convict you?—No, what I am suggesting is that they could have asked him an ambiguous question—suggested how his fingerprints could have got on the axe. That Brady handed it to him or something like that.

There is no evidence of Smith's fingerprints on the axe, is there?—I don't know. I don't know why he said it.

Do you agree that you never expected that it would take so many blows to kill Evans?—I wouldn't know. I said something like —

You never expected it to be such a bloody business?—I wouldn't say that.

What did you say 'like —'?—I said I thought he would drop when I hit him the first time.

That was when you were boasting about your killings after the murder, was it not?—No.

It fits in exactly with what Smith says, if not in precise words? —Yes.

You in fact said: 'That is the messiest yet,' did you not?—I said: 'It is a messy job,' in reference to cleaning up the blood on the floor.

If what you say is true, that Smith was working in cahoots with you, you could have together silenced this boy in a few seconds?—Yes.

May I suggest how you could have done so?—It is all right to suggest now, but that is how it happened, so there is no point.

Let me suggest how it could have been done. By gagging him as you did Lesley Ann Downey. That is a very effective way, is it not?—I suppose so.

And you are good at it?—No.

Exactly what you did to Lesley Ann Downey?—Yes.

Yes—with the assistance of Myra Hindley?—No.

Now I want you to look at the statement you made to the police between 9.33 am and 10.04 am on 7 October. Let us see what you said. 'Last night I met Eddie in Manchester. We were drinking.'—I did not use the word 'Eddie'. They used that. Sergeant Carr would say: 'Did something happen?' and I would say 'Yes', and he would write it down.

Under what terms did you know him, as Eddie or Evans, or what?—I just knew him as a person. I never called anybody by the first name until I knew them very well.

You familiarise slowly, do you?—I —

Never mind. 'Last night I met Eddie in Manchester. We were drinking.'—I pointed out to Carr specifically twice that I had offered him drink in the car and house and he refused. I don't know why he has put this.

Can you think of any reason why?—I don't know. I don't see that it matters anyway.

It may matter a great deal. You see, if you were drinking together, you must have been drinking before closing time, must you not, before 10.30?—He did not drink anything in my presence.

The difficulty, I suggest to you, that you are now trying to get out of is the statement of Hindley that you had both gone to Glossop?—I don't know anything about that. We were going to Glossop in the beginning of the evening.

I think you told the court that you had met Evans before. I

am interested in the club which you claimed on Friday was frequented by homosexuals. You were a visitor there?—I have been there about three times.

What were you doing in that hive of homosexuals?—Watching the antics of them.

Was the accused Hindley with you?—No.

I thought you always went out together. 'Whatever he did, I did. Wherever he went, I went.'—That is what Myra said. When I had a motor bike I used to go all over the place without Myra.

Evans was a very strange choice if the purpose was to rob him, was he not?—I wouldn't know. He looked older than he was. His face was covered with acne—whatever you call it.

Did you have the faintest idea that this boy had any money worth stealing?—No, I was going on appearances.

What appearances? Of wealth?—People walk around in rags nowadays and may have £20 or £30 in their pockets.

Rolling a penniless queer. That is a very odd exercise, is it not?—I thought he would have money, but I wasn't interested in the amount. I am saying that from my point of view, it was an activity. It was a hotting-up.

What was the point of the hotting-up exercise?—Just the atmosphere of it. Robbing is robbing.

Getting Evans there was a sort of hotting-up practice for a robbery with violence—with guns?—Yes, and that itself was only —the Electricity Board was only another practice for another job.

Oh, really. What was the other job?—A payroll.

So you were to start in the quiet foothills of the Electricity Board and then advance to raid a bank proper. Was that your great plan?—There was no question of robbing banks.

What I want to come to is this: some homosexual activity took place between you and Evans in the living room that night, did it not?—No.

Did he not have his trousers and underpants down at some stage?—He went to the toilet.

His fly buttons, when his body was found, were open from top to bottom. That is because you had been interfering with him.—No.

And there were dog hairs on his bare skin and on the inside of his underpants that came from the couch where you and he were engaged in some form of homosexual activity.—No.

What attraction did you hold out to lure—I had better use a neutral phrase—to get Evans to come to Wardle Brook Avenue? —I should think from the conversation that he thought there would be some sort of sexual activity.

This conversation was in the presence and hearing of the accused Hindley, was it not?—She was outside the station in the car.

Did this conversation not also continue in the car?—No. Just small talk in the car. Myra didn't take any part. She was short on replies.

Was any arrangement made as to how Evans was to get back to Ardwick that night?—There was some talk about dropping him off.

You were going to rob him and take him back in the car?—No.

What was he to do?—Walk.

Ten miles back to Ardwick after being robbed by you and Smith?—Yes, that was it.

Making no complaint to anyone on the way?—That is what we counted on.

You had in mind to commit a murder that night and to bury the victim where you had buried the others?—No. That night I came home and took the dog out for half an hour as normal. Then I took some photographs of the dog and Myra and the neighbour next door. I told the police this and they developed the photographs.

Going down the statement again: 'When the argument started, David was at the front door and Myra called him in. Eddie was on the floor by the living room door.'—Yes, but they missed out other small details. This is out of context. It is all stuck together.

Let me put another sentence to you. 'Eddie kicked me at the beginning on my ankle and there was a hatchet at the fireplace which I hit Eddie with.' Is that accurate?—That is accurate without the details, yes.

What detail is missing?—The fact that Smith came in.

MR JUSTICE FENTON ATKINSON: Why was the hatchet at the fireplace?—It may have been Myra's grandmother; she was in all night. She could have been using it.

THE ATTORNEY-GENERAL: You had, in fact, placed that hatchet

behind that settee in a bag in preparation for Evans sitting there, and for your using it in attacking him from the back, had you not?—No.

Now, just one other matter on the statement. If it was the case that Evans had been brought to the house so that Smith could rob him—roll a queer—why did you not tell the police that?—Because I did not want Myra's family and my own family—I didn't want the sordid details to come out.

Murder is pretty sordid, is it not?—Yes. It just depends how you think.

You seem to question the proposition that murder is sordid.—I think it is sordid, yes.

You do not go with the views of the Marquis de Sade on murder, for instance?—I have read de Sade, and that is Smith's book.

You have read de Sade?—Yes.

Enjoyed it?—Yes.

Approved of it?—Some of it.

The bits about murder?—No.

'Murder is a horror but a horror often necessary; never criminal, and essential to tolerate in a republic.' I suggest that is precisely what you were indoctrinating Smith in.—I was not indoctrinating him in anything. That book is Smith's book. I don't know why he denied it—he has got worse ones than that.

This was the diet you were consuming. Pornographic books, books on violence and murder?—No pornographic books. You can buy them at any bookstall.

They are dirty books, Brady?—It depends on the dirty mind. It depends on your mind.

Let me give you the names of one or two —

MR JUSTICE FENTON ATKINSON: *Uses of the Torture Chamber, Sexual Anomalies and Perversions.*

THE WITNESS: These are written by doctors. They are supposed to be social.

THE ATTORNEY-GENERAL: Was your interest in them on a high medical plane?—No, for erotic reasons.

Of course. This is the atmosphere of your mind. A sink of pornography, was it not?—No. There are better collections than that in lords' manors all over the country.

You did not have a bad collection as collections go, for a very

No all list ? up $\frac{1}{+2}$.   Destroy all
Note how many pages. EACH   lists.

O.B	DET	CARR	STH	END
HAT ×	Clean before wipe & to place in papers container which has been cleaned........ After use replace in container .	×		Burn shaft bury head.
CAR ×	Remove all moveable objects, clean cover floor and seat fresh Poly. at night. Cover all moveables tent etc		×	Destroy Poly. inspect car for spots.
GN ×	Polish, Balls Polish.	×		Dave
TICK ×	Place P/B.		×	
PIEC	Check periodically unmoved			W/H
PROP	1. STIMULATE			
CARR ×	for thtch, papers bag.			Destroy

The disposal plan

| N° all List 1 up | | 1+2 | | Destroy all lists |

Note how many pages EACH

OB	DET	CARR	STN	END
HAT	Clean before wipe pts place in paper container which has been cleaned After use, replace in container	×		Burn shaft bury head
CAR	Remove all moveable objects, clean cover floor and seat fresh Poly. at night Count all moveables, Keys ect.		×	Destroy Poly. inspect car for spots
GN	Polish, Bulls Polish	×		Dave
TICK	Place P/B		×	
REC	Check periodically unmoved			W/H
PRO P	STIMULATE			
CARR	For Hatch, paper bag			Destroy

Second sheet:

OB	DET	CARR	STN	END
ALI WE HOME THEN HEYWOOD	Period of termination? Dave Carr 7–8.30 Use bus, pick-up end CARR Belle Vue, bus back HATCH		×	14 days. Vague no memory after 14
METH	Drop me off, pass agreed Point ever five mins		×	
Dump	have container Hatch for Dave Carr Discuss		×	
CLOTH	Check & Polish all buttons & clasps. Brush hairs, clean shoes, wear glov Packamac?	× 10 BUT		
KEYS	Delete key ngt. 1 Pen			

Third sheet, no columns: *Verso of third sheet, no columns:*

2 GN	5 Bulls EA	money	
MATCHES			IF 1 AP Store Gn &
CIGS		WALLET	Bulls where? New
WATCH		10/- Note	Story
GLVES			
2 PR Shoes			Dist Why

humble collector?—I had a very poor selection. There are better.

I want you to look now at something you say you wrote shortly after the killing of Evans. Let us look at what is in the columns. Start with the top. 'No. all list 1 up. Note how many pages.' What does that mean?—How many pages were included in the list.

'Destroy all lists'?—These. This list. There is two pages.

Does that mean when the plan of eliminating all clues to link the murder of Evans with you had been completed?—Yes.

Then we come to the first column. 'OB'. What does that mean? —Object.

Then 'DET'.—Details.

'CARR'?—Carriage. Anything that is being carried, either from the house or from the car. This is only rough. There is stacks of detail left off.

What details have you left out? There is hardly anything to leave out, is there?—The train of thought is different now. There is no incentive to think of details.

What is different in your train of thought now?—The train of thought now is that I will be convicted anyway.

'STN'. What does that mean?—Stationary, anything that does not move.

'END'. That speaks for itself, does it not?—That is the end. It means the final action in respect of each item.

'HAT'. What does that mean?—Hatchet.

Detail—'clean before'?—Before leaving the house with it.

Just let us read the rest and come back to that answer. 'Clean before'. 'Wipe'. What does 'pts' mean?—Fingerprints.

'Clean before. Wipe fingerprints. Place in paper container which has been cleaned.' Read out, please, what follows.— 'After use, replace in container'.

What you wrote down previously were instructions as to what was to be done before?—Yes.

Clean the fingerprints before use?—Yes, and after use.

You were preparing instructions here as to what to do with the hatchet before and after it was used?—Yes.

MR JUSTICE FENTON ATKINSON: Are we quite clear on this, Brady?—Yes, the hatchet was —

Would you listen for a moment?—Yes, I am listening. The hatchet was being used to dig with.

THE ATTORNEY-GENERAL: Before digging with?—Yes, digging the earth.

You had a spade that you used to take on the moors?—No, there is no spade on the list.

Why should you want to clean the fingerprints before using the hatchet to dig with?—In case it was dropped in the dark.

Were you going to use the hatchet to dig the moors to bury Evans in?—No. The places at Penistone—there is caves. This is where Smith showed the police and took photographs. They have never mentioned this. There is caves under the overhanging rock and the earth dug out from outside and scooped in on top.

We come to the next sentence. 'After use replace in container'?—Yes, a container we were taking with us. After the hatchet had been used to dig with. It would bear traces of the earth and we didn't want to leave that in the car.

The next is 'CARR'?—Yes.

'Remove all moveable objects. Clean cover, floor and seat. Fresh poly at night. Count all moveables'?—Yes.

First of all, when was that to be done?—The next night.

You see, at the end you have an 'X' against that 'STN'. What does that mean in relation to what has got to be done to the car?— That means that those objects would not need the car. They would be stationary. They would be in an enclosed container.

You were going to remove them, apparently. 'Remove all moveable objects'.—This is referring to anything which is in the car. The car had not been cleaned out.

Let us look at the last column. 'Destroy poly. Inspect car for spots'.—In case there was any blood. That was to be done at the end—after everything had been removed.

Then we come to the next. 'GN'. That is gun?—Yes.

'Polish, bulls polish'.—Polish bullets. In case the guns were used.

You mean to remove fingerprints?—Yes.

Why should the guns be used?—They were being taken along, depending on the circumstances. Taking them as insurance.

Against what?—Interference.

'TICK' is the next. What does that mean?—Ticket.

It says: 'Place P/B'.—Prayer book.

Place the left-luggage ticket in the prayer book?—Yes.

I do not want to take any advantage of an inadvertent answer. Do you understand that entry to mean 'Ticket to be placed in prayer book'?—Yes.

That means that this was written down in this plan before you took the ticket — (*Witness interrupts:*) Out of my wallet and put it in the prayer book. The last two things I did was count every button on my clothes and take the ticket out of the wallet and put it in the prayer book.

Whose idea was it to put it in the accused Hindley's prayer book?—Mine.

You did not choose the prayer book to get a kick out of it, did you?—No. The innocence connected with a prayer book, I suppose.

Let us go to the next entry. 'REC'. What does that mean?—Reconnoitre.

'Check periodically unmoved'. What were you going to check? —That nobody had found Evans.

Precisely what you were doing time and again in regard to the graves of Downey and Kilbride, was it not?—No. It was chiefly to see if anything had been left in the darkness or if there had been any traces left. Anything at all. We had to see it in daylight.

A simple means of recording where the body had been placed would be to have a photograph of the grave, would it not?— I suppose so. The point is, I know this place.

Very well. Opposite is 'W/H'. What does that mean?—Woodhead. It is on the way to Penistone.

What was the idea—were you going to bury the body in Woodhead?—It was going to be buried in a spit. I am calling this place Penistone. I know it to be Penistone or near Penistone, but I am not saying it is actually Penistone.

Penistone is miles away from Woodhead.—I am saying this place is on the road to Penistone. I am not saying it is Penistone itself or anywhere near. There is a long road between Penistone and Glossop.

Was not, in fact, 'W/H' a reference to Wessenden Head Moor, just to the east of Saddleworth?—I don't know any of these names.

Was the Saddleworth area known to you as Wessenden Head Moor?—That area was known to me as across from Crowden.

You were really referring to the place where you had already buried the other bodies as 'w/h', were you not?—No. I have never heard any of these names.

The next entry, 'PRO'.—Pro-plus. Something to get us through the extreme circumstances which lay ahead. After the tension and everything and what had to be done. There was no Pro-plus in the house. I had a sprained ankle. I felt drained. I felt green at times, in a cold sweat. I wanted something to get me through it.

According to the evidence of David Smith, you told him that part of your preparations for killing was to take a drug, Pro-plus, as a stimulant.—That is rubbish.

Here it is: Pro-plus.—It is there.

The next page—first item is 'ALI'.—Alibi.

An alibi for what?—For the next night.

'We home then Heywood'.—We were going to Heywood after everything had been completed the next night.

What was Heywood?—My parents. I was going to visit them.

That would not be an alibi, would it? Or were you going to try to get someone to say — (*Witness interrupts:*) Smith was meeting someone at Belle Vue. That is his alibi, while we took the body out. The next night between seven o'clock and 8.30, when it was dark.

You had been at Heywood with your parents—was that the story you were planning to concoct?—Yes, and Smith was supposed to be at Belle Vue.

What about the previous night—the actual killing night? Did you prepare an alibi for that?—No, nothing could be done about that.

Very well. Let us see what was to be done. 'Details. Period of termination'. What does that mean?—How long everybody's recollection would last.

'End. 14 days. Vague no memory after 14 days'. What does that mean?—It means if something cropped up after fourteen days, you wouldn't say Heywood or Belle Vue. It would just be you couldn't remember.

Is that 'Carr 7 to 8.30'?—Yes.

'Use bus, pick up'?—Yes.

'Belle Vue, bus back'. Who was to do that?—I can't rememb
the details of this. This was being discussed between us as it wa
being written down.

What does 'Carr hatch' mean?—I don't know. I don't thin
that had been agreed.

'METH'. Is that method in relation to the alibi?—That is
the place where Evans was going to be buried.

What are the details? 'Drop me off. Pass agreed point ever
5 mins'. What does that mean?—In the dark, we had to find th
place. I would be dropped off from the car and the car would g
on.

What does 'picnic' mean?—The picnic place where the cav
were.

Was Hindley to come back every five minutes to see all wa
well? She was the sort of watch dog, was she?—No, just in ca
somebody stopped by a stationary car. There are not offici
parking places and things.

You had rather a bitter experience of leaving a vehicle on th
road with a body in it, had you not?—No. Myra pointed out th
in this area police patrols had stopped while I was shooting wi
a revolver. It was a mile past this picnic spot.

Next item. What does 'Dump' mean?—That is the actu
place. The spot where Evans was going to be buried.

'Have container'.—The container for carrying the hatch
instead of taking it back.

'Hatch for Dave'. He was to burn the shaft and bury the hea
—That was the end. Yes.

Why is the word 'discuss' here?—That is in regard to carryin
to get the body out to the car and out of the van. Carriage in ca

This was something you were going to discuss with Smith?-
Yes.

I thought your case was that you were going over this, ite
by item with Smith, after the killing of Evans?—I have alread
pointed out there was a lot of detail still to be discussed.

This was a bit of unfinished business?—Yes.

'CLOTH'. 'Check and polish all buttons and clasps. Brush hair
clean shoes, wear glov, Packamac'. Does that refer to you
clothing?—That refers to everybody's clothing, particular
Smith and I. Anyone who would leave the car.

So that night, after this killing in that room, there you are, checking the number of buttons on your coat? On your waist-coat, too?—It was the last thing I did.

'Brush hairs'. Animal hairs, I suppose?—Yes.

'Clean shoes'. Why?—There is two pairs of shoes each in case where we had been digging we carried soil back into the car. They were to be changed before getting into the car.

There is that detail on the next page. This armoury—the equipment, rather—that you were needing. '2 pr shoes' one sees there?—Yes.

'Gloves, watch, cigs, matches' I see on that page. '2 GN': guns? —Yes.

Five bullets each?—Yes.

And the '10 BUT'—what are they?—That is my buttons on my clothes.

Is it other than a mere coincidence that there were ten buttons on the jacket of Evans?—Unless the police have torn one or two off to make it suit them, it was a coincidence. Was there any more buttons on?

Are you suggesting that the police have concocted the asser-tion that there were ten buttons on the coat of Evans so that they can damage you by reason of that entry '10 BUT' on that docu-ment?—I don't know. There is no mention of the jacket in this. It is not just jacket, it is every button—and I had ten buttons. There is only one on my jacket.

Over the page of these lists there are the words 'If I AP'. What does that mean?—I couldn't say. It could be 'apprehended'.

'Store gun and bulls where?'—I don't know the train of thought.

What is the word that follows that?—'New story'.

What was the new story to be?—I don't know the train of thought when I made this. I just jotted things down.

What does 'Dist' mean?—That is something to do with the district. Why we were in the district of Penistone and Woodhead.

'New story'—you see, that relates to what is to happen. What is to be done either by you or your confederate or confederates in the event of your being arrested. That is your train of thought there, is it not?—I think it was something to do with if we had to run on the moors. I know that is what that 10s note was for. In

case we were left without transport and we would have to ha~
some money—carry something with us.

Is this right, Mr Brady—that that plan was prepared befo~
Evans was killed?—It was prepared between two and a quart~
to four in the morning.

Whenever it was prepared, you were preparing a scheme ~
hide from the police the fact that you were involved in the mu~
der of Evans, were you not?—Yes.

Do you find anything wrong in that, looking back at it?—~
was a case of self-survival.

Smith did go to the police, did he not?—Yes.

Do you blame him for doing that?—Yes.

Why?—For what has now occurred.

You were not able to carry out the perfect murder, is th~
right?—I didn't attempt to.

And, of course, you have hated Smith ever since he went ~
the police?—I don't think he is worth hating.

Would you agree with me—or perhaps this is a matter ~
comment, and if my learned friend objects to the question, ~
can. Would you agree with me that —

MR HOOSON: Surely my learned friend is not going to put ~
question which he thinks is comment and then ask me to obje~
to it?

THE ATTORNEY-GENERAL: Is this right, that you have admitt~
that you planned carefully before committing any crime?—
Robbery, yes.

Robbery and murder?—No.

You see, before the Evans murder you removed all the i~
criminating material, did you not?—For the coming Saturday ~
the Saturday afterwards.

The tape recording and the photographs of the naked Lesl~
Ann Downey would be highly incriminating if anything with ~
sexual element was contemplated as a crime, would they not?~
Yes.

That is why you removed them on Tuesday, to clear the grou~
for Wednesday?—No.

The exercise that you were staging, in part at any rate ~
impress Smith that you could kill without a conscience.—No.

You knew he was just a boy, a youth?—No. He spoke abo~

his age at different times, saying it was an asset in case anything happened. In case he was apprehended for anything. Youth—he would probably get Borstal or something like that.

You were a Borstal boy yourself, with a record for dishonesty, and Smith had a record of minor violence as a juvenile?—Using a knife on a man, I don't know if that was minor.

I don't know if that was put to him, but never mind. What was the bond between you?—Business. Anything that would bring in money.

By 6 October his whole future had become very much involved in yours, had it not?—Yes, but about three days before that there was an argument because he kept calling in so much he was a nuisance.

Not such a nuisance that you were unwilling to take pornographic pictures of a little girl of ten so that he could make some money out of it?—Yes, and I was going to get some.

How much?—The arrangement was 60-40. He wanted it three ways and I would have 10 per cent more.

You worked out the percentages as though it was some literary transaction. You had yourself taken many pornographic photographs for sale, had you not?—No. Otherwise the police would have found them.

On how many occasions had you taken pornographic pictures? —I think twice. About three years ago.

Long before that little girl was brought to 16 Wardle Brook Avenue?—Smith also took photographs with his polaroid camera.

Three years ago?—No. Up to September when his father stole his camera.

You are now doing your best to blacken Smith at all stages, are you not?—No. You brought up pornographic pictures.

Why do you think Smith went to the police station?—I haven't the slightest. Ask him.

Leaving aside the Evans murder for the moment, can you think of any reason why David Smith would want to implicate you and the accused Hindley in other murders?—No.

Smith has told the court that you told him you picked your victims from the fifteen to twenty-one age group because these young people, when they disappeared, tended to be listed as missing persons, whereas you had had experience that with small children like John Kilbride and Lesley Ann Downey, there is a hue and cry?—No.

The whole community is worried about the safety of those children when they disappear, is it not?—I wouldn't know.

MR JUSTICE FENTON ATKINSON: You mean that, do you?—Pardon?

You really mean what you have just said?—I know that it would cause a hue and cry, I suppose. I have heard this so many times —

THE ATTORNEY-GENERAL: What have you heard so many times?—This sort of thing that you are saying.

What you are saying is that all Smith has told the court of your statements to him is a pack of lies?—Yes. I have not read his statements.

You heard him giving evidence?—I have heard him talking, yes.

I want to ask you some questions now about Lesley Ann Downey. You told the court a few minutes ago that the arrangement was that you and Smith were to get a share of the proceeds of the sales of pornographic pictures taken of that little girl?—No, the original arrangement was in reference to a girl called Madeleine.

You say that Myra Hindley was a reluctant participant in what happened to that child?—Yes.

You have said that her role was to placate the child, as I understand it?—Yes, and be a witness that only photographs were taken.

Why be a witness of that?—In case the girl made complaints or in case the seller or Smith interfered with the girl after she left.

What was the purpose of the tape recording?—I just wanted a safeguard.

Safeguard of what?—Against Smith.

Why against Smith?—Against anybody. Against the police if they eventually traced the photographs back to me.

That tape recording is a record of a brutal sexual attack on a little girl of ten, is it not?—No. She was not undressed when that tape was on.

At what point was she undressed?—When Smith came upstairs.

We hear in the recording the child protesting: 'Please don't undress me'?—She isn't protesting—she is asking.

Did you believe that this child had agreed for 10s to be photographed in the nude?—Smith was saying it in front of the girl. I believed it. I asked the girl if she was all right.

During any of the period of this tape recording—it lasted thirteen or fourteen minutes—is there any word of concern there, if the child was all right, from you?—I haven't read the complete transcript.

What was the effect of reading it on you, and hearing it played in the court, Brady?—The effect now is embarrassing.

It was made on Boxing Day, 1964, and we find it in October 1965. Why did you keep it all that time?—Because it was unusual.

Is that the best adjective you can apply to that, Brady?—Yes. that is the best adjective I can find at the moment.

For those interested in perversion and horror it was something of a connoisseur's piece, was it not?—I wouldn't know.

Worth making two copies of, for those that way inclined?—No.

The child asks you at the end: 'What are you going to do with me?' This is the child that had apparently consented to be photographed for 10s?—Yes.

Then: 'Put it in,' you say. Then she said: 'Don't undress me, will you?' and you said: 'No, put it in.'—I don't think I said that.

That is what the transcript says, you know.—There are quite a few mistakes in this transcript and the transcript of the other tape. He has put names in of people who don't even exist.

There is not a whisper or a sign of a male voice other than yours throughout the whole of this recording, is there?—There is sounds in the background which they can't read.

For your interest to secure a recording of the fact that nothing untoward happened to that child, the key moment would be to record Smith saying something when he is taking the child away.—I didn't know what was going to take place when I put the tape recorder on.

There is nothing in this recording to give you any protection at all.—No, Myra wanted me to destroy it.

And you dare not let that child out of the house alive after what you had done to her?—Yes.

You see, looking down at page 4 of the transcript, this is your contribution. When the child is refusing to be gagged, 'Put it in.' you say. 'If you don't keep that hand down, I'll slit your neck.' —Again, I think that is a wrong translation. I can't tell what I am saying on the tape—I don't know how he can.

You reduced that little child to utter terror, did you not?— No. Towards the end she was crying. There was no sound at all.

Of course there was no sound at all when she was gagged. That was the point of gagging her.—Yes, but she kept pulling it down.

That is why you ultimately tied the scarf so tight that she could not pull it down.—The scarf was not tied tight.

Towards the end, the accused Hindley says: 'Put that in your mouth again, packed more solid.' Of course, you appreciated, did you not, that the more solidly the handkerchief was packed into the mouth of that little girl, she could be suffocated in a matter of seconds by merely putting your hand over her little nose?—No.

Suffocation of that child then became child's play, I was going to say, rather unattractively, but that is right, is it not?—No.

You said in evidence on Friday: 'After completion, we all got dressed and went downstairs.'—I didn't answer that.

Is that what happened?—I didn't utter those words. I don't know where you have got that.

MR HOOSON: I am bound to say I was examining him and I do not recollect that answer at all. I am sure I would have done if that reply had been made.

THE ATTORNEY-GENERAL: Both my learned friends have a note of it.

MR MARS-JONES: That is so, my Lord.

MR JUSTICE FENTON ATKINSON: And Mr Waterhouse?

MR WATERHOUSE: Yes, my Lord.

MR JUSTICE FENTON ATKINSON: You say that is not right?

THE WITNESS: I didn't say that. I said the girl got dressed and we all went downstairs. The girl. The girl.

MR JUSTICE FENTON ATKINSON: I do not know what the jury's recollection is.

A MEMBER OF THE JURY: He said that, sir.

THE ATTORNEY-GENERAL: That was a slip of the tongue? It revealed the truth, did it not?—No. I said the girl got dressed.

Did you know of the hue and cry when the child disappeared?
—The name on the tape is Westford.

You and Hindley had actually drawn the attention of Pat Hodges to the publicity about this little child. You showed her the *Gorton Reporter*?—I didn't show her anything.

You are there; your voice is heard.—That tape lasted about half an hour and it is about all sorts of things.

It is about the *Gorton and Openshaw Reporter*.—What is the rest of the half hour? What is the rest of it?

I am interested in what is relevant to this murder trial.—I cannot remember anything about the section you are talking about.

You were there.—The only detail I can remember about it is a joke about Hamlet.

You knew they were talking about the missing child?—I didn't, no.

MR JUSTICE FENTON ATKINSON: Mr Attorney, can we enquire whether Brady ever passed any of the Downey photographs over to Smith?

THE WITNESS: No. That New Year's Eve—by that time I had decided not to distribute the photographs. I showed him a part of a developed film and told him this was how it had turned out.

THE ATTORNEY-GENERAL: On 18 October you were asked by Mr Benfield: 'Where did you meet Lesley Ann Downey?' and he says you said: 'I met her at the house. I don't know how she got there.'—Yes, I know.

Just a moment. 'I don't know how she got there.' Did you say that?—No, I didn't. No.

He is lying, is he?—Haigh is. It is Haigh's notes. Every time I asked for my solicitor, he puts down some fictitious question and answer.

Did Mr Benfield say: 'Who brought her?' and you said: 'Two men'?—He was asking for the names all along. 'We want to help you. Don't get your solicitor. We are the people to help you. We have the facilities, etc.' This is how he was going on. I was willing to give the facts to the solicitor, and if he advised me to give them to the police, I would have given them to the police. I told Benfield this and told him it repeatedly. Obviously he knew I would be advised against giving them.

Why should a solicitor advise you against — (*Witness interrupts:*) I am taking it from the attitude of the police.

Were you trying to help them?—Yes. I was trying to help them and Myra.

MR JUSTICE FENTON ATKINSON: You say you were trying to help them and Myra?—Yes. As soon as Myra was arrested, I stopped co-operating with the police. As far as I was concerned, that was it.

THE ATTORNEY-GENERAL: In the interviews by the police, there was no violence or threats?—There was threats. There was one which was by Mounsey. At one point he said: 'I don't think you have any feelings at all. The only feelings you have got are for your dog. We will destroy your dog, and maybe you will realise what it is like to lose something you love.' They also brought in the *Manchester Evening News* where there was a photograph of Downey's uncle struggling with two policemen. He says: 'How would you like him to get hold of you? We can arrange that.'

Are you suggesting the police deliberately got that dog put to death in order to threaten or impress you or Hindley?—It is a coincidence, we will say.

You made visits to the grave of Lesley Ann Downey, did you not?—No. I have been up in that area.

Pat Hodges has pointed out the very spot. Between the two signposts. That was your favourite rendezvous, was it not?—No. She didn't go often to that place. She has been all over the moors.

Is she not telling the truth? Is she another liar?—Mistaken.

The night that little Lesley Ann Downey disappeared, Mr Burns has given evidence that the accused Hindley came later than usual—about half-past eleven—to say that she could not take her grandmother back home that night. You were in the car, were you not?—I don't know what the hour was. I was in the van about three-quarters of a mile away.

And the reason why you did not want the old lady about was that you either had the body of that child in the van or you had it in the house and were going to dispose of it that night. That is the reason, is it not?—The roads were unmanageable.

You had, of course, been up on the moors on Christmas Eve, had you not?—Glossop, yes.

Glossop?—Glossop.

You had been to this very place?—Glossop.

With the little girl Pat Hodges?—Glossop.

She told the jury that on Christmas Eve this was the very place you went to?—Glossop.

What were you doing up on the moors on Christmas Eve—getting the grave ready?—We were at Glossop after stopping at a building site at the top of Hattersley.

You took the little girl home about half-past one and went back on the moors, did you not?—No.

Getting ready for the disposal of a body on Boxing Day?—No.

Now I want to ask you some questions about John Kilbride. A car was hired by the accused Hindley for a day on 23 November. What was the hiring for?—For going for a run in it.

The accused Hindley had a second hiring on 27 November. What did you want the car for on the second occasion?—The same. To go for a run. That's all.

Check body not moved?—No.

Body disposal plan?—No.

Why does John Kilbride's name appear in the exercise book?—Why are all the others there?

Are you saying you were just writing down?—The explanation I give to you was I must have been testing the pen. This book was used seven years ago.

And it is a pure coincidence it happens to be the name of a little boy who was found buried 400 yards from Lesley Ann Downey, who had been in your house? A pure coincidence?—Yes.

ELEVENTH DAY   *Tuesday, 3 May*

IAN BRADY (*recalled*); *cross-examination continued by* THE ATTORNEY-GENERAL:

Mr Brady, yesterday we were discussing the Kilbride case, which arose in 1963. I want to ask you this: as long ago as 1963 were you planning a payroll snatch or some similar criminal enterprise?—Yes.

Is it your case that the accused Hindley knew nothing of your criminal activities and aspirations?—She knew my views, but no details.

I want you to look at one of the letters which was found in one of the suitcases which was deposited by you at the railway station. (*Exhibit produced to the witness.*) It is your letter to Miss M. Hindley, and it is dated 16 April 1963. You say: 'I have sprained my ankle,' then at the bottom of the page: 'Let's capitalise on the situation. I shall grasp this opportunity to view the investment establishment situated at Stockport Road next Friday. I will contact you before then to give other details.' What was that about? —That was a reference to buying a car at a used car lot on Stockport Road.

That is a very curious way of describing an investment establishment?—That is a very curious letter; it was written three years ago.

You were doing a reconnaissance of somewhere where there was money, were you not?—No.

And you were going to contact the accused Hindley to go over details before you did it?—No.

Of course, at that time the vehicle which you had was a motor cycle. The accused Hindley used to accompany you on the pillion?—Yes. We went all over the place.

Why did you need to hire a car for the 23rd November?—No need.

It is because it is not sufficiently easy to carry a body on a motor cycle?—I would not know.

And it is not convenient when you are doing reconnaissance for a grave to do it on a motor cycle?—It could be done.

I want you to look now at this photograph of the accused Myra Hindley crouching over the grave of John Kilbride. Are you saying to my Lord and the jury that it was upon the purest coincidence that out of that vast area of moorland you happened to take a photograph of Myra Hindley at the grave of John Kilbride?— I am saying that this is a snapshot, that is all.

Will you answer my question, please?—Well, I will say it is a coincidence.

When was the photograph taken?—About two or three years ago.

According to Mr Mounsey, you said: 'I took it about eighteen months ago.'—I said: 'Two or three years ago.'

You said: 'The reason I said eighteen months ago, it is the age of the dog.' Did you say to him: 'It is approximately eighteen months old'?—Two or three years old. The information can be checked with members of the family. My mother knew the age of the dog.

What was the accused Hindley doing in the photograph?—Looking at the dog or the ground. There is another photograph where she appears to be looking at the ground which the police have not brought in, and there is nobody there.

Never mind about the other photograph. What expression do you detect on her face in that photograph?—Pleasant.

It is a very strange expression, half smile, half mourning, perhaps?—I cannot say.

Will you look at this photograph of the body of John Kilbride? Do you see that the trousers are pulled down below the knees, or round the knees?—I cannot make anything out on the photograph.

Just try, will you? It is obvious that there is naked skin between the knees and the thigh, save for the earth that covers the flesh?—You can see something which appears to be cloth at the bottom.

We have been told they were his jeans. Now look at this photograph of the body after the clothes had been removed at the mortuary. Do you see, just above the knees, there is rolled down in a roll his underpants?—Yes, I can see cloth.

It is the Prosecution's case from those photographs, that that boy was in some way homosexually assaulted. That was something which you were ready and willing to do, was it not?—No.

That is what you did to that boy on that moor or some other place on 23 November 1963, was it not?—No.

And you buried him in that grave?—No.

MR JUSTICE FENTON ATKINSON: I want to be quite clear about what you are saying about Lesley Ann Downey. This is your case, that in the end the girl readily agreed to take her clothes off and pose, and went off reasonably happy; is that it?—Not happily; I would say 'tense'.

She said she would not complain?—I asked her, and she said she would not.

It is right that you kept a recording, or wanted to make a recording, in case she made a complaint and you were taken into custody for assaulting the girl? The recording would be of some assistance in your defence?—That was the idea before the recording, but not after.

Then why did you keep it, that is what I want to understand?—Well, because it was unusual.

Re-examined by MR HOOSON:

Mr Brady, you told my learned friend the Attorney-General just a few moments ago that you had taken many other photographs, and in particular you had taken one that you referred to as being of Myra looking at the ground?—Apparently looking at the ground.

Just look at these photographs. Can you find the photograph there? Where is that taken?—At the Snake Pass.

Is that a photograph of Myra holding a dog in her hands, apparently looking at the ground?—Yes. This is a slide, not a photograph. They are all slides except one. They are photographs of the moors.

Without any subject matter on them?—Yes. They pointed out something and said: 'This is a head in one of them, sticking out of the water.'

These photographs were all shown to you by the police at different interviews?—Every slide and every photograph was shown to me.

Was there any particular scenic interest for you in those photographs?—The mist effect in black and white.

How many tapes had you kept in all?—There were about twenty.

And when you said that the Downey tape was unusual, what did you mean?—Unusual—I cannot think of any other word.

Had you yourself seen a copy of the *Gorton Reporter* dated 1 January 1965?—I have no recollection of that edition until this case came up.

You told the members of the jury from the start that you killed Evans. Had you anything to do with the deaths of Kilbride or Downey?—No.

MR HOOSON: Thank you. Will you come back into the dock. (*To* MR JUSTICE FENTON ATKINSON:) I wonder if you would allow the next witness not to give her address publicly? I will put it on paper.

MR JUSTICE FENTON ATKINSON: I think that is fair enough.

NELLIE HINDLEY *examined by* MR HOOSON: I am the mother of Myra Hindley and Maureen Smith. I remember Boxing Day, 1964. At that time I was living in Eaton Street with my husband; since then we have separated. On Christmas Eve, a Thursday, Maureen and her husband, Dave Smith, asked me if I would mind their baby at the night time as they were having a party. Well, they brought her round to me in the evening and she was with me then until I took her home at dinner-time on Christmas Day. Then Maureen said: 'Will you mind her at night-time?'— while they went for a drink, like. I said I would do. They brought her round at eightish and I kept her until the Boxing Day morning. Maureen came for the baby. I think she wanted me to mind it at the night-time, but I used to go out to work and her father had had a stroke just before that, and I asked her would she stay in or get somebody to mind the baby if she wanted to go out again. I would not have the baby for Boxing Night. I didn't see anybody that night; I just spent it quiet. I had the baby the following day, Sunday, for an hour and a half in the evening. Because Boxing Day had fallen on a Saturday, I had the Monday off from work. I had the baby on the Monday night for an hour and a half. It was not late because I was going to work next day.

Cross-examined by MR HEILPERN:

Did Maureen seem frightened of her husband?—She was. I don't know if she still is, but she used to be very frightened.

Was he something of a bully towards her?—He was if he wasn't getting his own way all the while, yes.

Was she rather under his thumb?—Yes.

Mrs Hindley, if Myra in 1963, the last part of 1963, and the beginning of 1964, had been shopping regularly at Ashton Market, do you think you would have known about it?—Oh yes, definitely.

Cross-examined by THE ATTORNEY-GENERAL:

Mrs Hindley, you, I take it, do not like Mr Smith?—I have always done my best for them both.

Do you think, whether rightly or wrongly, that he is responsible for your daughter Myra being in the dock?—He could be. He is that kind of person.

You would be prepared to say a good word for David Smith?—Oh, he is good when he wants to be.

I suggest you are mistaken, and that it was Boxing Night when the baby was brought around so that Maureen and her husband could go and have a short visit to a pub?—No, I didn't have her on Boxing Night. I can remember that very well, it was my step-brother's birthday. I had the baby with me on Christmas Eve and Christmas Day, not Boxing Night. Then I had her for a short time on the next two nights, and then I had her again on the following Thursday.

And they collected her on the evening of Boxing Day and took her home?—No, sir, it was the night afterwards.

MR HOOSON: That is my case, my Lord.

MR HEILPERN: The accused Myra Hindley is my sole witness.

MR JUSTICE FENTON ATKINSON: Do you wish to take the oath in the normal form or do you want to affirm?

THE WITNESS: I want to affirm.

MR JUSTICE FENTON ATKINSON: That is because you have no religious beliefs?

THE WITNESS: Yes.

MYRA HINDLEY, *affirmed; examined by* MR HEILPERN:

Could you tell us, Miss Hindley, what were your feelings for Ian Brady?—I became very fond of him. I loved him. I still—I love him.

Did you and he always go together on his motor cycle or were there occasions when he would go alone?—He often preferred to go out by himself.

Can you tell us when it was you passed your driving test?—7 November 1963.

How many vehicles had you had by October 1965?—I had had three vehicles altogether. The first one was an Austin A40, February 1964; the second was a Morris Mini, May 1964; and the third one was an Austin Mini-traveller, April 1965.

I would like to come now, Miss Hindley, to the time about the beginning of October 1965. Round about then did you get any kind of idea that there was something in the wind between Ian Brady and David Smith?—About what?

About any plan that they might have?—No, they were talking together. Smith was always coming round and saying 'would I go and sit with Maureen' because he wanted to talk.

We have heard about Ian Brady's plan and views about getting money by robbery and so on. Had you some sort of idea that something was afoot?—I did when the suitcases were taken to Central Station.

What sort of thing did you think was afoot?—Committing a robbery.

Whose idea was it that things should be put in the suitcases?—Ian's and Smith's, I suppose.

Whose idea was it that they should be taken out of the house to Central Station?—Smith came walking down the stairs carrying the suitcases and I asked him what they were doing with them, and Ian said he wanted me to drive down to the left-luggage office and deposit them. I asked Ian: 'What for?' and he said: 'Never mind, just take them down.' And I asked again, and Smith said: 'Don't ask any questions and you won't get told any lies.' I kept on asking because it was unusual, and Smith said it was something to do with the robbery that they had been talking about, and I didn't ask any more questions, and that was it.

If Ian Brady told you not to ask any more questions, were you in the habit of asking questions?—If I asked questions, he would say: 'Drop it.'

What happened?—I would drop it.

The next night, 6 October, did Smith come to your house?—Yes. He came round looking for my grandmother at about six to six-thirty and he went home again. He came back about half-past seven, and he left with us around eight.

Whom did he talk to?—Ian, because I was tidying up the tea things.

Did you know about any plans for doing anything that night?—No, it was just an ordinary night to me, as far as I was concerned. There was nothing on the television so we decided to go out, which we often do when there is not much on TV, and we were going to a usual spot which we frequented.

In which direction did you drive off?—Initially the road to Glossop. We decided to get some more wine and turned back.

And that would send you back on the way to Manchester?—Yes.

Then where did you go?—We just drove around all over Manchester, cruising about and occasionally stopping and parking off the main road and talking, just as we would have done.

Did you go to Central Station that evening?—Yes. We were passing there and Ian said we could get a drink in the bar. It was about twenty-five past ten, so instead of trying to park the car, he said that I should wait for him.

MR JUSTICE FENTON ATKINSON: Where did you park? In the station yard?—Just on the road. Actually, I waited in a 'No Parking' street.

MR HEILPERN: Then Ian Brady came back with someone?—Yes.

Did you know him at that time?—No. I know now it was Edward Evans.

Did he say anything?—No. Ian said: 'This is a friend, and I have just brought him back for a drink.'

When you got back to Hattersley, did you all three go into the house?—Yes. When I walked in, the dog ran up as it always does, and I stayed on the front door step. I went into the front garden. Then Ian came to the front door and told me to slip round and bring Dave.

You went up to the flat at Underwood Court? When you got there did you press the buzzer of the internal telephone system?—Yes.

Who was it who answered the 'phone?—David Smith. I said: 'It is me,' and he pressed the electrical thing to open the front door.

Who opened the door to you?—David Smith.

How was he dressed?—He was fully dressed except for his shoes and jacket.

What did you say to him?—I said: 'Ian wants you,' and he said: 'Right, I'll just put my shoes on,' and I followed him into the hall.

Did you ask about Maureen?—I said: 'Where's the dog?' He said: 'In the bedroom with Maureen.' I shouted and Maureen came out with the dog.

At that moment, was anything said about a note?—Maureen said: 'Dave, show Myra the note.' I said when I had read it: 'Where are you going to get this from for Saturday morning?'

Maureen said: 'We will have to get it from somewhere because Page, the caretaker of the flats, wants the slightest opportunity to get rid of us.' I said: 'Why don't you try for a tap off the old man?'—meaning my father who had just had a compensation award from his firm. It was a standing joke that you could not get a tap off the old man. I said to Smith: 'What about your own father?' and he said his own father did not have it to give him.

Did you deliver any message to Maureen?—Maureen pointed to my shoes, which were these white ones, and she said my mother was asking for them. I said: 'I am bringing them tomorrow, because I want her to bleach my hair.'

Tell us what happened then.—David Smith stood up and put his shoes on. He picked his jacket off the back of the chair and said: 'I am going out to Ian's, don't wait up,' and Maureen said: 'All right, I will leave you some supper out.' He said: 'I am not taking the dog, I will just take the stick,' and he went into the hall. I said: 'Hang on, and I will walk along with you in case the lights go off.'

Did you on the way back say anything to him about miniature wine bottles?—No, I never mentioned them at all to him.

Did you say anything about flashing lights on and off?—No, I never mentioned lights at all.

You came to the house. Did you go in?—We both went to the side of the house. I had left my key inside, and I knocked on the door and Ian opened it.

What did you do?—One door was to the kitchen, and I took him into the kitchen and closed the door so that the dog could not run out. I was going to feed him.

And then did you see or hear anything?—I was just about to open a tin of dog food, and I heard a shout from inside, so I ran, and as I opened the kitchen door, the living room door was open and momentarily I saw Ian and Evans grappling with each other, and I thought they were fighting. I shouted: 'Dave,' meaning him to come and see what was wrong. He came running past me. As soon as he ran in, there was a loud cry, and I ran into the kitchen. There was a terrible noise, and I put my hands over my ears.

When you took your hands away from your ears, were there still some noises?—It was relatively quiet.

What did you do?—I just opened the kitchen door to go to the living room and stopped dead in the doorway.

What did you see?—A pool of blood. Evans was lying on the floor half under the table and Smith was kicking him and jabbing at him with his stick. As soon as I saw that, I ran back into the kitchen.

Where was Ian?—I didn't see Ian.

Did someone come in to you in the kitchen?—Yes, Smith. He wanted some string. He asked me had I a mop and bucket, and I told him to get it himself, and he went to get it.

Did Ian ask you to get some materials?—Yes, some cloths.

Can you tell us how you were?—I was sick through seeing the blood, I was crying, I was horrified, I was frightened.

Who were you concerned about?—Ian.

The body was taken into the bedroom. What was your general condition at this stage?—I was asking what had happened, and I was crying and worried to death.

Who were you worried for?—Ian.

Did Ian say to you: 'It is the messiest yet'?—No.

Did you say: 'You should have seen his face, the blow registered in his eyes'?—No, because I didn't see any blow.

After the body had been put in the bedroom, can you recall what Ian and Smith started to do?—I said I would make a cup of tea and I went into the kitchen. I was in and out of the living room, and Ian and Smith were sitting on the couch with the coffee table brought up in front of them. There was a shorthand pad and papers all over the place. They were talking and Ian was writing. I said: 'What are you doing?' and Ian said: 'It doesn't matter,' in other words, 'don't ask,' because they didn't want to tell me.

Was there some discussion about what should be done with the body?—Yes. I was asking what they were going to do, and Smith said: 'The best thing to do is to bury him.' I said: 'Where —in the back garden?' I thought he was joking or being sarcastic. He said: 'No, not in the back garden, you fool.' I said: 'Where, then?' He said: 'What about the place where we shoot?' I referred to that as Mossley. He said: 'That's as good a place as any.' I said that if they did bury it up there and it was discovered, too many people knew we had been up there, and I said that the girl next door but one knows, because she has been up there five or six times with us, and I said it would be stupid to contemplate going up there.

Did you say anything about having been up there with a body in the car whilst Ian was digging a grave?—No, I did not say that. After I said about Mossley, Smith said: 'Where else is there?' Ian said: 'What about Penistone?' and I said: 'There's police patrols up there.' I said: 'Don't you remember when we went to Barnsley for some ammunition, and on the way back you went down to try it?' I was waiting for him and a police car came down the road, and I was hoping they would not hear the shots. He stopped and asked me if anything was wrong, and there was a box of ammunition on the seat beside me and Ian hadn't a gun licence, and I didn't know what to say. I just said about drying my sparking plugs.

For how long did they discuss, with Ian writing, before Smith left?—I think it was until about three o'clock, and then Smith said: 'I will be going now.' And after Smith had gone, Ian was still sitting writing and thinking, and it was about a quarter to four. I remembered that the car wasn't locked and I said: 'You go,' so he took the papers he was writing and went off and locked the car. I was on the doorstep.

How did you spend the remaining hours before the police arrived some hours later?—Until about five I was trying to tidy up, and finally I lay down on the divan.

Did you sleep?—No. I was worried and thinking what would happen, and what had happened, and how the hell it had happened.

We know that the police arrived and Ian was taken away. You were pressed about where you went that evening, and you said you went to Glossop. It was not true?—No.

Why did you say that?—Because I was still frightened. It was stupidity, I suppose, but that was the original intention.

Did you play any part at all in the killing of Evans?—No.

Did you know anything of any plan to kill him?—No.

Did you know anything about any plan to rob him?—No.

Did you know anything about any intention on the part of anyone to do him any harm?—No.

Miss Hindley, I am turning now to the case of Lesley Ann Downey—Boxing Day, 1964. Did you know anything about any arrangement between Brady and Smith about bringing anyone to the house?—No.

Did Ian tell you something?—Yes. It was approximately half-past six. He came into the living room and he said: 'Dave's brought a girl and he wants me to take some photographs, but she is a lot younger than I was given to expect and I want you to be present while I take them.' I did not want him to take the photographs. I said: 'What do you want to take photographs for?' and he said: 'For money.'

You have heard that recording played and you have had a copy of the transcript. What are your feelings about that?—I am ashamed.

Can you help us about why you took part?—Because Ian asked me and Smith kept saying: 'We have come all this way and Ian has agreed, and don't you start poking your nose in.' It was not for me to start arguing, but when I saw the girl I said she was too young. I said it was not right. Smith said he had just had an argument with Ian about it, and he didn't want another.

Was the child willing, or reluctant, or what?—She was quiet downstairs, and then Ian went upstairs and Smith was in the garden. Ian shouted: 'Ready,' and I shouted to Smith: 'Right, Dave.' He said: 'You go up. I'll be up in a minute.' I took the girl upstairs and told her to go into the bedroom. I came down again and said to Smith: 'Hurry up, Ian's ready.' Then the girl screamed. She was very frightened. She was upset. She was crying. The front door was wide open, and the bedroom door was open, and the bedroom window was open, and I was frightened someone would hear her. I started to panic. I was worried. That's why I was so brusque and cruel in my attitude to her.

At what stage did the child get undressed?—I had been down-stairs. It is on the tape recording. You can hear me going down-stairs. He said: 'It will be all over in a second.' Shortly after this, Smith came up. Just then she was sat on the bed and she was quiet, and I switched the radio on because I was hoping that she would remain quiet. I thought the radio would help to alleviate her fears.

The suggestion about the music, Miss Hindley, is that there

was another tape recorder being played at the same time.—It was the radio, not the tape recorder, that I switched on.

What happened then?—Smith told her to get dressed again and she did, and we went downstairs.

MR JUSTICE FENTON ATKINSON: Do you mean that Smith was in the room when the photographs were taken?—Just in the doorway. He could not get into the room because Ian was there with the tripod.

MR HEILPERN: Was there any other person present, or just outside the house, at that time?—Smith said he had come all this way and it would only take half an hour and his mate was waiting outside in the van. He was talking from our garden down on to the road, and there was a small van. He was talking to somebody, but I could not see who it was.

We have got to the stage when the child got dressed.—We went downstairs then. I said to the girl: 'Are you all right?' and she said: 'Yes.' She walked out of the house with Smith.

On that night, of course, your grandmother was still up at the Burns' house in Dukinfield? What was the weather like?—It was snowing still and the roads were covered with snow. I hadn't driven in such conditions before. I was very tense and Ian was a back-seat driver and complaining. I stopped short. About a mile.

Did you go to Mr Burns's house?—Yes, we walked. I said to my gran: 'Can you stay here the night, because Ian and I are abandoning the car and walking.' My uncle kept insisting that she could not sleep upstairs. When he kept on about it, grandmother said she would sleep on the floor, and I said: 'All right, I will call for you in the morning,' and I left.

What was the walk like?—It was just as bad as going. Ian said he would keep quiet and let me drive at my own speed. We eventually abandoned the car again and walked home.

Do you remember your sister Maureen gave some evidence of a conversation she had with you about a missing girl at the beginning of March 1965?—Yes.

Was there any such conversation?—Never.

We have heard evidence from the young girl, Pat Hodges, that you went up on the moors on Christmas Eve of 1964. Is that right?—Yes, to the same place that we were going to on 6 October—Glossop.

I want to ask you about the tape recording of Pat Hodges. Did you particularly draw her attention to any item in the paper?—Not as far as I can remember. She was always reading the paper, and she finished the paper she was reading, and there was a whole pile of papers on the waste paper basket in the living room. There always is by gran's chair, and I remember seeing the *Reporter* lying on the top, which I just passed to her to keep her occupied. We did not get it; it was brought by my uncle every week. He always used to bring a load of newspapers.

Did you draw her attention to any particular item?—No, I just gave her the paper and she was reading it.

Did anybody call at your house on the evening of Boxing Day?—Yes, Pat Hodges.

About what time?—I think about half-past eight. She was round practically every night. It was when she came and I had to go to the door that I first noticed how bad the snow was.

Turning to the Kilbride matter, Miss Hindley, first of all, do you know anything about John Kilbride?—No.

Apart from the wish to hire a car to get experience of driving, had you any special reason for hiring a car on 23 November 1963?—No.

Can you recall where you went?—Whaley Bridge. With Ian.

Was it in a particularly dirty condition when you returned it?—No. If it had been, I would have made some attempt to clean it so as to remain on good terms with the firm. Nobody mentioned it.

Round about this time, where did you normally do your shopping?—At Adsega's supermarket.

What day of the week?—Saturday. Sometimes on my own and mostly with my mother.

In general, would you have cause to go to Ashton Market?—No, it was too far away, and I had no car until 1964. The bus stop was about half a mile away. It would be pointless to go six or seven miles when I could get the stuff from Adsega's.

What about stockings? In general, which would you prefer to buy?—Plain nylon. They were cheaper than the other ones, and where I worked the yard was always strewn with wires and cables, and I used to go through several pairs a week.

How many times have you been to Ashton Market?—Twice.

It is said that at some stage in the interview on 14 October 1965 at Risley, Mr Tyrrell mentioned the girl Lesley Ann Downey by name?—No. Nothing at all was said to me about her then.

MR JUSTICE FENTON ATKINSON: Did you know at that time that she was the girl who had come to the house when photographs had been taken?—No, I was not told until I think it was the 18th.

MR HEILPERN: 18 October is the interview in the evening with Mr Haigh and Mr Benfield about photographs and the recording? —Yes.

Did you in the course of your interview ever ask for your solicitor?—I asked every time Mr Benfield mentioned Ann Downey. I must have asked dozens of times in all the hours I was there.

In the course of the interview, you had some tea and Mr Mattin remained with you. You said, according to him: 'I made all my own decisions. People go through several stages in their life and after discussions they change their mind. Ian never made me do anything I didn't want to do. All that about killing is bloody rubbish.' Is it entirely right: 'Ian never made me do anything I did not want to'?—No. I really was talking about religion when I made my own mind up. He was suggesting that because Ian had no religious beliefs, I had not either. I said: 'Just because Ian had not any, it didn't mean that I could not, and it was just Ian that made me change.'

Did Ian ever persuade you in any way to do things that you did not want to do?—He asked me to do some things, and if I objected, we argued, and I would do them eventually and go along with him.

Miss Hindley, why?—Because I just did.

Can you help us with the reason?—I cannot.

MR HOOSON: I have no questions, my Lord.

Cross-examined by THE ATTORNEY-GENERAL:

This is the truth about the matter, you are not merely clay in the hands of the potter, are you?—No.

Did you guard any secrets from Brady?—I didn't have any secrets.

So far as you know, did he guard any secrets from you?— Yes, I know now that he did.

What secrets?—Secrets about his plans for robberies.

The letter which I showed Mr Brady this morning related to plans to do a pay-roll robbery, did it not?—It related to the buying of a car.

What does 'investment establishment' mean?—A car lot.

How do you think that that can be reasonably described as an investment establishment?—(*No reply*.)

There is not a word about a car, is there?—No, and there is not a word about banks.

You bought two revolvers and ammunition?—Yes.

What for?—I joined a club, and there were hundreds lying about and being used.

What did you want to buy revolvers for?—For the same reason that everybody else did, so that we could use them on Sunday. They used to spend the whole of Sunday afternoon with these guns, firing them. I mentioned it to Ian, and he asked me to get them.

To be used in connection with a robbery?—No.

We know that there were two loaded revolvers in your bedroom on the morning that Evans's body was found. What were they there for—loaded?—They were always loaded because we used to carry them in the car.

If you were going to take them for shooting practice, you would not take them loaded, would you?—I didn't know whether they were loaded or not.

You knew perfectly well—five rounds in each revolver. It was part of the body disposal plan, was it not?—No.

And, like Brady, you would have shot without pity if necessary, if you had been disturbed trying to bury Evans, would you not?—No.

I suggest to you that you were playing a very important part in the proposed robberies?—No.

You were the only driver in the team, were you not?—I was a driver, but not in the team.

Did you take part in revolver practice?—No. Smith and Ian.

It was part of the rehearsal?—No, as far as I was concerned, they were going pigeon shooting.

You, of course, had the same ideas as Brady had on practically everything, did you not?—Obviously not, if he was going to rob a bank.

The same ideas—ultimately, at any rate—on religion?—Yes.
On politics?—Yes.

On marriage?—Yes.

On sex?—Yes.

On people in general?—Yes.

The same literary tastes?—No, not quite.

If it was not quite, you wish to qualify the similarity?—I didn't have any enjoyment from pornography.

Or from books on sadism?—No.

You knew that Brady was a taker of pornographic pictures?—Yes.

Did you disapprove?—No.

Now I come to the Evans case. When Brady introduced you to the young man, did he not say to Evans: 'This is my sister'?—No, he was told before he reached the car.

You were a completely innocent agent in Evans being brought to the house; is that what you are saying?—Yes.

And what you are saying is that Smith was the evil genius in this thing?—I am not saying it.

You were in that room when that boy was being killed almost all the time, were you not?—No, I was not.

And with your feet calmly on the mantelpiece when it was all over?—No.

'We never left each other, we never do'—and you were near Brady's side when he was hammering the boy's head with the hatchet, were you not?—No.

'What happened last night was an accident.' Did you say that to Detective Policewoman Campion?—Yes.

Do you think that that was an adequate description of what had happened?—Well, it was an accident. Someone was killed who should never have been.

Was there a lot of screaming?—There was a lot of noise. I put my hands over my ears.

This court has heard more than one scream in the room where you were?—Yes.

The screams of a little girl of ten—of your sex, madam. Did you put your hands over your ears when you heard the screams of Lesley Ann Downey?—No.

Why not?—I wanted her to be quiet.

Or get the child out of the room and see that she was treated as a woman should treat a female child, or any other child?—I should have done, but I didn't. I have no defence to that.

No defence?—It was indefensible. I was cruel.

I put it to you that the screams of this boy no more affected you that night than the screams of Lesley Ann Downey?—I didn't hear any screams from Evans. I put my hands over my ears.

You had a conversation with gran, did you not?—No, she shouted down: 'What is all the noise?' I said: 'It is just the dog barking'—not that the tape recorder had dropped on my toes as was alleged I had said.

But this was during the shouting?—No, it wasn't.

It is very odd that she should ask the question after the noise had ceased.—No; she was probably awakened from her sleep and had got out of bed to come to the bedroom door.

You were quite determined that the old lady should not interfere?—Yes, I shouted up so that she would not come down. If she had come down she might well have dropped dead with shock.

There were spots of blood on your shoes?—Yes. It was probably splashed on. Possibly because the shoes had been left in the living room. I had been out in my high-heeled shoes.

This trial is now in its eleventh day. Have we heard this suggestion before, that the shoes were in the room, and that you were not wearing them that night?—No.

Let me see the shoes, please. Is there any trace of blood inside those shoes, so far as you know?—No.

Your feet were inside the shoes and your feet were taking whatever blood fell upon that area?—No.

Are you now wearing the high-heeled shoes that you were wearing that night?—Yes.

May I see one of them, please? (*Shoe handed to* THE ATTORNEY-GENERAL.) Is that the shoe that you were wearing to go on the moors?—Yes, I went in the car. I always wear high-heels outside. We were not going to walk on the moors. We were just going to park.

On 7 October did you tell Policewoman Campion that your statement would be the same as Brady's?—Yes.

Why did you say that? Is it because you saw precisely what he saw and were therefore able to speak of the same facts, Miss Hindley?—No.

You never suggested at any stage that day that you were not in the living room when Evans was killed?—I said I didn't see the attack.

Why did you go on foot to Smith's flat?—Because I had left my car keys in the house, and I was in the garden when Ian asked me to go for Smith. It is only five minutes away, and I have often walked to Smith's.

If you had gone in the car, you would have had no excuse for inviting Smith to walk you home?—There was no excuse; I went there to ask him to come.

On the way to 16 Wardle Brook Avenue you said that Ian had some miniature wine bottles to give to Smith, did you?—No. I went to give him a message, and there was no reason to mention wine bottles.

That was your inducement to get Smith into the house?—There was no inducement to get Smith into the house.

Do you agree that there was a signal of the flashing lights?—There was not.

The signal was necessary because your colleague Brady had to get things ready; he had to get the stage set, had he not, Miss Hindley?—No.

And part of the setting of the stage was the availability of the hatchet. Why was the hatchet in the living room? Can you help us about that?—It could have been there for a number of reasons.

Suggest some, if you would?—Well, the table in the living room—I am sure the police would notice—one of the leaves of it was broken and I had to hammer it back into place. Grandmother could have used it for that.

It was a tidy little house, if I may say so?—It was not really tidy.

Did you notice the hatchet in the fireplace that evening?—No.

Had you ever seen it in the fireplace?—I had seen it in the wastepaper basket at the side of the fireplace.

From the time you brought Evans back to the house, you were not in or near the living room until it was all over; is that what you are saying?—Yes.

You were involved in the so-called body disposal plan, were you not?—No.

Were you consulted about what was proposed in that plan?—Yes, I was told about picking up the pram of Smith's, and I knew that they were going to bury the body.

Where?—At Penistone.

'Drop me off, pass agreed points every five minutes.' The plan was that you were to go driving round the country with a body in the back of the van, and then at some timely moment stop so that Brady could take it over, was it not?—No.

Were you consulted about the proposed alibi?—I wasn't consulted about anything on the plan.

Well, did you know about it?—No.

Were you anxious to know what was going to happen to the body?—I was anxious to know what was going to happen to my husband.

Were you not told that it was going to be buried in Penistone?—Smith wanted to bury Evans at the place where we shot.

It was you who was objecting to that idea?—Yes. As I say, we had been there often and we would be known.

You were playing your part as the master criminal there, were you, in trying to eliminate any link back?—I just thought that people knew we had been there.

I put it to you that you had had rather a nasty experience when you were up on the moors in the car?—Yes, but not in the same context. In so far as that Ian was digging a grave—no; but Ian was shooting the revolver.

If Smith is not telling the truth about that, it is a pretty dreadful thing to say about you, is it not—that after the murder of this boy you were really rather boasting to him of having got away with an earlier murder? It is a dreadful allegation to make?—He has made quite a few dreadful allegations.

Why, do you think?—I don't know.

He has also said that after the killing Brady said: 'It's the messiest yet.' Did you hear that said?—No.

And then the so-called jokes. According to Brady this time—he says that Smith said: 'He is a brainy bloke.'—I heard him say: 'He is a brainy swine.' He said that when he was mopping blood.

Was he referring to the intellectual attainments of the dead boy, or his brains that were scattered on the floor?—I don't know.

If it was said by Smith — (*Witness interrupts:*) It was said by Smith.

'Eddie is a dead weight'—did you hear that said?—Yes, by David Smith.

Did you think it funny?—No, but Smith did.

Smith says that you said to the accused Brady: 'You should have seen the look on his face. The blow registered in his eyes.' —I didn't say that at all. I didn't see any blow.

This again is a terrible invention of Smith's?—He is a liar.

The day before the Evans murder, did you know why the suitcases were taken to the station?—Yes. Ian didn't tell me at first, so I asked him again, and he said he and Smith wanted them out of the house because they were thinking of robbing someone.

You were perfectly willing to play your part, were you?— Yes; Ian asked me would I take them.

Had Smith not gone to the police that morning, you would still have been living with Brady as his faithful ally and supporter in all he did, would you not, Miss Hindley?—I don't know.

TWELFTH DAY *Wednesday, 4 May*

MYRA HINDLEY (*recalled*); *cross-examination continued by* THE ATTORNEY-GENERAL:

Miss Hindley, you have said that until October 1965, when Mr Benfield spoke to you about it, you did not know that that naked girl that Brady photographed in your presence was Lesley Ann Downey?—Yes.

Were you aware, when that little girl disappeared, of the hue and cry that was raised to try and find her?—No.

But what we do know is that on New Year's Day, a few days after the girl disappeared, you were examining a newspaper showing her photograph and all the details about her, were you

Gorton & Openshaw Reporter

No. 2723 99th Year — (and the Droylsden and Clayton Herald) — JANUARY 1, 1965 — Price 4d

Have you seen 10-year-old Lesley?

BIG SEARCH FOR LOST GIRL

Last seen on fairground on Boxing Day

Little friend makes appeal on television

CHRISTMAS ended in tears and anguish for attractive Mrs Ann Downey of Charnley Walk, Ancoats. On Boxing Day, her 10-year-old daughter Lesley disappeared and all this week there has been an intensive search for her in the East Manchester area.

Lesley was last seen on Boxing night after spending her last sixpence on a five-minute ride on the "Cyclone" roundabout on the fair at Holland Street recreation ground, only a short distance from her home.

Lesley's friend, Anne Clark and her sister Linda, who live in the same block of flats as the Downey family rode on the "Cyclone" with her.

Lesley set off for home—five minutes away—after the fairground ride but suddenly turned to her friends and said "I'm going back."

Boy 'kneed' in face

— alleged

YOUTH BROKE ICE TO RESCUE DOG

Swam 30 yards in freezing water

FOR 15 minutes a 17-year-old Droylsden boy smashed his way through the ice rescuing Gorton Upper Reservoir to get to a dog which was struggling in the water 30 yards out from the bank on Sunday.

HOW TO HELP

A century of road deaths in 1964

Spinster burned

Car and bus collide

The Editor and Staff wish all Readers a Happy New Year

not?—No. The recording was approximately three weeks after the New Year.

Let me remind you of the newspaper that was referred to, *The Gorton & Openshaw Reporter.* (*Exhibit produced to the witness.*) Do you see in rather small print under that: *and the Droylsden and Clayton Herald?*—Yes.

It is dated 1 January 1965. Then what is written in the head-lines? 'Have you seen 10-year-old Lesley?' That was the name, as you knew, of the little girl that Brady photographed naked. At any rate, you knew her name was Lesley Ann?—I wasn't in the room when the name was given. I didn't know till afterwards.

Oh, Miss Hindley, you have heard the recording?—Yes.

And you heard her say that to Brady?—No.

You saw this newspaper?—I saw the newspaper. I passed it to the girl, but I didn't read it.

You pointed out to her what was in the small print immediately above the headline—*The Droylsden and Clayton Herald.* You are not saying you did not notice, in the boldest possible head-line print: 'Have you seen 10-year-old Lesley?' It was something immensely noticeable, was it not?—Yes, I think it was. It was a big headline.

There is a description of the clothing of the child, and you knew from that description that this was an account of the little child that you had had in your house and that had been gagged and photographed naked, did you not?—No. The newspaper was not bought by me. It is not circulated in Hyde.

It matters not who it was bought by. You saw it?—Yes.

And you took particular pleasure when Pat Hodges was talking about the little girl from Ancoats, did you not?—No, I didn't hardly take any interest.

Did that give you and Brady some sort of morbid satisfaction? —No.

A kick?—No.

MR JUSTICE FENTON ATKINSON: You said that this was three weeks after the New Year?—Approximately, yes.

It is obvious it is happening on a Friday, and New Year's Day was a Friday, was it not?—I don't remember.

THE ATTORNEY-GENERAL: At one point on the tape, the little girl says: 'Oh, it's Friday, isn't it?'—Yes.

On this particular New Year's Eve you went to the Smiths' house at Gorton and you had an all-night party?—Yes.

And on this New Year's Day you had actually bought this newspaper yourself at seven o'clock in the morning?—No.

On the tape you say: 'This morning when I went to the paper shop about seven o'clock, I didn't know whether it was this morning or last night because I had just come back from the village'?—Yes.

Why did you go to the paper shop at seven o'clock in the morning?—To get a paper—not this paper. They don't sell this paper in Hyde at all.

You were at Gorton at the Smiths' party until you went to buy a paper?—No, that was New Year's Eve.

The morning after?—No.

So you invited the little girl to read this paper, did you not?—Yes. She had been reading the *Sun* and she had finished with it and I passed her *that* to keep her occupied.

Are you really saying that, Miss Hindley?—Yes.

After you had pointed out the full title of the newspaper, Pat Hodges said: 'You see that girl there of Ancoats?' Then you said: 'Yes, just near'? What did you mean by that?—I don't know.

You see, the address is given—'Christmas ended in tears and anguish for attractive Mrs Ann Downey of Charnley Walk, Ancoats.' What does 'Yes, just near' refer to, please?—I can't remember.

The little girl is pointing out to you the very photograph of Lesley Ann Downey?—No.

What did those words mean—'You see that girl there of Ancoats'?—She was probably just talking as she was reading the paper. I was answering casually—idly. She was talking on and on and on.

Then the little girl says: 'She lives near my friend.' Then something unreadable follows, and you say: 'And she lives near here.' You were interested, were you not?—No, I was just speaking casually to her. That is all I was doing. I was making idle answers.

Let us see what idle answers you gave. You then ask her: 'Did she know her?' You were interested to know if Pat Hodges happened to have a friend who knew Lesley Ann Downey. That intrigued you, Miss Hindley, did it not?—No.

And it was because of that bit of conversation that this tape was kept by you and Brady, was it not?—No.

If you had realised that it was the missing girl who had been photographed naked, what would you have done?—I can't say because I didn't realise.

The fact is that you did nothing because you and Brady killed that child. That is the explanation, is it not?—No.

After the conversation about the paper, there is a bit about the Beatles, then something about Paul getting married. Then one gets a male voice, very loud, saying: 'Bitte.' Whose voice is that? —I don't know.

Don't you?—No.

Don't you?—No.

Was 'bitte' one of Brady's favourite expressions?—It is a German word.

That I understand. Further on, a male voice is recorded as saying: 'Yes. No taking photographs.' Was that Brady's voice?— Oh, yes, yes.

But what you will not have is that the male voice, very loud, saying 'bitte' is his?—No, I think that came on the tape.

Will you look, please, at the photographs of the naked child? (*Exhibits produced to the witness.*) You were present, were you, when every single one of those photographs was taken?—Yes.

Were you entertained by the photograph of the naked child in the pornographic attitude in prayer?—No, I didn't see any of these poses when they were being taken.

Where were you?—I was in the room, but I was looking out of the window because I was embarrassed at what was going on.

I suppose the curtains would have been drawn over the window, would they?—Yes.

Were you looking at the curtains?—No, I was the other side of the curtains, looking out of the window, which was wide open. I didn't want to be there in the first place, but Ian asked me to. She started getting undressed and I went in there.

A pretty rotten witness you would have been, looking out of the window.—I was not a witness. I was in the room. Ian was in the doorway with his camera, and Smith was stood behind him. I would have known or heard if anyone had crossed the room.

Were you concerned that something unpleasant might have happened to this child?—No. Nothing would happen after the taking of the photographs that was unpleasant.

The taking of the photographs was unpleasant?—Yes.

'Unpleasant.' Is that the best adjective you can find for them? —No, you can find much better adjectives and I will agree with you.

They are shameful and disgusting, are they not?—Yes, they are.

Who was it who got the child to pose?—I don't know. The radio was on.

It is not the Albert Hall; it is a small room and you were there. How was the child made to pose?—I don't know. I didn't want anything to do with it. I was embarrassed and ashamed. The radio was on and I was really listening to the radio.

What was the purpose of switching on the radio, please?—I switched it on eventually just to ease the tension that was in the room previously.

There was only one way of easing that child's tension, and that was to get her dressed and get her out quickly. Why did you not do that?—I don't know. I am ashamed. There's no defence for what I did. I think it was cruel, criminal, and I am ashamed.

Was this not a carefully taped recording of children's voices singing Christmas carols?—No.

This was a piece of cruel refinement in what you were doing to that child, was it not?—No.

Supposing the child had had the strength to refuse to pose, what would you have done?—I don't know.

We know, do we not, what you did when she was refusing to be gagged? 'Shut up or I'll forget myself and hit you one.'— I don't remember saying that. If it is on the transcript, I must have.

That was your contribution to placating the child, was it not?— I was desperate that no one should hear. The doors and windows were open. I was panic struck.

On three of the photographs your fingerprints appear. You examined them from time to time for your delectation and amusement, did you not?—No, I was shown them at the end, when the child left, and that was the last I saw of them.

You knew a good deal about the sale and distribution of pornographic pictures, did you not?—No.

About the taking of them?—Yes.

How did you know that?—Because Brady had took them of me.

I want you for a moment to look at the transcript of the tape recording. The first recognisable human sound on the tape is of the little child screaming and saying: 'Don't. Mum.' Why was she saying: 'Mum'?—I don't know. It wasn't me, this woman. It was all Ian, because he was in the room with her at first.

This woman was all Ian? It was a woman's voice.—No. When he went to take her coat, she scuffled and screamed, and this is right at the beginning of the tape.

What immediately follows it? 'Child screaming. "Don't. Mum." ' Then the very next words are: 'Shut up.' Was that your voice?—No, this wasn't me at all in the room with her.

MR JUSTICE FENTON ATKINSON: This is very serious. Just think. Are you telling the jury that when this transcript shows it was a woman speaking, it was not you at all, it was Ian Brady?—No, in the beginning it is all in whispers. It is not my voice at all, I am sure.

THE ATTORNEY-GENERAL: I am not talking about whispers. When the child screamed, a woman's voice said: 'Shut up,' and that was you, was it not?—No. It was Ian. I am sure this was Ian because I was not in the room. I am not disputing that the rest of it is my voice.

Let us see at what point you admit it is yours.—'Quick footsteps mounting stairs, then entering room.' That is when I come into the room.

What woman could it be other than you?—Nobody, but it was all in whispers. It was Ian's voice, because I did not enter the room until after footsteps are heard on the stairs, and I had just come up from telling Smith to come up.

Now we are on common ground. Then it is you and Brady?—Yes.

What was he doing?—I think he was putting a handkerchief in her mouth.

'Woman: "Hush, hush. Go on." ' Go on—what?—'Put it in.'

I could hear the noise from downstairs. As soon as I went into the room, I just told her to be quiet.

That is why you gagged her, is it not?—I didn't gag her.

You told the court a moment ago that 'Go on' means 'Go on putting the handkerchief in her mouth'. Was that not gagging her?—No, it was just to stop the screaming.

Further on, the woman says: 'Shut up or I'll forget myself and hit you one.' Was that you?—Yes, I remember saying that.

You were then trying to force the gag into the child's mouth, were you not?—No, I was trying to move her hand so Ian could put the handkerchief in her mouth.

If she had not moved her hand, you would have had no compunction in hitting her?—I wouldn't have hit her much. I never touched her. I never harmed her.

You would have hit her more readily than hitting a dog?—No.

Do you still say, in the light of that terrible sentence, that you were reluctant to take part in what was going on?—I was reluctant originally, but when she started crying and shouting and screaming, I just wanted her to be quiet.

Just as Brady wanted Evans to be quiet when he was striking him on the head with the axe?—I don't know.

The child was trying to pull the gag out of her mouth all the time, was she not?—No, she was trying to stop it going in.

Time and again you were driving into this child's ears your orders: 'Put it in.'—I just wanted her not to make a noise.

Then you say: 'Will you stop it. Stop it.' Did you think there was the most terrible threatening tone in the second order to 'stop it', Miss Hindley?—No, it was a desperate tone.

Then one hears the poor little child making a retching noise. This thing was being pushed down her throat, was it not?—No.

Later the man says: 'Why don't you keep it in?' Then the child says: 'Why? What are you going to do with me?' Does that sound like a child who had agreed to be photographed for 10s?—No. That is why Ian asked Smith, didn't she know what she was there for.

Who do you say undressed this child?—Herself.

Can you therefore explain the child's saying: 'Don't undress me, will you?' That was precisely what you were trying to do to the child?—No, I was not.

Let us see what else goes on. 'Child: "I've got to go because I'm going out with my mamma. Leave me, please. Help me, will you?"' Did not that strike a chord of pity in you?—I wasn't there then. Shortly afterwards, I went downstairs again to tell Smith to come up.

But you see, this tape recording has picked up a lot of steps. It is not until after 'Honest to God'_and 'Yes' from the man that there are quick footsteps of a woman leaving the room. It was then that you went downstairs.—I must have been on the landing to see if Smith was still where I had left him. That is why I went downstairs to tell him.

A little further on, Brady is saying: 'If you don't keep that hand down, I'll slit your neck.' That is why you do not want to be landed with hearing that, is it not?—No.

If you had heard that, would it have shaken you?—I don't think he said that.

MR JUSTICE FENTON ATKINSON: That was not really what you were asked.

THE ATTORNEY-GENERAL: I suggest to you, another reason why you are seeking to say you were not in the room at that time is because the child gives her name.—I told you before, I wasn't in the room when the name was given. The only time I heard the name was when the tape was played afterwards.

The child says: 'Westford.' Then the little girl says: 'I have to get home before eight o'clock.' Was that why you were saying to the court yesterday that Pat Hodges had come to your house at half-past eight that night?—I told the court Pat Hodges came to my house at half past eight that night because she was round practically every night and she said she did.

Towards the end of the transcript it says: 'Quick footsteps of woman leaving room.' Then a click. The sound of a door closing. Then footsteps coming upstairs. Then eight longer strides.— I went downstairs to tell Smith to come in and I went in the living room and switched the lights on. The dogs were barking. I switched them on and then came upstairs again.

There is nothing to indicate that you told Brady that Smith was coming in or that Smith was anywhere near the place.— No, because Ian had told me to go downstairs to tell Smith.

This is a wicked invention on your part, is it not?—No.

What was Smith doing in the garden?—He was talking to a man in a van—in a car—in the road.

In this street in an estate where anybody could see him if they were walking by when he had brought a ten-year-old child to be pornographically photographed? Very remarkable conduct on Smith's part, was it not?—Yes. That is Smith.

Now, you are back in the room. The child, crying, says: 'It hurts me on me —' Then would you read what follows that, please?—'Hush, shut up. Now put it in. Pull that hand away and don't dally and just keep your mouth shut, please.'

Did you say that?—I suppose I must have, but 'don't dally' is something I don't use.

Then you say: 'Wait a bit, I'll put this on again.' What did you mean?—I was putting the scarf on because it had slipped down.

Then the child was whining and you say: 'Shh. Hush. Put that in your mouth and again —' Then there follow the words: 'packed more solid.' Why did you want the mouth to be packed more solid?—I wanted her to put the handkerchief in her mouth.

Why more solid?—I don't know.

That was preparatory to suffocating her in due course, was it not?—No.

And you knew that, Hindley?—No.

Then, when the photographs were taken, according to what Brady said the day before yesterday: 'We all got dressed.'—No. The girl was undressed and we all went downstairs. We weren't undressed.

Did you indulge in any pleasures while these things were happening to the child?—No.

That child, had she been allowed to live, would have been a most dangerous witness against you and Brady, would she not?—No, because Smith said she didn't know where she was.

You confessed yesterday to having been ashamed of what had happened to that child. Do you remember a conversation with your sister Maureen?—No, I don't remember because there was no such conversation.

Are you saying that not a word was said by your sister about Lesley Ann?—I am.

It is a wicked lie, if that is right?—It must be.

From your own sister?—Yes, from my own sister. Yes.

It was the truth, you know, Miss Hindley.—No.

And it reflected your callousness about the whole of this matter.
—No.

Until the moment of discovery came.—No.

And your shame is a counterfeit shame, Miss Hindley, is it
not?—No.

On the Christmas Eve, two days before Lesley Ann Downey
was killed, you had been up on the moors, had you not?—Yes.

Is Pat Hodges right when she says you intended spending the
night there?—No.

You went to Saddleworth Moor on Christmas Eve?—No, I
went to the moors at Glossop.

You went there to lay the preliminaries of a murder to be
committed on Boxing Day?—No.

Then, on Boxing Day, you had the problem of Mrs Maybury
on your hands, did you not?—No.

I do not want to go into the whole of that evidence, but Mr
Burns, your uncle, said that, after argument, you said: 'I can't
take you home, gran, and that's that.'—No. I said: 'Are you
staying or aren't you?' and my auntie said: 'Of course she's
staying.'

Are you saying now that you wanted to take Mrs Maybury
home?—No, she wanted me to take her because my uncle
wouldn't let her sleep upstairs—otherwise she would have wanted
to stay.

You know why that upstairs bedroom was not available?—
Yes. I only know she was invited to sleep in the bedroom two
weeks after my cousin died.

Why did not Mrs Maybury leave the house that night?—
Because I asked her would she stay because the roads were too bad.

Now will you look, please, at this photograph of Brady. Who
took that?—I did.

That photograph was taken when Brady was standing less
than 50yd from Downey's grave, was it not?—No, he was
standing on some rocks.

Where?—Near where I now know Lesley Ann Downey's
body was found.

With a great smile on his face?—No, with a smile on his face.

Very well, a mood of relaxed enjoyment?—Yes.

Then we see you in a similar mood in this photograph that was taken nearby. Not the most attractive picture ever taken of you, Miss Hindley, is it? Why was it kept?—It wasn't kept. It's a photograph. There are lots of unattractive pictures of me in the album.

What shoes were you wearing in that photograph?—I don't know.

High-heeled shoes?—No. They are hardly the thing to go walking about the moors in, but ideal for going around in the car in.

Indeed. Now look at this photograph of a stretch of waste land. Were you there when Brady took it?—I was with him on the occasion.

Has it any merit?—Not particularly, no. There's other photographs in the album have no particular merit.

I suggest to you that the merit it had was that it was a picture taken of a piece of ground within a few feet of the grave of Lesley Ann Downey.—I don't know where the grave of Lesley Ann Downey is.

Did you know when that photograph was taken that it was of a piece of ground near the grave of Lesley Ann Downey?—No. These photographs, as far as I remember, were taken in 1964, because in October 1965 Ian was taking photographs made with slides; and also the coat I am wearing was left by me at Bannock Street when I moved to Hattersley, because I put it in a box when my dog had pups.

What you are saying is that by some amazing coincidence a photograph happened to be taken of the grave before the child was dead. Is that what you are saying?—No. I am sure it was taken in 1964.

I move now to Kilbride's case. I ask you to look at this photograph. The interest in the particular subject, of you with the dog, to you and the photographer, was that you were looking down, as you well know, at the grave of John Kilbride?—No.

Do you deny it was taken early in 1964?- -I don't deny it, but I don't confirm it. As far as I know, it was two or three years ago.

If it was taken three years ago, it was taken before the death of John Kilbride. So the coincidence would be more amazing than ever—that you were being photographed in a place where, some months later, somebody buried John Kilbride?—Yes, but I didn't know this was the grave of John Kilbride.

Your dog is a little puppy in the photograph?—Yes.

It was born in January 1964, was it not?—I can't remember.

That is what you told the police, you know.—So they say.

Do you deny it?—I can't remember what I told them. I was there for nine hours when I was being questioned and I wasn't taking notes.

You were very fond of this dog, we have been told. You were very distressed when it died?—Yes.

Are you really saying that you cannot remember which year the little puppy was born in?—Yes, because my dog had quite a few litters of pups.

Very well. There are just one or two other matters I want to ask you about. Your sister Maureen has said that you shopped regularly at Ashton Market on Saturdays before you moved to Hattersley.—That is what she said.

Is that true?—No, it is not true.

I suggest to you that you knew that Ashton Market was frequented by little boys who used to run errands.—No, I did not know that.

I suggest to you that you performed the same function in regard to John Kilbride as you did in regard to Evans in that you took the car there and took the boy to where he was killed.—No.

You hired that car to play your part in a planned murder, did you not?—No.

Is it right that you denied to the police that you had ever been to Ashton Market?—No, it is not right. I told them I had only been there twice in my whole life. I was so astonished at Maureen's remark that I went there every week.

There was a good reason why you should choose not to be associated with Ashton Market, Miss Hindley, was there not?—No, no reason.

It was from there that you and Brady picked up this little boy John Kilbride.—No.

It was from there that, ultimately, with your assistance, his body ended in that lonely grave on the moors.—No, I was nowhere near Ashton at all.

MR HEILPERN: I have no re-examination. That is the case for the accused, my Lord.

CLOSING SPEECH FOR THE CROWN

THE ATTORNEY-GENERAL *began by reminding the jury that the case had to be decided upon the evidence that they had heard in the court, and upon nothing else*: 'May I say this, that it is very easy to be swayed by emotion and swayed by passion. For my part, speaking for the Crown, I do not call those emotions in aid. My submission on behalf of the Crown is that the case against these two accused and each of them on each of these three charges of murder has been established beyond any shadow of doubt.' *Mr Hooson, for Brady, had submitted that the prosecution's case was founded on the evidence of one witness, David Smith, but that submission would not call for any detailed comment*: 'There is, in fact, a mass of evidence from sources other than the mouth of David Smith, pointing inescapably to the guilt of these two accused on these three charges of murder. . . . I do not now invite you to the conclusion that David Smith was a young man unsullied by the world in which he lived before he met the accused Brady. He told his story frankly, and my submission is that he told the story exactly; but of course his story is a very unattractive one. . . . Mr Hooson suggested in a vivid phrase that the prosecution put Smith forward as a sort of devil's disciple or sorcerer's apprentice. By now, having heard all the evidence, do you think that this might not, in fact, be a dramatically accurate description of David Smith in relation to the accused Brady? David Smith is certainly no angel. Do you think he comes near the standards of criminality which have been disclosed in respect of the accused Brady? On his own admission, Brady has told you that he worked and worked on means of committing crime so that no trace of its commitment could be discovered or detected. He worked on it, perfected it. Who was the devil in the piece, who was the disciple?' *Even on his own evidence, Smith must be regarded as being implicated in the murder of Edward Evans; whatever the circumstances by which he was induced to be present at the killing of Evans, he saw the killing and did nothing to prevent it*: 'But I would not ask you to find either of the accused guilty on any charge on the evidence of David

Smith unless you were able to find substantial corroboration of what he said in evidence.'

THE ATTORNEY-GENERAL *went on*: 'Smith has told you that he was informed by Brady in the small hours of the morning, after much wine had been drunk on 28 September 1965, that he, Brady, had already done three or four murders and buried the bodies on the moors. Smith told you further that Brady told him that he had photographic proof of this. The fact, I submit, is that you now know that the photographs admittedly taken by Brady show the exact location of the graves of John Kilbride and Lesley Ann Downey. How could Smith possibly know of the photographic proof that Brady had, that he had committed murders, unless Brady had told him?'

THE ATTORNEY-GENERAL *said that Hindley and Brady* 'formed an evil partnership together and co-operated together in all that they did'. *On 6 October 1965 Hindley went out with Brady and drove the car which carried Evans to her home. She brought Smith to her home just before Evans was killed. Plans for disposing of the body were well and truly laid. The accused were going to take it up on to the moor, but according to Hindley there was a suggestion that it should be buried on the moors where they used to shoot. She was not keen on that because people might have seen her.* 'Do you think that fits in with a distraught, hysterical, tearful woman that she has described herself as that night? Doesn't it rather suggest the calculated, pretty cool co-operator in murder?'

Referring to the disappearance of Lesley Ann Downey, THE ATTORNEY-GENERAL *said that after the* 'uttermost indignities' *to which she had been submitted by the two accused,* 'they could not dare to let her leave that house alive—and they did not'.

THE ATTORNEY-GENERAL *gave* 'trademarks' *of similarity between the three murders: the victims were all young, all disappeared from public places in the same area, and there was evidence of abnormal sexual activity involving all three victims shortly before they died. Other 'trademarks' were that a car was an essential requirement in all three cases; the mode of killing was almost certainly asphyxiation in two cases and possibly in the third; the accused had preserved records relating to the murders.*

'My submission is that the same pairs of hands killed all three of these victims, Evans, Downey and Kilbride, and these are the pairs of hands of the two accused in this dock.'

CLOSING SPEECH ON BEHALF OF THE ACCUSED BRADY

MR HOOSON *said that it was the submission of the prosecution that this was an open and shut case, but there were matters that had been under the consideration of the jury that were bound to cause very considerable doubt in their minds. The great danger in this case was that one was carried away by the oft-repeated thesis with which the Attorney-General concluded—that because Brady killed Evans, and because there were certain similarities, then it must be concluded that the same hand killed Kilbride and Downey.*

Brady had admitted planning a bank robbery. The jury had heard of the preparations, but no one had ever suggested that the bank robbery or a robbery of any kind was committed. That might cause the jury to reflect.

MR HOOSON *said that he adhered to the view that the prosecution's case was largely founded on the evidence of David Smith. It had been asked how Smith could have known there was photographic proof, but on the evidence of Superintendent Talbot there were photographs all round the house, where Smith was a frequent visitor.*

MR HOOSON *pointed out that Smith had helped for two hours or more in cleaning up the blood after the Evans murder.* 'Would that help you in determining whether the evidence by Smith is corroborated—or do you think he was involved far more than he has admitted and took part in that assault?'

MR JUSTICE FENTON ATKINSON: Are you submitting there is a legal ground for a lesser verdict in the Evans case?

MR HOOSON: No.

THIRTEENTH DAY *Thursday, 5 May*

CLOSING SPEECH ON BEHALF OF THE ACCUSED BRADY *(continued)*

MR HOOSON *said that John Kilbride disappeared on 23 November 1963; although it was the third charge against the accused, it was the first in time. The prosecution said that Hindley was a frequenter of Ashton Market; this was evidence against Hindley, not against Brady. The evidence had come from Hindley's sister:* 'How reliable a witness was Maureen Smith? If I follow the example of the Attorney-General and use plain words, she told lies in the witness box without any doubt at all.' *Could the jury accept her as a reliable witness?*

Then there was the exercise book with the name of John Kilbride written in it; the name was a doodle and various other names were written in the book. 'That is the flimsiest possible evidence on a charge of murder. You cannot guess whether a man committed murder. It must be established beyond all reasonable doubt.'

If the photograph of Kilbride's grave were the only photograph, it might have the compulsive significance suggested by the prosecution, but there were other photographs which were not said to have any sinister significance.

'What the prosecution really says is that the evidence on Kilbride, thin and unsatisfactory though it is, is made credible by the evidence on Evans and Downey. The question you have to ask is: "Have the prosecution satisfied us, or have they proved to our satisfaction, that Brady or Hindley murdered Kilbride?" '

MR HOOSON *said that the conduct of Brady and Hindley relating to the pornographic photographing of Lesley Ann Downey was absolutely disgraceful. The jury might think they both deserved punishment for that; but that was not what they were being tried for. It was one thing to say that the accused were so ruthless that they were prepared to photograph the little girl; it was quite another to say they killed her to dispose of her as a deadly witness against them. When one looked at the photographs, what perhaps was a little astonishing was how calm the little girl looked. The child appeared to be reasonably composed, and that might give the jury some idea of what went on at the time of the tape recording.* 'Of these photographs, one would say there was grave suspicion of Brady and Hindley, but that does not amount to proof of murder.'

The jury's assessment of David Smith was vital in the Downey case because both Brady and Hindley alleged that Smith brought the girl to the house. Smith said that he was not there, but the jury might think that he would, of course, deny being at the house as a matter of self-protection. Here was a plain clash of evidence between Smith and Brady and Hindley.

MR HOOSON *then turned to the Evans case*: 'It has never been doubted that Brady wielded the axe, and I cannot suggest to you, on Brady's own evidence, that in law this could be other than murder.'

MR HOOSON *submitted that Smith's involvement in the murder was much greater than he was prepared to admit in the witness box.* 'Smith is facing no charges. It cannot, and should not, be suggested by the defence that Smith went to the police because he had an arrangement with that newspaper. He went to the police on 7 October, before he had seen anybody from any newspaper. Thereafter, in a short time he acquired a financial interest in the conviction of both Brady and Hindley. I am not suggesting that a newspaper man would improperly get Smith to change his evidence, but there is great danger in a long conversation between a witness and an outside person interested in the case. It may well be that in the course of those conversations a witness may see different ways of strengthening his evidence, improving his case.'

CLOSING SPEECH ON BEHALF OF THE ACCUSED HINDLEY

MR HEILPERN *said that the case was loaded with a mass of evidence which in no circumstances constituted evidence against Hindley. The jury must consider two matters. First, was she involved in the killing? If the jury was not satisfied about that, was she an accessory after the fact? The jury must look for, and find, real and reliable evidence connecting Hindley with each and every charge laid against her. The case consisted of links in a chain; if there was a doubtful link, the jury must resolve that doubt in favour of the accused and throw the link away.* 'It is my submission that the prosecution case against Hindley is an insubstantial structure.'

The prosecution's speculation that Hindley was fully aware of what was going on was really based on the fact that she and Brady lived together. Hindley had some inkling, some rough idea, of what was in the wind at the vital time, but did not know the details. There was no evidence that she knew of the plan to pick up and rob anyone, or that she knew that anyone was to be brought to the house to be killed; there was no evidence that she took part in the compilation of the body disposal plan.

MR HEILPERN *said of the Downey case*: 'No one, least of all those appearing for the defence in this case, could listen to that tape recording, that transcript that was read out, and see the photographs of that little girl, without the most intense feelings of abhorrence and revulsion. You must not allow your natural and human feelings of indignation and horror to cloud your judgment about the real issues in this charge.' *Hindley's case was extremely simple: she knew nothing of the child's death; she had no hand in it and no hand in burying the child.* 'I suggest there is no evidence in relation to Myra Hindley.'

Turning to the Kilbride case, MR HEILPERN *said that the evidence was of the flimsiest kind. Hindley's case could be expressed in half a dozen words:* 'I know nothing about it.'

THE SUMMING-UP

MR JUSTICE FENTON ATKINSON *told the jury*: 'You must not convict either of these two of any offence unless all of you are sure of guilt. You must be as sure of guilt as you can be about anything in ordinary human affairs. . . .

'From the outset this truly horrible case attracted an immense press publicity. The committal proceedings were reported very widely. I expect you had probably read all about one side of the case before you had any idea you might find yourself on the jury. I know I had read all about it before I had the slightest idea I might have to sit here to try it. . . . Happily, inside this court, at least, thanks to the way all counsel have performed their duties, we have been able to avoid all unnecessary sensationalism in the way the case has been conducted and to do our best, to do our job, to see that the accused have a fair trial and that just verdicts are arrived at. Anything you may have read or heard or discussed about the case in days gone by will have sunk to the bottom of your minds or you will have forgotten all about it.'

MR JUSTICE FENTON ATKINSON *said that in the case of Evans, if it was proved to the jury's satisfaction that Brady struck the boy fourteen blows about the head with the axe, there could be no question that he must have intended to kill or to do really serious injury*: 'As he advances no slight justification or excuse for what he did, that would on the face of it be a plain case of murder. The intention to kill is really the necessary inference from the nature of the violence employed and the wounds inflicted.

'The other two cases, of course, are different. Those two children's bodies had been buried so long they were decomposed to the state they were in when they were found, and it is not possible for the doctors to ascertain any definite cause of death. . . . Exercising the discretion I have, I thought it right that these three charges should be tried together, because it appeared to me that although, of course, you have to consider each case separately, with a separate verdict on each, that they were so interconnected that you certainly do not have to consider them, so to speak, in water-tight compartments. . . . In every case, what weight you attach to the evidence of the other cases is a matter entirely for you, members of the jury. You should not attach too much.'

Referring to police evidence of interviews, MR JUSTICE FENTON ATKINSON *said*: 'If you are not satisfied that the police are speaking the truth—if you think Brady or Hindley again and again were saying: "I want my solicitor," and the police were not allowing them to see him—you should not attach any weight to what they are alleged to have said. I would only add this, that the police were investigating some desperately serious matters, were they not? They are not engaged on some polite game or exercise. They do not have to invite the accused to have the solicitor there, and that is what the police say was the position, broadly speaking; Brady and Hindley were taking the attitude that they were capable of looking after themselves and were quite content to answer the questions put to them. . . .

'From first to last in this case there has not been the smallest suggestion that either of these two was in any way mentally abnormal or not fully responsible for his or her actions. That leads on to this, does it not—that if (and I am saying that, so to speak, underlined)—if the prosecution is right, you are dealing here with two sadistic killers of the utmost depravity? There is no escape from that, and, as was said in another very well known murder trial of some years ago, they are entitled to the unusual incredulity which such terrible offences must raise in the mind of any normal person. Could anybody be as wicked as that? That is what the prosecution are setting out to prove. . . .'

FOURTEENTH DAY *Friday, 6 May*

THE SUMMING-UP (*continued*)

In recapitulating the evidence, MR JUSTICE FENTON ATKINSON *rarely allowed his own views to emerge. Referring to the absence of blood on the rugs in the living room, he pointed out that* 'the room was virtually swimming in blood [as a result of the killing of Evans]. Well, apparently the rugs escaped completely, and the prosecution, I think, would still invite you to take the view that Smith is probably wrong and that that is a sign that before this event took place somebody had taken the precaution of removing these rugs.'

The exercise book containing the name '*John Kilbride*': 'The prosecution seems to make something of that, but I wonder if you really think there is much in it? When you look at the book, you see that it is full of doodles and scribbling. . . . On this page there are all sorts of names. It is not suggested that any one of the other names is the name of a missing child.'

The photographing of Downey: 'When the photographing was over we have that answer: 'We all got dressed' [from Brady in examination-in-chief]. It possibly casts a flood of light on the nature of the activities that were going on.'

The part played by Hindley: 'You have a picture of her being very closely in Brady's confidence. . . . Brady was quite dependent upon her for transport. That must lead to this, members of the jury, that if you were to conclude, for example in the Downey case, that Brady had buried Downey's body on the moors, the prosecution can say this, can they not, that he could not very well have done that without motor transport available, and nobody has suggested that he had anyone with whom he would have shared such an operation other than Hindley. . . .

'You may take the view that the really crucial case from her point of view is the Downey case. There the prosecution have a strong case against her, because you heard her voice speaking on that recording and know so much of what was going on on that occasion, and if you are satisfied that she was guilty there and has really told a lying story to try and put the blame on to Smith, that may throw light in your minds on the Kilbride case, having regard to the marked similarity between those two cases. If you think she was a party to both of those, it may colour your view as to whether she was in on that with Brady as a willing participant or whether it was a complete surprise to her and she was in the kitchen when it all happened, covering her ears, with no sort of advanced knowledge of what was being planned by Brady and by Smith.'

MR JUSTICE FENTON ATKINSON *made the following comments regarding David Smith:* 'Mr Hooson has told you that the prosecution case is founded upon Smith, and that a case founded upon Smith can be likened to a house built upon sand. Is he closing his eyes to the reality of the situation? . . . No words have been too strong for the defence to apply to Smith. They have used such terms as unprincipled, without scruple, without mercy, and so on and so forth, and, of course, a lot of that was clearly justified. . . . He had previous convictions for violence. He was asked for details, and it appeared that if some young man had called him a bastard, his reaction was a violent one and he retaliated in no uncertain manner; but as yet he has not killed anybody with an axe, or anything so extreme as that. . . .

'Then there is this unfortunate affair with the newspaper. I am sure they did not intend to do so, but they have handed the defence a stick with which to beat Smith and his wife Maureen. You have heard that this youth at the time was pretty desperate for money, and he has been promised £1,000 for his story. I understood him to say it was going to be something like a series of articles about his times with Brady—something of a defamatory nature which could only be published if there was a conviction. . . . It is the sort of temptation to which he should never have been exposed for a moment. . . . I do not think it is really suggested that the substance of his evidence has been substantially affected by this quite extraordinary arrangement that he had with this newspaper.

'Something further about Smith is this: on his own saying, he is there in the room when Evans was killed. He does nothing, says nothing; he helps to clean up the mess afterwards; he helps to tie and wrap up the body. It is the string off his own stick which was used to tie the boy's legs to his chest. There was apparently just as much blood on his clothing as there was on Brady's. There is blood on that stick, and he says that that must have happened when he dropped his stick on the floor. . . . You will have to consider the question as to whether he did take some part in that attack. And in that case he is what the law calls an accomplice. . . . If you think he was in it, he would have the temptation to minimise his share and exaggerate Brady's. . . . Knowing so much of his background, that he was planning a bank robbery and had a lot of unpleasant views which you have heard, you will probably think it is safest to say: "We will not act upon his evidence unless we can find something outside it to support it." '

MR JUSTICE FENTON ATKINSON *outlined the jury's duty thus*: 'Have you any doubt of Brady's guilt in any of these three cases? Of course, you say "Guilty" in relation to Evans; a verdict of "Not guilty" is not possible. But on Downey or Kilbride have you any doubt about it? If you have, then of course you say: "Not guilty." If you think the cases of Kilbride and Downey are proved against him beyond any doubt, it follows that there must be a verdict of guilty.

'The first thing to remember in considering Hindley is this—that a great deal of the evidence against Brady is not evidence against her; and, in particular, Brady's statement to Smith about killing people and burying them on the moors. That is something said behind her back, and that is no evidence against her. Anything that Brady may have said to the police by way of an apparent admission is not evidence against her. The disposal plan is only evidence against her if you think that from the whole of the evidence she must have seen it and known the substance of its contents. It is very important to remember this. . . .

MR JUSTICE FENTON ATKINSON *concluded*: 'There it is; you have listened very long and very patiently to all the evidence in the case, and you must go now and consider your verdict. You will come back and your foreman will be asked to give the verdict of you all. He will be asked to deal with each count separately, and each accused separately, and tell the court your verdicts.'

The jury retired at 2.40 pm and returned at 4.20 pm to ask two questions:

1. When did Myra Hindley purchase the guns?

MR MARS-JONES: It was before the end of 1963, if my recollection is right. John Boland sold the Webley 0·45, in my note, in 1963. He thought it was some time in the summer of 1963. The other weapon was in the autumn of 1963. Certainly before you get to 23 November 1963 in both cases.

2. What was the date of the letter referring to 'the investment establishment'?

MR JUSTICE FENTON ATKINSON: It was 16 April 1963.

The jury retired at 4.27 pm and returned at 5 pm.

VERDICTS AND SENTENCES

THE CLERK: Members of the jury, will your foreman please stand? Mr Foreman of the jury, are you agreed upon your verdict?

THE FOREMAN: We are, my Lord.

THE CLERK: Do you find Ian Brady guilty or not guilty of the murder of Edward Evans?

THE FOREMAN: Guilty.

THE CLERK: Do you find Myra Hindley guilty or not guilty of the murder of Edward Evans?

THE FOREMAN: Guilty, my Lord.

THE CLERK: Do you find Ian Brady guilty or not guilty of the murder of Lesley Ann Downey?

THE FOREMAN: Guilty, my Lord.

THE CLERK: Do you find Myra Hindley guilty or not guilty of the murder of Lesley Ann Downey?

THE FOREMAN: Guilty, my Lord.

THE CLERK: Do you find Ian Brady guilty or not guilty of the murder of John Kilbride?

THE FOREMAN: Guilty, my Lord.

THE CLERK: Do you find Myra Hindley guilty or not guilty of the murder of John Kilbride?

THE FOREMAN: Not guilty.

THE CLERK: Do you find Myra Hindley guilty or not guilty that she, well knowing that Ian Brady had murdered John

Kilbride, did receive, comfort, harbour, assist and maintain the said Ian Brady?

THE FOREMAN: Guilty, my Lord.

THE CLERK: Are those the verdicts of you all?

THE FOREMAN: Yes, my Lord.

MR JUSTICE FENTON ATKINSON: Call upon them.

THE CLERK: Ian Brady and Myra Hindley, you have been convicted of a felony on the verdict of the jury. Have you anything to say why the court should not pass sentence upon you according to law? Have you, Ian Brady?

THE ACCUSED (BRADY): No—except the revolvers were bought in July 1964.

THE CLERK: And you, Myra Hindley?

THE ACCUSED (HINDLEY): No.

MR JUSTICE FENTON ATKINSON: Ian Brady, these were three calculated, cruel, cold-blooded murders. In your case I pass the only sentences which the law now allows, which is three concurrent sentences of life imprisonment.

Put him down.

In your case, Hindley, you have been found guilty of two equally horrible murders, and in the third as an accessory after the fact. On the two murders the sentence is two concurrent sentences of life imprisonment, and on the charge of being an accessory after the fact to the death of Kilbride, a concurrent sentence of seven years' imprisonment.

Put her down.

Mr Attorney-General, I think it should be said here that these matters clearly were only brought to light by a police investigation of the utmost skill and patience. I forget who it was who found that little ticket tucked into the back of that book, but that is the sort of thoroughness which has led to this case being tried, and I think we should be extremely grateful to all of them for the way in which they have dealt with it.

Also, I would like to thank the police and all those responsible for the wholly admirable arrangements which have been made in this court for this trial, which have greatly facilitated the conduct of the case.

THE ATTORNEY-GENERAL: I am most grateful, my Lord.

APPENDIX 1

From *The Times*, 18 October 1966:

Court of Appeal: Criminal Divison
Regina v. *Hindley*

Before the Lord Chief Justice, Lord Justice Winn and Mr Justice Widgery

The Court dismissed this appeal by Myra Hindley, aged 23, at present detained in Holloway prison, against conviction, on 6 May 1966, at Chester Assizes (after a trial beginning on 19 April before Mr Justice Fenton Atkinson and a jury) on a single indictment jointly with Ian Brady—who did not appeal—of the murder of Edward Evans, aged 17, and Leslie Ann Downey, aged 10, and of being accessory after the fact to the murder of John Kilbride, aged 12, by harbouring Brady knowing that he had murdered Kilbride. The appellant was sentenced to concurrent sentences of life imprisonment on the charges of murder and a further concurrent sentence of seven years' imprisonment on the accessory charge.

The Court dismissed an application for leave to appeal against the sentence of seven years' imprisonment.

Mr Godfrey Heilpern, QC, and Mr Philip Curtis appeared for the appellant; the Attorney-General (Sir Elwyn Jones, QC), Mr W. L. Mars-Jones, QC, and Mr R. G. Waterhouse for the Crown.

Mr Heilpern said that in addition to the charges on which the appellant was convicted she was indicted also with the murder of Kilbride; the charge of being accessory was alternative. Before the pleas were taken submissions were made by counsel for Brady that there was still a rule of practice against joinder of counts for murder; that, in any event, the evidence in relation to the three separate counts did not in fact relate to matters based on the same or similar facts; and that, further and in any event, the three counts, as a matter of discretion, should not be dealt with together because it would be prejudicial to the defence. On behalf of the appellant he (counsel) adopted and added to those submissions and had further submitted that she should be granted a separate trial from Brady. Mr Justice Fenton Atkinson had ruled against all the submissions.

They were reflected in the notice of appeal but both counsel for the appellant had most anxiously considered them, and the one ground pursued on this appeal was that a separate trial of the appellant ought to have been ordered. It was immediately conceded that the question of ordering a separate trial for one accused charged jointly with another was wholly a matter for the discretion of the Judge at trial. There was here, however, so much vital, fundamental evidence going to the whole root of the question of Brady's guilt, which was evidence against him and not evidence against her, that separate trials should have been ordered in the exercise of the Judge's discretion, particularly because he had ruled that the jury could properly consider all the counts.

Where there was, as here, in relation to each of the counts the most damaging evidence against one of the accused which was not evidence against the other it must produce overwhelming prejudice in the minds of the jury however careful

252

the Judge was to point out in the summing-up that certain evidence was evidence against only the one accused. In the circumstances of this case it was impossible for a direction to have been given to the jury which would have realistically enabled them to go through the mental gymnastics involved and to separate the cases in their minds; the situation was incurable *ab initio* since the counts were to be dealt with together.

There was very little law to assist the Court. The principle, and the cases, set out in Archbold *Pleading, Evidence and Practice in Criminal Cases*, 36th ed. (1966), paragraph 129, was that 'Separate trials are sometimes ordered where evidence admissible against one of the accused would not be admissible against the others'.

Even on a separate trial the fact that Hindley was living with Brady could not have been excluded and would have emerged as part of the background, and prejudice was bound to have been created, but, in a separate trial, the admissions he made, vital matters, would have been excluded. If the background itself was likely to create prejudice how much more important was it, therefore, to exclude matters which would aggravate the situation.

In spite of his researches counsel had been unable to discover any case really parallel to the present in which there was such a volume of evidence admissible against one and not the other accused.

Counsel, concluding his submissions in opening, said that if the proposition in paragraph 129 of Archbold (*supra*) had any validity at all then this was a classic case in which the principle should be applied.

CROWN'S REPLY

The Attorney-General said that Mr Justice Fenton Atkinson was entitled to exercise his discretion as he did, and was absolutely right in the interests of justice in exercising it as he did. Recent cases showed that the Courts had been increasingly taking the view that the evidence as a whole should be considered. That was eminently important in this case. From the point of view of the appellant in this case it was by no means a one-way operation since she was advantaged in some respects. If she had been tried separately she would have had to call Brady who then would have been known to the jury as a cruel, sadistic murderer of little children.

The appellant was in an inescapable difficulty by which, of course, she was prejudiced. On her own showing she was intimately involved with Brady and that was a situation of her own making and choice.

In the Downey case there was the most overwhelming evidence against her and he (counsel) did not suppose that any of his learned friends who heard that tape recording would ever forget it—it was a most painful experience.

The Court stopped counsel from continuing his submissions.

Mr Heilpern, in reply, referred to an editorial comment in (1963) *Criminal Law Review*, 786, 787, reading: 'Our law of evidence frequently assumes that jurors are capable of considering evidence for one purpose and excluding it entirely from their minds for others. . . . Whether any jury is capable of performing these feats of mental agility may well be doubted. Teachers of law know well that students find these distinctions difficult to grasp. It is unreasonable to suppose that the juror finds it any easier; and, in any case, grasping the distinction is one thing, applying it is quite another.'

JUDGMENT

The Lord Chief Justice, giving the judgment of the Court, said that it was unnecessary to go into any of the details of this horrible case. Indeed, they were only too well known already.

Mr Heilpern said that the direction was impeccable and could not have been put better or stronger, but that the evidence which was inadmissible against the appellant was such as was bound to create such overwhelming prejudice that no direction could possibly have cured the matter.

The Court had carefully considered his arguments and was quite satisfied that there was no ground for saying that Mr Justice Fenton Atkinson erred in the exercise of his discretion or that any miscarriage of justice had resulted. The evidence complained of, of course, was very damaging evidence against Brady, but the important thing to observe was that it was not evidence which directly at any rate sought to implicate the appellant. Indeed Brady at all times sought to exonerate her from any part in his activities. To that extent it was a benefit for her to be tried with Brady, who had given evidence seeking to exonerate her.

It might be said that that inadmissable evidence did impliedly implicate her in that it clearly showed, for example, the taking of bodies to the moor and the confession that he could not drive—but it was not implicating her in any matter in dispute because she, throughout, said that he could not drive the car.

Any implication against her that was to be found in the inadmissible evidence could certainly have been put right by an adequate direction from the Judge.

There was, no doubt, in this case a danger of grave prejudice from the fact that that man was a really terrible murderer and that she had throughout admitted a very close association with him, taking part in all his activities and, indeed, being in the house if not in the room on the occasion of two of the murders. That was, no doubt, grave prejudice if nothing more to an appellant in those circumstances, but that was a prejudice which was inevitable, and was there just as much, if not to a greater extent, if she were tried separately. This Court was quite satisfied that there was no miscarriage of justice. The evidence against her was overwhelming, and the appeal and application was dismissed.

Solicitors—Messrs Bostock, Yates & Chronnell, Hyde; Director of Public Prosecutions.

APPENDIX 2

Following the trial, the Press Council issued the following Declaration of Principle:

1. No payment or offer of payment should be made by a newspaper to any person known or reasonably expected to be a witness in criminal proceedings already begun in exchange for any story or information in connection with the proceedings until they have been concluded.
2. No witness in committal proceedings should be questioned on behalf of any newspaper about the subject matter of his evidence until the trial has been concluded.
3. No payment should be made for feature articles to persons engaged in crime or other notorious misbehaviour where the public interest does not warrant it; as the Council has previously declared, it deplores publication of personal articles of an unsavoury nature by persons who have been concerned in criminal acts or vicious conduct.

In making this declaration the Press Council acknowledges the wide support given by editors to the broad principles set out.

The Council does not intend that the principles enunciated shall preclude reasonable contemporaneous inquiries in relation to the commission of crime when these are carried out with due regard to the administration of justice. There may be occasions on which the activities of newspapers are affected by over-riding questions of public interest, such as the exposure of wrongdoing.

No code can cover every case. Satisfactory observance of the principles must depend upon the discretion and sense of responsibility of editors and newspaper proprietors.

APPENDIX 3

From *The Times*, 18 July 1969:

Moors trial witness sent to prison

David Smith, one of the chief witnesses in the Moors murder trial, was sentenced at Chester Assizes yesterday to three years' imprisonment.

Mr Smith, aged 21, labourer, of Slater Way, Hattersley, Cheshire, pleaded Guilty to wounding William Lees with intent to do grievous bodily harm at Hattersley on 8 June. He appeared yesterday in the same court as Ian Brady and Myra Hindley (defendants in the Moors case).

Mr D. Morgan Hughes, for the defence, said Mr Smith's act was a direct consequence of the Moors murder story, which the people of the neighbourhood could not forget.

Mr Alan Lees, for the prosecution, said there had been trouble in Hattersley Labour Club in which Mr Smith and Mr Lees were concerned. The next night Mr Lees was on his way home when Mr Smith pulled a knife from his pocket and stabbed him several times.

Mr Hughes said: 'Had he not been involved in the murder trial he might not have been in trouble.

'For most of the time he has been out of work. He got a job in a foundry but when the employees heard of it they either walked out or threatened to do so.'

Mr Justice Veale said he expected Mr Smith had been subjected to sustained hostility and that there had been difficulties for him, but this was not the first time he had been in trouble. He had been before the court four times for assault.

From *The Times*, 8 November 1972:

Moors case witness cleared

David Smith . . . was acquitted by a jury at Manchester Crown Court yesterday of the murder of his father. He pleaded guilty to the manslaughter of Mr John James Smith, who was suffering from incurable cancer . . .

Mr Justice Kilner Brown heard Mr Smith's counsel describe his appearance at the trial eight years ago as a searing and blistering experience which had had a profound effect on him. He sentenced Mr Smith to two days' imprisonment, which meant his immediate release.

Mr Reginald Haulker, for the prosecution, said Mr Smith had crushed 20 sodium amytal tablets, mixed them with milk, and given the drink to his father, who died several hours later.

(According to a report in the *Daily Telegraph*, 'As he left the court after the case, Smith kissed the girl with whom he is now living . . . and who is expecting his child . . . He said that he was now hoping to divorce his wife, Maureen. The couple have been living apart for some time.')